THE

CUBANS

ALSO BY ANTHONY DePALMA

Here: A Biography of the New American Continent

The Man Who Invented Fidel

City of Dust: Illness, Arrogance, and 9/11

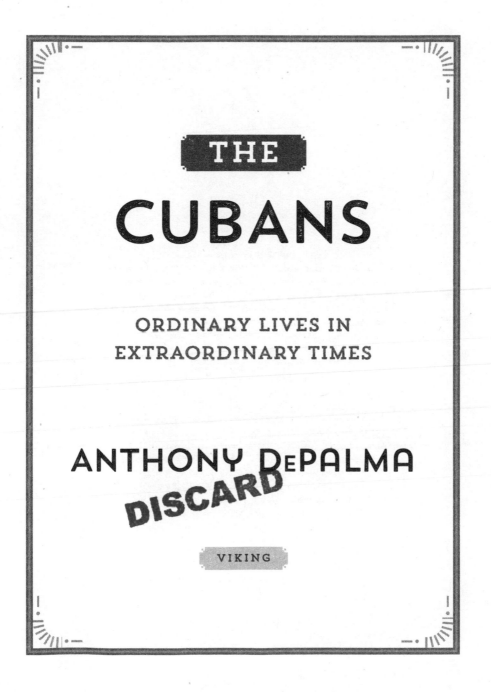

THE
CUBANS

ORDINARY LIVES IN
EXTRAORDINARY TIMES

ANTHONY DePALMA

VIKING

VIKING

An imprint of Penguin Random House LLC
penguinrandomhouse.com

Library of Congress Cataloging-in-Publication Data

Names: DePalma, Anthony, author.
Title: The Cubans : ordinary lives in extraordinary times / Anthony DePalma.
Description: [New York] : Viking, [2020] | Includes index.
Identifiers: LCCN 2019052262 (print) | LCCN 2019052263 (ebook) |
ISBN 9780525522447 (hardcover) | ISBN 9780525522454 (ebook)
Subjects: LCSH: Guanabacoa (Havana, Cuba)—Biography. | Havana
(Cuba)—Biography. | Cuba—History—1959–1990. | Cuba—History—1990–
Classification: LCC F1799.H353 A293 2020 (print) |
LCC F1799.H353 (ebook) | DDC 972.91/23—dc23
LC record available at https://lccn.loc.gov/2019052262
LC ebook record available at https://lccn.loc.gov/2019052263

Printed in the United States of America
1 3 5 7 9 10 8 6 4 2

Designed by Cassandra Garruzzo
Maps by Jeffrey L. Ward

For Miriam

It is not for glory that I struggle since
all the glory in the world
fits inside a kernel of corn.

JOSÉ MARTÍ

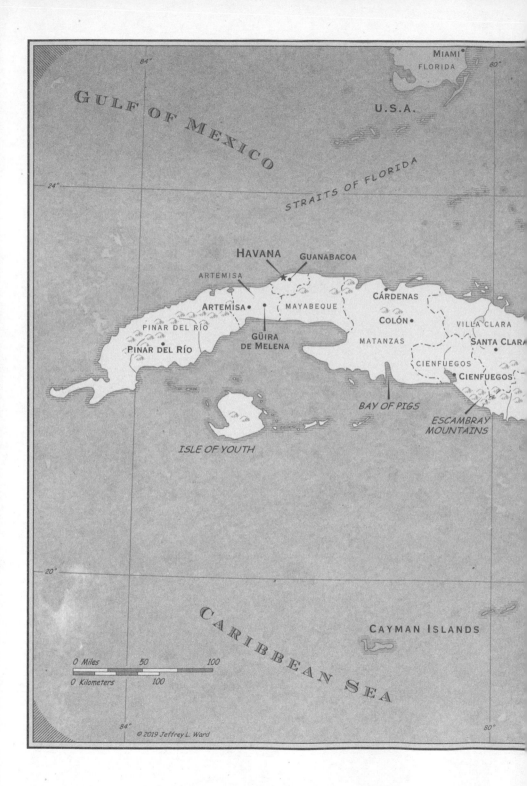

MIAMI
FLORIDA

GULF OF MEXICO

U.S.A.

STRAITS OF FLORIDA

HAVANA   GUANABACOA

ARTEMISA

ARTEMISA   CÁRDENAS
                MAYABEQUE
PINAR DEL RÍO   COLÓN   VILLA CLARA
                GÜIRA
PINAR DEL RÍO   DE MELENA   MATANZAS   SANTA CLARA

                                CIENFUEGOS
                                        CIENFUEGOS
                        BAY OF PIGS
                                        ESCAMBRAY
                                        MOUNTAINS

ISLE OF YOUTH

CARIBBEAN SEA

CAYMAN ISLANDS

0 Miles   50   100

0 Kilometers   100

© 2019 Jeffrey L. Ward

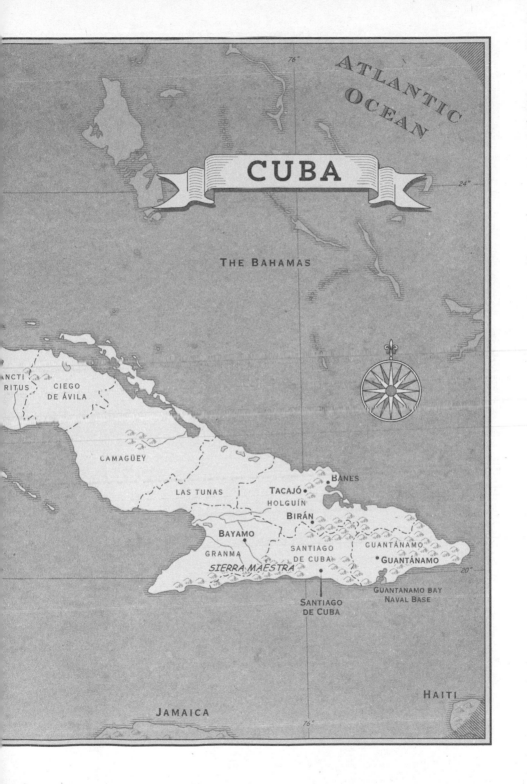

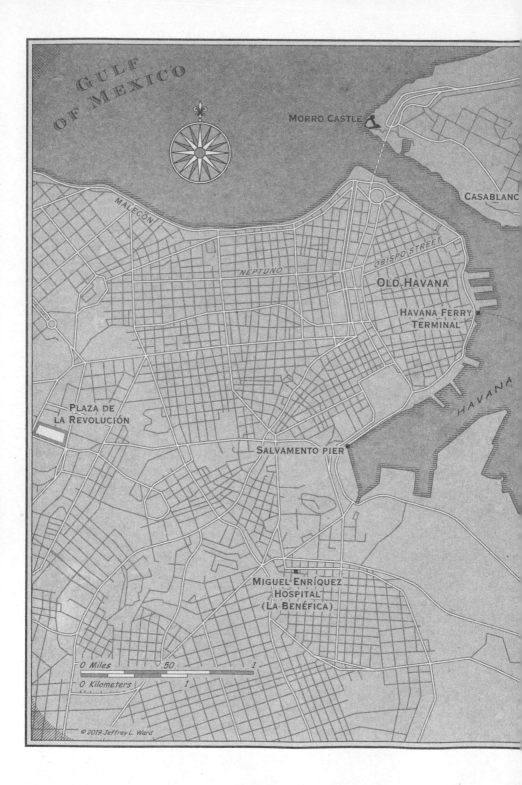

GULF
OF MEXICO

MORRO CASTLE

CASABLANC

MALECÓN

NEPTUNO

OBISPO STREET

OLD HAVANA

HAVANA FERRY
TERMINAL

PLAZA DE
LA REVOLUCIÓN

SALVAMENTO PIER

HAVANA

MIGUEL ENRÍQUEZ
HOSPITAL
(LA BENÉFICA)

0 Miles   50   1
0 Kilometers   1

© 2019 Jeffrey L. Ward

PROLOGUE

September 9, 2017

When the lights went out around five that afternoon, and the television swallowed itself dark, the lone fan in the house, the white plastic one from China with the brand name Hopeful, slowed to a dead stop. That's when Cary, Pipo, and Oscar, along with Faru, their scrawny Pekingese with a bad underbite, knew it was time to hide. Cubans are no strangers to hurricanes, but this one made even the most storm-scarred of them shudder: a category five monster named Irma, with 165-mile-an-hour winds, torrential rain, and 16-foot-high waves, which was scheduled—if it kept to the timetable delivered by the gloomy TV meteorologists—to smash into Guanabacoa, their quirky hometown across the harbor from Old Havana, between two and three the next morning. The electricity surely wouldn't return by then, but how long they'd be in the dark, or what they'd find when the lights came back on, nobody could say.

They'd developed and refined their own drill to prepare for big storms like this one, with every member of the family assigned specific tasks. Oscar was just twenty-six, so it was up to him to climb up to the roof and tie down everything that could blow away. His father, Jesús, who everyone knew as Pipo, scoured the neighborhood for food while his mom, Cary, was in charge of everything else. She taped the windows, closed the shutters, and filled enough old soda bottles with purified water to last a few days. When she was done, she took a minute to call Cuka, her lifelong friend in Tacajó, the little sugar town in eastern Cuba where both of them grew up, to make sure everyone there was prepared for the nightmare headed toward them.

Cuka picked up right away. Yes, she was all right. Everyone else too. She'd already done all she could, and there was nothing left to do but hunker down and wait. Waiting was a skill that Cubans mastered no matter where they lived or what they were doing. At first, Cary and Pipo thought of riding out the storm where they often did, in Oscar's bedroom. Their house was big and solid—a prerevolution midcentury modern that had been split into two apartments; their upstairs neighbors had even built a clandestine metalworking shop on the roof. But the coming storm threatened to be so bad they might be stuck inside for a long time. Oscar's room was the smallest in the house, and there was nothing but louvers in the windows to keep out the wind and rain. There wasn't enough room for them in the kitchen or storeroom, and the parlor, facing the street, was far too exposed. That left their own bedroom, with its lone window facing south, away from Irma.

They were getting the bedroom ready when the phone rang, surprising them. It was Pipo's younger sister Luz María calling from Cárdenas, ninety miles away, to let them know that, despite the storm, her son's girlfriend had gone to the hospital to give birth to their first child. After that, the phone too went dead. Their only radio, a hand-cranked one that Pipo had given Cary one Valentine's Day, was broken, leaving them almost as cut off from the outside as if they were stranded in Cuba's remote Sierra Maestra mountains.

Not long after they had settled into the bedroom for the night, the rain started. Not a downpour but bulging drops so fat and heavy they could almost hear them fall one at a time, splashing into the dirt but doing nothing to cool things off. With all three of them in there, and Faru panting frantically on the floor, the bedroom soon was stifling. Cary got up to open the casement window, and the musty smell of rain and dirt washed in. From where they lay, with their heads at the foot of the bed and their feet pointing toward the open window, they had a clear view of the blood-orange sky. For Cary, the strange light and evocative scents brought back harrowing reminders of another storm. She was just a girl then, living with her mother and twin sister in a rooming house near Cuka in Tacajó. When Hurricane Flora tore through, what little they had was nearly blown away.

With the three of them so close, Oscar soon got antsy and started complaining about the heat. Pipo was hot too, but what bothered him more was the metal roof of the warehouse across the street. Several times already, he'd said that if it blew off, they'd be right in its path. Cary told both of them to cut it out. Their house was made of concrete, wasn't it? And though their pantry wasn't full, there was some food in there, wasn't there? "Just calm down. We'll be all right."

Through the open window all she could see were the dark clouds that blotted out the stars. That gave her an idea. When she was a girl in Tacajó she'd learned a song about stars that always helped her calm down whenever she was frightened.

"Do you two want to hear a song?"

Through tempests and turmoil, Cary—Caridad Luisa Limonta Ewen— was always helping others. They joked that she'd been born first so she could show her twin sister the way. And like her late mother, Zenaida, she tackled whatever Cuba threw at her with confidence and courage.

With the wind kicking up, and the warehouse roof clattering, Cary sang the melancholy old song in a low, sweet voice that her husband and son could barely hear, a lullaby in the storm.

Pregúntale a las estrellas si por las noches me ven llorar
Ask the stars if at night they see me cry
Ask if I do not seek to love you, how lonely am I
Ask the gentle river if it sees my tears running
Ask all the world the depth of my own suffering.

Just as Cary hoped, the song helped settle them down. As Irma drew closer, Pipo and Oscar fell into an uneasy sleep. But not Cary. She couldn't stop thinking about Cuka and Tacajó and the terrible hurricane she'd lived through when she was a child. Nor could she forget the innocent baby being born into this monstrous storm. They knew it was a girl; the tests had shown that months before, and the date for the cesarean had been long planned. But what terrible timing! Would they name her Irma? Or would they stick with tradition and check the church calendar of saints, cursing her with a name like Wilfreda? She'd rather be named for a night of terror.

As the hours passed, Cary was bone tired, but she kept staring at the open window, listening to the wind tugging at the warehouse roof and looking for the stars that she knew were there though she couldn't see them.

All of Guanabacoa (wan-ah-ba-COE-ah) was on edge that night. Just down the street from Cary and Pipo, Lili Durand Hernández went around her apartment shutting all the windows and doors as much to keep out the storm as to keep in her elderly father, who had started to wander. About a mile away, in the rundown center of Guanabacoa, María del Carmen López Álvarez remembered what her own father had always told her about their sturdy little house, which the family had owned for more than a century. If it survived the big ones in 1926 and 1944, he'd say whenever a storm approached, it'll make it through any others. She had so much faith in the old house that the only precautions she took were to have the TV antenna taken down and the big clay pot, called a *tinajón*, in the patio filled with fresh water. And just to be safe, she asked her son to take the life-size busts of Julius Caesar and Raphael off their pedestals and lay them on the floor.

A block away from María del Carmen, on the opposite side of the church of Los Escolapios, Arturo Montoto worried about Irma's approach in a way that nobody else in Guanabacoa could imagine. His biggest concern was not the art studio and extensive garden he had spent so much time and money building, but a six-foot-tall resin foam sculpture of a baseball, completely black with stitches of bright red thread, that was sitting in his courtyard. It was so big and so round that once he had bonded the two halves together, he could not get it back inside. His assistants had lugged it under an awning, but they had no way to tie it down. He checked to make sure it was protected from the rain, then he took one last look around his property, ending at the orchard he had planted with his own hands: lush mango trees, a lissome lemon tree, a banana tree with its floppy leaves waving wildly as the winds picked up. He would have loved to plant a *mamoncillo* tree too, like the ones he remembered as a boy, but they took such a long time to mature that he knew he'd never taste its fruit.

And although Jorge García was awaiting the storm 230 miles away from Guanabacoa, in a dumpy ranch house across the street from a Miami boatyard, he was keeping a close eye on his old hometown. He'd escaped from Cuba twenty years earlier, but his grandson was still there, and whenever a big storm threatened Guanabacoa, Jorge worried. He'd already lost far too much to Cuba.

IRMA WAS JUST ONE FLASHPOINT of concern for Cubans in the stormy year between Fidel Castro's death in November 2016 and his brother Raúl's staged departure from office in 2018. Those two events seemed to draw the curtain on the long-running Castro era and presage the dawn of a new, uncertain, and not yet fully formed act in Cuba's long history. With the revolution sagging under the weight of six decades of grand promises—some realized, many others still a dream—the communist government was toying with capitalism the way a tiger plays with its prey: tapping it lightly one minute, squeezing the life out of it the next. Socialist officials urged would-be Cuban capitalists to go ahead and open their small businesses, then they erected layers of burdensome regulations to limit profit and handicap success. Their real goal was not to lift millions out of poverty. It was to prevent anyone from making millions.

Despite those constraints, half a million Cubans preferred to work for themselves rather than the state. But then just as they were getting used to living without a man named Castro leading the nation, the political and economic feud with the United States flared up again. Donald Trump reversed parts of Barack Obama's historic opening of a few years earlier, frightening away American tourists and making the short trip to Cuba once again seem forbidding. Washington then lumped Cuba together with Venezuela and Nicaragua in what it called a "troika of tyranny" and put crosshairs on all three countries. Ordinary Cubans had no choice but to brace for another "special period" that they feared could turn out to be even worse than the shortages and desperation they suffered in the 1990s, when the Soviet Union disappeared, taking with it the billions Cuba relied on to keep the revolution alive.

In Guanabacoa, as in most other parts of Cuba, the Obama opening had raised hopes, and the Trump reversal dashed them. The sensually restored Old Havana that Americans discovered during the brief tourism boom was the cartoon fantasy version of Cuba. Guanabacoa is the gritty 3-D reality most Cubans live with—broken streets, collapsing buildings, more garbage than flowers. Hot. Smelly. Noisy. Raw. The proud old town predates every U.S. city, and in its nearly 500-year history it has experienced many ups and downs. Officially a part of Havana, it sits on the other side of the city's fabled harbor, but it could be any place along the 760 miles of the main Cuban island, each with its own unique culture and identity. Its 120,000 residents are no more likely to say they live in Havana than residents of Brooklyn are to describe where they live as New York.

"*Después del triunfo*," "after the triumph," is Cuban shorthand for everything that has happened since Fidel and Raúl Castro grabbed power in 1959. Everyone knows that Fidel remade Cuba's political, economic, and social structures, putting the state in charge of and above everything and everyone but him. During most of Cuba's six decades of revolution, the real people of Cuba have largely been hidden behind his king-size image.

As Cuba starts to move from the Castro era to whatever comes next, it is changing in many ways—even if the images of old cars and ancient buildings suggest that time is standing still. Some of Cuba's leaders have ideas about business and property that are radically different from Fidel's, but it's not at all clear whether this represents a desperate attempt to prop up an exhausted revolution, or the genuine beginning of a new nation. For decades, analysts and correspondents routinely referred to "Fidel Castro's Cuba," as if the country he controlled since 1959 belonged entirely to him. When he died in 2016, state-run media in Cuba proclaimed, "*Fidel es Patria*," "Fidel is the fatherland," while schoolchildren were encouraged to repeat, "I am Fidel."

But those children and their parents are not Fidel any more than the dead Fidel ever was Cuba. They are ordinary people like Cary, Arturo, Lili,

Jorge, and María del Carmen. Real Cubans, living in real places like Guanabacoa where the old cars are not prized classics, but just ugly hunks of battered metal, held together by wire and running on hope. Where the rum is cheap and comes in small cardboard boxes. Where there are no robocalls, no fad diets, no supermarket flyers or commercial billboards. Where daily life depends not on tourist dollars but on the courage, confidence, and inventiveness of people living with an excess of prohibitions and a minimum of inhibitions. Where people have become masters at masking their misery with vibrant music and rapturous dancing, disguising their frustrations with layers of disrespectful mocking, making a joke of almost everything and taking almost nothing so seriously that it merits their protest.

For their entire lives, Cary and the others have had no choice but to be minor characters in Cuba's never-ending passion play, forced to take one of only three paths the revolution left open to them: They could join the masses and comply with the Castros' dictates whether or not they believed in them. They could take the heroic path and resist, accepting that to do so was suicide. Or they could flee.

If it sometimes seems that all Cubans are, as they say of themselves, *un poco loco*, a little crazy, it is because they live in an impossible country. They have been on what amounts to war footing for three generations now. Their government constantly reminds them of the imperialist peril from the north, yet it also demands that the empire drop its embargo so that Cuba can do more business with America and its allies. The regime has used the perpetual threat of American intervention as cover for every misstep, failed program, food shortage, or power blackout over the last six decades, but it also depends on the billions of American dollars that exiles send back in remittances to keep Cuba afloat. State-run media presents the United States as a hellhole of drug addiction, mass murder and runaway consumerism, while portraying Cuba as an egalitarian paradise run by a government that can do no wrong. And yet, when Cubans compare their own lives with what they hear from relatives in Miami or with what they see on the internet, they know it isn't so.

That would be enough to drive anyone mad, but it accounts for only part of the Cubans' precarious hold on the reality of their lives. They have long been cursed by their own greatest strength—their indomitable adaptability and their bottomless capacity to make do. That's why the U.S. embargo hasn't worked, and never will. The idea of making conditions on the island so intolerable that the people will rise up and crush the Castro regime ignores the Cubans' innate ability to find a way to survive. People who can turn a plastic soda bottle into a gas tank for a motorcycle, or use an old piston heated in a kitchen stove to repair a flat tire, see the world differently from other more conventional societies. When adversity is a constant, survival is a process of adjustment. Perhaps living on an island routinely hit by hurricanes has helped them develop this aspect of their national character. After all, nothing can stop a hurricane or prevent it from doing damage. The only option is to pick up the pieces and figure out how to reuse them.

Unlike Fidel, whose millions of words have been heard, recorded, and replayed ad infinitum, these ordinary Cubans are never heard from. Their voices have few outlets inside Cuba, and fewer still outside the island. When they speak out, it usually is in small rooms where they hope that the whoosh of a table fan or the tinny sound of an old TV keeps their remarks from prying ears. Most never get involved in public protests for fear of retribution from a state system of surveillance that they believe watches over their every move. Only the bravest or most desperate risk everything to join the small number of outspoken dissidents that the government stalks, harasses, and sometimes imprisons. But it is undoubtedly the complicated silence of their ordinary lives—their personal histories of living with an interminable revolution, their changing priorities and shifting alliances, their triumphs and their tragedies from one moment to the next in an endless stream of warm days under a brilliant sun—that tell the remarkable story of Cuba best.

PART ONE

REALIZATION

CHAPTER 1

TACAJÓ, ORIENTE PROVINCE
1940

Anyone who lived in the Cuban jungle in the 1940s knew that with the humidity and infernal heat seeping under, around, and into everything, ants would get into the bread no matter what you did. Tie it in a bag and hang it from a nail, and before long there'd be a conga line of ants climbing straight up the wall like they had formal invitations to dinner. As a poor black teenager in the sugar-mill town of Tacajó, deep in Cuba's wild eastern end, Zenaida Ewen went only as far as the sixth grade in the local school, where classes were taught in English and a little Spanish for the children of the Jamaicans who worked there. But she had watched her mother put bread on the stove, and she knew that keeping it close to but not in the flames would drive out the ants before dinner was served.

Jamaicans had lived in Tacajó since the mill began grinding sugarcane in 1917. They came during the boom years following the Spanish-American War when foreign money—mostly American dollars—poured into the island. Cuba hadn't come out of its war as the fully independent nation that many had fought for, but for those who did business with the North Americans, times were good, especially in Oriente province. The fertile mixture of sun, soil, and rain made land there ideal for growing things, including the dense fields of sugarcane that for a time made Cuba the world's biggest supplier, and

cemented sugar so firmly into the economy of the country that people grew
fond of saying, "Without sugar, there is no country."

Turning oceans of green stalks into the white sugar crystals that sweeten
coffee and cake around the world has been backbreaking work since the first
cane fields were harvested centuries ago. By the early nineteenth century,
African slaves were dragged in to do the work, but Spain, Cuba's colonial
master for five hundred years, never allowed as many slaves into Cuba as were
brought to other Caribbean islands. The slave trade was abolished in Cuba in
1820, but it wasn't until 1879 that the institution of slavery ended. British historian Hugh Thomas surmised that the Cuban upper class almost certainly
would have pushed harder for full independence from Spain "had it not been
for anxiety about their slaves, and the specter of Haiti." After the USS *Maine*
was sunk in Havana Harbor in 1898, and the United States jumped into
Cuba's long-running war of independence, Spain was forced to give up its
prized colony. Cuba became a republic but one saddled with ambiguous democracy, incompetent leadership, and a legacy of racial prejudice that has never
been fully erased.

With the influx of foreign investment in the early twentieth century, the
Tacajó Sugar Corporation, headquartered in New York, grew rapidly and
prospered. The United Fruit Company, with operations nearby, also expanded
aggressively, buying from local growers such as Ángel Castro, a Spanish sol-
dier who had settled in Cuba after the war ended and was amassing a fortune
on Manacas, his twenty-thousand-acre plantation not far from Tacajó. Such a
shortage of labor developed that the Cuban government in 1922 authorized
Tacajó Sugar and United Fruit to import thousands of contract workers to
help with the harvest, expecting to send them back home after the season
ended. Most were Haitians or Jamaicans. Many never left.

Zenaida's mother, Sarah Ann Ewen, was twenty-nine when she received
her Jamaican passport in 1922 and made the trip from Kingston to Cuba,
drawn by the image of a Cuba filled with opportunity. She landed in Santiago
and then made her way overland to Tacajó, where she had heard she might
find the good life that Jamaicans had discovered in Cuba. The lush valley
around the sugar mill reminded her of home, but it was no paradise, espe-

cially for a single mother with little education and no skills. Most of the streets were unpaved, sanitation was crude, and the cycle of work at the sugar mill meant periods of intense labor followed by months of dead time. That was if you had a job. Sarah needed to find one, and fast. Women didn't work in the mills then, but they cooked and cleaned, which Sarah surely could do. She started washing clothes for the single men who lived in broken-down dorms. Later, the mill's Cuban doctor took her in as a domestic servant to help his wife run their big house near the main entrance to the mill. It was a step up for Sarah, an opportunity to create a better life for her children, and she was determined to make the best of it. But in 1941, when she was just forty-seven, she suffered a fatal heart attack that left Zenaida and her brother, Cleveland, orphans. Neighbors in Tacajó took them in.

Whether out of pity or necessity, the Cuban doctor agreed to let Zenaida take her mother's place even though she was only thirteen, spoke halting Spanish, and had never worked as a domestic servant. One day, Zenaida was cleaning a crystal bowl filled with candy when she noticed ants crawling inside. Knowing she'd be punished if the doctor's wife saw the ants, she remembered what her mother had told her about putting bread near the stove. She reasoned that if flames worked for bread, she could do the same thing with the candy dish. The flames drove away the ants all right, but the heat shattered the crystal. When the doctor's wife found out what happened, she scolded Zenaida harshly and called her a stupid, stupid girl.

Zenaida swore she'd never be humiliated like that again.

When the doctor left his job, Zenaida worked for the new medic's family. Her life continued that way, moving from family to family, secretly harboring a dream to one day become a doctor herself. When one of the families she worked for moved to Havana in 1947, Zenaida decided to go with them. She was nineteen and believed life would be better in the capital. It didn't take her long to realize that a young black woman with no education had no business dreaming of becoming a doctor no matter where she lived. After a few years in Havana she'd had enough, but instead of returning to Tacajó she tried her luck in the city of Guantánamo. She'd heard that the U.S. naval base there hired Cubans and treated them well, especially if they spoke English.

Zenaida found work at a nursery school on the base. Every day, she took a ferry across the bay to the American side, being sure to sit in the seats reserved for blacks. She made good money and spent some of it on gold jewelry that she kept as insurance, just in case things did not work out. She caught the eye of a young cabinetmaker from Haiti named Aristede Limonta who also worked with the Americans. He was dark and handsome, with a husky sex appeal that years later she'd compare to the American singer Barry White. They fell in love and moved into a small wooden house on the corner of Céspedes and Eighth, on the south side of the city of Guantánamo. When Zenaida became pregnant, she made a sacred vow to the Virgen de la Caridad del Cobre, Cuba's patron saint, whose sanctuary sits on a hill outside the city of Santiago. If the baby is a girl, she promised, her name will be Caridad.

For a short time, Zenaida believed she had succeeded in putting the humiliation at the doctor's house behind her, but there was trouble ahead. Aristede started making eyes at other pretty young women. Zenaida tried to ignore it. When her water broke, Aristede hired a horse and buggy and rushed her to the hospital in Guantánamo. On December 18, 1956, she delivered the baby—a girl—but then the midwife told her another baby was on the way.

I can't have another one, not now, she told the nurse. I'm having trouble with the father.

Trouble or not, she was having twins.

Ten minutes later, a second baby girl was born. For Aristede's family, having twins was nothing unusual. His great-grandmother María was said to have given birth to five sets of them.

SEVENTEEN DAYS BEFORE THE TWINS WERE BORN, Fidel Castro and eighty-one of his rebels had beached an old American yacht called *Granma* in an almost impenetrable mangrove swamp on Cuba's southern coast. It was the calamitous start of their armed struggle to overthrow Fulgencio Batista, Cuba's dictator, who, with the solid backing of Washington, had ruled for decades. Then, at the same time that Aristede was promising to help Zenaida care for their infant daughters, Batista was boasting that the troublemaking

Castro brothers had been killed in the landing along with nearly all the invaders.

Both Aristede and Batista were lying.

Zenaida fulfilled her vow to the Virgen de la Caridad and named her first baby girl Caridad Luisa. She called the other Esperanza Caridad. Hope and Charity. Charity and Hope. By now, she was well aware of Aristede's womanizing and felt betrayed by his infidelities. But with twins to care for, she was willing to turn her cheek and give him another chance. All four of them lived together for about three months. Then one night, after he'd had too much to drink, Aristede hit her.

Hurt, angry, and feeling like she'd been humiliated once again, Zenaida put her babies in a basket and went around the tiny house grabbing what she could of their possessions. But the gold jewelry that she had scrimped to buy, which was supposed to be her insurance just in case something like this happened, sat in a cabinet on the other side of the bed, where the drunken Aristede was passed out. She couldn't chance waking him and getting hit again. Or worse, getting into a fight over the babies.

Zenaida slipped out without the jewelry and took the girls to the house of one of her mother's Jamaican friends. When the babies were a few months old, she tried to go back to work, but on her first day she ran into Aristede on the ferry. He started yelling so everybody could hear, accusing her of running away with his babies and keeping him from seeing them.

Let me off, she shouted, and the ferry pilot slowed the engine. Back on shore, she sent a telegram to her brother, Cleveland, telling him to meet her at the train stop at Manguito, outside Tacajó, because she was coming home. She never recovered her jewelry and she never married, but she would always insist that Aristede had been the first and only true love of her life. Still, for decades afterward, whenever she heard any song by Barry White on the radio, she'd leave the room.

A single mother, twenty-seven, with no job, no skills, and no place to live, she was left with nothing but her two girls and her own determination that they would never be abused the way she had been. Reluctantly, she went back to the house of Carmen Caro, the woman who had taken her in after her mother's death, and knocked on the door. She was embarrassed to admit that she had failed in everything she'd tried since she had left Tacajó years before, and now she had no one else to turn to. Carmen had a large family of her own, with many children—including a little girl they called Cuka—and grandchildren all living under the same roof. But she was a generous soul and made room in the big, old house for them.

IN THE MOUNTAINS not far from Tacajó, Fidel had revealed to the world that Batista had lied about the landing. He and most of the men with him had indeed been strafed as they wrestled through the mangroves, but once they gained their footing on the beach, they managed to make it into the dense forest of the Sierra Maestra, where they regrouped. Early in 1957, he called dozens of his followers together to finalize plans for an armed uprising to overthrow Batista, leaving somewhat vague just what would happen if, against all odds, they managed to oust the dictator. Before that meeting started, Fidel talked to an American newspaper correspondent from the *New York Times* whom his men had smuggled into the mountains. When the reporter, Herbert L. Matthews, returned to New York days later, he wrote a series of sensational articles that revealed to the world not only that Fidel was alive, but that he was winning the war against Batista—a gross exaggeration in 1957. Matthews portrayed Fidel in glowing terms, painting him as a Cuban Robin Hood, a heroically impressive young lawyer with a scraggly beard who promised to restore constitutional government and hold elections.

Some of the fighting was taking place in the mountains around Tacajó, but Zenaida was too busy taking in laundry for mill workers and raising her girls to get involved in Castro's struggle. He and his movement were attracting many followers, and by the middle of 1958, when the United States finally cut off arms sales to Batista's government, there was little doubt that the dictator's days were numbered. Early on the morning of January 1, 1959, Batista loaded a few planes with as much as $400 million that Castro claimed had been looted from the national treasury and, with his family and a few aides, fled to safety in the Dominican Republic.

Like most Cubans, Zenaida rooted for Fidel, then just thirty-two, as he took over the entire country. She believed him when he promised that he was going to make life better for all the people of Cuba, regardless of their race or gender. When Fidel set up his national system of watchdogs and called it the Committee for the Defense of the Revolution (CDR), she became an active member. She also joined the Federation of Cuban Women, founded by Raúl's guerrilla wife, Vilma Espín. When the government opened a small health clinic inside the home of the former director of the sugar mill, she got a job mopping floors and changing sheets. It wasn't much compared with her dream of becoming a doctor, but for her and her little family, it was a step up, a big one.

The Americans who had run things in Tacajó scurried home when the mill was nationalized in 1960. The Cubans who took over made sure its bellowing smokestacks and daily rhythms continued to dominate life there. They kept the phone system linking the home of every worker to the central office functioning and saw to it that the mill's whistle bellowed at the start and end of every shift, a deep *vruuuum*—like a hole in a gigantic muffler—that, in the dim light of dawn, with roosters crowing and frogs croaking, woke Zenaida and the girls to the challenges of each new day.

They lived in a *cuartería*, a long row of ten tiny apartments, each no more than a single room. The latrine was in the woods a few steps away. That was their home when Hurricane Flora came crashing toward them in 1963. It was a powerful storm, one of the deadliest ever. By the time Zenaida heard the warnings on her little transistor radio, the wind and rain were almost on top of them. The clinic needed her, so she snatched the girls, not yet seven, from the wooden *cuartería* and brought them to a friend who lived in a sturdy masonry house near the clinic. The girls watched from the open front door as she inched her way up the wind-blown street toward the clinic, grabbing a bougainvillea fence to keep from being blown off her feet. Frightened that she might never come back, they tried to comfort each other through the long night. As the sky churned with gray clouds and the stars disappeared, Cary sang a song that Mr. Pedrozo, her fourth-grade teacher, had taught the children in chorus: *Ask the stars if at night they see me cry.*

When Flora finally veered off into the Atlantic, and Zenaida was allowed to leave the clinic, she collected the girls and took them home. Flora had completely flattened one end of the *cuartería*. The walls of their section were still standing, but the roof had been torn off and the heavy rains had soaked the big armoire that was packed with everything they owned. They gathered what they could save and, once again, moved in with friends.

As Tacajó rebuilt, Zenaida became a fixture in the clinic. In 1968, she enrolled in a training program for nurses' assistants at a hospital in the city of Holguín. When the nine-month program ended, she returned to Tacajó with a new title and a plan for the future. In the local clinic where she once washed floors, she now had a job as an auxiliary nurse. She came to be known, and feared, for ruthlessly giving injections to all, sticking everyone from the bravest to the most squeamish without the slightest hesitation or sympathy. But she also endeared herself to the people of Tacajó for the big heart she opened to everyone.

FROM THE TIME CARY AND ESPERANZA were little girls, their mother tried to dress them alike. But Cary was determined to be who she wanted to be. Once, when she and Esperanza were invited to Cuka's birthday party, Zenaida wanted them to wear identical blue dresses with matching hair bows. Cary had other plans. She dragged a stool into the closet, took out a red dress, and begged her mother to let her wear it instead of the blue one. Headstrong as she was, she lost the argument that day. But by the time she turned fifteen— usually a big celebration for Cuban girls—she was more often getting her way. It took some arguing, but when Zenaida prepared the girls for their joint *quinceañera* celebration, she sewed a pink dress with long sleeves for Esperanza, and a blue dress with short sleeves for Cary.

They were fraternal twins, both five feet four and blessed with the same lustrous mahogany skin, high cheekbones, and broad smile. But Esperanza's face was fuller, which made her look more like their mother. Cary had inherited Zenaida's gap-toothed smile, along with her resolute character. She always was more organized than her sister, filled with passion and dramatic flair. "Look at what an actress she is," Zenaida would say when she found Cary crying, "her tears are flowing out of only one eye."

The United States was one of the first countries to recognize the new post-Batista government that Fidel organized, but the relationship between the two countries soon soured. After Fidel nationalized parts of the economy, including American oil refineries and sugar mills like the one in Tacajó, without compensating their owners, President Dwight Eisenhower sharply reduced sugar quotas and stopped exports. In 1962, President John F. Kennedy expanded the sanctions to a total trade embargo, which has been in place ever since.

It became difficult for Cuba to get spare parts to keep the mill in Tacajó running. But the Cubans managed to continue grinding cane and exporting processed sugar, mostly to the Soviet Union, which paid well for it. Fidel's government empowered Tacajó and its people. The big houses on Second of April Avenue that had been owned by the American directors were chopped up into apartments. Cary and Esperanza were free to walk into the social club in Tacajó that had been restricted to the American owners of the mill and the white Cuban managers who ran it. The girls also were able to sign up for music lessons in the house of culture that had been off-limits to black youngsters like them. The drastic changes filled Zenaida with hope that the revolution could actually sweep away the lingering racial discrimination that she had endured. They were being sent a clear message, one that Zenaida and many Cubans had been waiting to hear: young people like her twins would not be held back because of the color of their skin. Nor would being girls in a macho Latino society keep them from realizing their dreams, so long as they worked hard and got an education.

In 1970, Zenaida and the girls joined countless other Cubans who cut cane in the frenzied national effort to meet Fidel's goal of bringing in an unprecedented ten-million-ton harvest. The harvest fell short, and an uneasy political and economic reality seemed to settle over Cuba. The revolution, mighty as Fidel made it seem, had limits. And Zenaida realized that her little sugar town was a dead end. With the girls in a government boarding school, working in the fields during the day and studying at night, she decided to return to Havana. As soon as she found steady work and a place to live, she'd bring Caridad and Esperanza to live with her.

It wasn't as easy as she'd imagined, but with her certification as a nurses' assistant she eventually found a job at a Havana hospital. She reunited the family and enrolled the girls in Havana schools. They did well enough to qualify for select universities, but they weren't sure that continuing to study was the right thing to do. Their mother was working twelve-hour shifts at the hospital and coming home dead tired, all for them. They came up with a bold plan. Esperanza could become a hairdresser, and Cary was willing to do manicures. It couldn't be a business, not even a small business, not in their Cuba. A nationwide effort in 1968 that Fidel called the Revolutionary Offensive had taken ownership of every remaining private business, no matter how small, and outlawed any kind of private enterprise, even beauty parlors. But the girls knew that Cuban women would always be willing to pay for beauty. They would cut hair and polish nails at home, and if anyone asked, they'd say they were just helping friends.

They proudly laid out their plans for Zenaida, but she didn't react at all the way they expected. "Absolutely not," she told them, leaving no doubt that she was not to be disobeyed. She reminded them how she had been humiliated at the doctor's house in Tacajó. "That happened to me because I was a poor black girl without much education," she said. History was not going to repeat itself. Laying out for her girls the harsh truth of Cuban life, she told them, "You have disadvantages as young women, and even more so because you're black. You'll always have to work harder and give one hundred and fifty percent to everything you do, just to be seen as doing it right."

They were going to go to university, and that was that.

Esperanza decided to study architecture in one of Havana's universities, a sensible course for a young Cuban communist. But once Cary was exposed to the music, literature, and art of Havana, she couldn't get enough culture. She fell in love with literature, in particular the works of Honoré de Balzac and the Spanish poet Gustavo Adolfo Bécquer. They filled her with such courage that when difficulties arose, as they often did for her family, she turned to them for comfort. Once, when she watched her mother defend herself in front of the community against unfounded charges of mistreating a handicapped girl she was caring for, Cary recalled Bécquer's bleak lines, and felt better about her own family's troubles:

> My life is a wasteland;
> flower that I touch is undressed,
> there, in my fatal way,
> someone is sowing evil for me to gather.

Cary's grades weren't as good as Esperanza's. Spelling and grammar tortured her, but she did well enough on all the rest to qualify for a new program that allowed college-age Cubans, as members of the socialist bloc, to study in foreign universities. She had her heart set on the art history program in East Germany, but when the selections came out, she learned she'd be sent to Ukraine, where art history wasn't available. An academic adviser suggested economic engineering instead. "What's that?" she had to ask. Economic engineering was a popular course of study in Eastern Europe that applied economic principles to real-world problems. But few people in Cuba had any idea what it meant, and that included Zenaida. It didn't sound to her like something a proper young Cuban woman ought to pursue. Nor, in her opinion, did it hold much promise.

"Probably something they have there that will be useless here," she complained. Esperanza had chosen a more realistic path that kept her in Cuba. Why couldn't Cary do the same?

Zenaida refused to sign the parental consent form, forcing Cary to ask relatives to persuade her that studying in the Soviet Union was something to be proud of. And they had to convince her that what happened to the *Titanic* did not necessarily mean every ship that crossed the Atlantic was doomed. Reluctantly, she gave in and signed the papers. While Cary went through a year of language training in Cuba, the government picked over her background. Inquiries were made with the local CDR to find out how much of her young life she had dedicated to the new Cuba, and whether she had any contacts with the enemy in the United States who might persuade her to defect. Her long-absent father, Aristede, had escaped to the United States in 1970. Cary hadn't seen him since she was five and hadn't had contact in years. But she decided it was best to tell the truth. After a fellow student lost his chance to study overseas because he withheld the information that his father lived in Florida, she was glad she'd revealed everything.

When Cary underwent a required medical checkup, a blood test showed she was anemic, a weakness that could have knocked her out of the program. By then, Zenaida had accepted Cary's decision to study on the other side of the world and she was willing to use her nursing skills to help her get there. She changed Cary's diet and fed her vitamins, nursing her back to health.

As for the *Titanic*, Zenaida reluctantly conceded she could do nothing to ensure Cary's safety but pray.

In mid-July 1976, just as the United States was celebrating its bicentennial, Cary waved to her mother and sister from the gangplank of the *Kazakhstan*, a large Soviet cruise ship docked in Havana Harbor that would carry her and two thousand other Cuban students across the ocean. "The ship was full of young people, Chinese, white, mulatto, black, all of us equal, with practically the same clothes, the same suitcases," she recalled fondly. The students shared the same vibrant sense of camaraderie as they departed for the land where communism had been founded and where, by all accounts Cary had read and heard, it was flourishing. More than sixty years after its own revolution, the U.S.S.R. represented an ideal that Cary, as a young believer in the new Cuba, whose family already had benefited from the changes that Castro imposed, aspired to. It was a dream come true, a tangible result of real social upheaval, not the kind of revolution the Beatles sang about, but one that changed the basic rules of society and made it possible for a poor black girl to get a degree at a foreign university.

As Cuban tugboats slowly pulled the *Kazakhstan* away from the dock, she could only imagine how much grander the ideal world she was heading to would be than the Cuba she was leaving behind.

CHAPTER 2

PINAR DEL RÍO

1958

The *mamoncillo* trees behind the house where Arturo Montoto lived with his five brothers and three sisters were mature enough to teach them a lesson in self-sufficiency. The children were already selling their mother's dried cod fritters and lemonade at construction sites. But their profits were limited because they had to buy the fish and lemons. When the *mamoncillos* in their yard were ripe enough to pick, they gathered bags of them without paying a centavo and boarded a bus to the city. The small tropical fruit the size of a large cherry was a favorite for city people who liked to crack open the tough outer skin with their teeth to get at the citrusy flesh inside.

They rode the bus past the large Catholic cemetery that marked the boundary between their neighborhood of Fenix and the city of Pinar del Río and continued up the tree-lined Alameda until they reached the top of Real Street. They jumped off there and walked down the hill, passing the India Hotel, the photo shops, and the Bank of Canada, until they came to El Fuego, the city's most elegant clothing emporium. Like other businesses, El Fuego had its name proudly embedded in the terrazzo floor. Arturo sat on the three steps leading to the store's main entrance, holding his bag of *mamoncillos*. He waited for the cool rush of air conditioning as the door opened and listened for the tap-tap-tap of women's high heels. "*¡Mamoncillos! ¡Mamoncillos!*" he then cried out, ready with a broad smile and the open bag of freshly harvested fruit that cost him nothing.

Arturo turned five when Fidel rode into Havana with his rebel army at the start of 1959, and for the first few years little changed in Fenix. Arturo's family lived in a humble wooden house with the *mamoncillo* trees in the yard and rain shutters on windows without glass. His father, Jesús, continued to repair shoes and, as a side business, make espadrilles out of canvas and rubber. His mother, Elena, was a domestic worker when she wasn't pregnant. Growing up the second youngest of nine children on the border where the city met the countryside, Arturo developed a sensitive eye for nature and an appreciation for physical labor and the tools used by those who work with their hands.

His curiosity and desire to learn sometimes led him to risky new worlds. In 1966, when he was thirteen, he found an English primer in a desk drawer in his school. At first, he didn't know what it was. He showed it to one of his teachers, who recognized it right away. The book was Leonardo Sorzano Jorrín's *Libro Primero de Inglés*. Generations of Cuban children had learned the fundamental rules of English from it before the revolution. But following the Bay of Pigs invasion in 1961 and the missile crisis the following year, English instruction had been replaced by Russian.

Arturo held the book in his hands, running his fingers over the cover. "I want to learn that," he told one of his teachers. "I want to learn English."

The teacher told him that he had studied the same book when he was a boy, but that using it was now forbidden. Still, seeing Arturo's interest, he agreed to teach him. In secret, they began with the first lesson: "Tom is a boy. Mary is a girl." Teaching the language of the enemy could cost the teacher his job, or worse, and there would also be repercussions for Arturo, but before either of them got into trouble, Arturo's father was given a job in a hospital in the mountains of Pinar del Río, and he moved the family there. Arturo lost contact with the teacher, but he stumbled on a different English instructor, one with a distinctly American accent.

From the northern coast of Pinar del Río, radio signals from Florida came in so loud and clear that even the old RCA Victor radio he listened to at home picked up broadcasts from Key West. Instead of tuning in to Cuban radio, with its heavy dose of Marxism, Arturo devoured American rock and roll even though it was a dangerous thing for a young Cuban to do. The Key West Hit Parade served as his instructor in both the English language and American pop culture. Arturo let his hair grow, hoping to look like the pictures of John Lennon he saw on the covers of albums that were smuggled into Cuba. Long hair or tight blue jeans made a young man suspect, either of being pro-yanqui or of being homosexual, and Castro's government jailed both.

He was constantly told that he had to fight against the enemy and to be on guard because that enemy could "come from within." Cubans who dared to think differently feared more than anything else their ever-present neighborhood CDR. The president of each local CDR was the person to whom neighborhood snitches reported. They kept track of who had not attended a May Day parade, who listened to the baseball game while Fidel was speaking on the radio, who had an illegal satellite dish hidden under a barrel on the roof, and passed along the information to Fidel's feared Stasi- and KGB-trained Interior Ministry. The CDR president had what some called the power of "*fusilamiento del dedo*," literally "to execute with a finger" by pointing out and denouncing anyone suspected of counterrevolutionary activities, depending on how the regime defined such things at the time. Simply allowing someone to use your telephone to call a relative in Miami could trigger a denunciation and ruin a life. The surveillance network was so pervasive that Cubans grew fearful of voicing any complaint. Even in their own homes, they refrained from mentioning the name Fidel, in case anyone was listening. Instead, they stroked an imaginary beard when they dared to criticize el comandante.

Arturo was uprooted again when the revolutionary government modified the educational system to force high school students to spend time in boarding schools, where they worked in the countryside while they studied. It was part of the revolution's idea of creating "the new man," an independent, self-sufficient individual—modeled after Ernesto "Che" Guevara—who was willing to work to the best of his abilities for the betterment of the whole society. Students at Arturo's school were given the assignment of planting trees on hills that had been denuded by charcoal burners. After a day spent outside, his classmates complained bitterly about the calluses on their hands and fell into deep sleep without bothering with the schoolwork they had been as-signed. Not Arturo. He took out paper and charcoal pencils and drew. He had no formal art training, but he had studied the comic-strip classics in the Sun-day newspapers and was intrigued by the visual way they told their tales. He marveled at how characters sometimes were drawn in profile as they spoke. In other panels, they faced the reader. And in some, they were not even shown on the page.

Years later, he applied to the provincial school of arts. His grades were excellent and his teachers wrote sterling recommendations. During an ad-mission interview, he was asked to name a few important artists he admired.

He thought for a few seconds before answering. Then, the poor kid from a poor neighborhood who'd never been to a museum admitted he couldn't think of any.

"None at all?"

He felt his opportunity slipping away. Desperate, he mentioned the names of the artists who drew the comic strips he admired.

"Those are not artists," the professor huffed. "They're illustrators. I'm talk-ing about an important person in the history of art."

The only art instruction he'd received was a correspondence course that had been advertised in the Cuban magazine *Bohemia*. How was he supposed to know anything about famous artists? He sat silently, desperately trying to think of a name. Then it came to him.

"Sure, *profe*. I know a famous artist," he said. "The Florentine Giant." That was the title of a comic strip based on the life of Leonardo da Vinci that he had read long before.

ARTURO WAS ADMITTED to the provincial art school and in 1973 won a schol-arship to Cuba's newly created National School of Art in Havana. A decade earlier, Fidel and Che Guevara had been playing golf at the Havana Country Club and, in the kind of spontaneous decision that was not unusual in those heady revolutionary days when they had an entire rich country to do with what they pleased, the two leaders decided that Cuba needed an art school.

Not used

And the posh country club that the revolutionary government had confiscated from its private owners was the perfect place for it. Cuban architect Ricardo Porro and two Italian architects came up with a fantastic design— outrageously sensuous—for interconnected schools of music, dance, and visual arts. To house the different schools, they had conceived of a series of Catalan domes that were said to suggest women's breasts. A fountain in an interior courtyard was shaped like a papaya, which has a sexual meaning in Cuba, and the passageways evoked fallopian tubes. The project design won international acclaim, but when spending priorities shifted toward defense after the Bay of Pigs, the project clashed with the Soviet-style functionalism that Cuba was embracing. The regime turned against the architects, arresting one of the Italians and charging him with spying. Porro went into exile in England, and the art school campus was never completed. By the time Arturo started taking classes there, Porro's brick buildings and connecting hallways had already started to deteriorate.

None of that mattered to the young artist. He was painting every day and enjoying a level of luxury he'd never imagined. The Havana Country Club had been one of the most exclusive venues in Cuba, a place once so rigidly aristocratic that even the dictator Batista, because he was a mulatto from a humble Oriente family, for a time had been denied full membership. The students lived in mansions that had been left vacant when their owners—wealthy businessmen, government officials, and others of the privileged classes—fled Cuba, leaving everything behind.

The grounds contained sprawling gardens that reminded Arturo of the Pinar del Río countryside. He spent much of his time in a huge attic experimenting with different styles while he explored color, light, and perspective. At the outset of the revolution, Fidel had made it clear that Cuban artists were free to create whatever they wanted so long as they did not contradict the ideological principles he had imposed. "*Dentro de la revolución, todo. Contra la revolución, nada*" was his mantra. "Within the revolution, everything. Against it, nothing." Cuban artists enjoyed greater artistic freedom than artists in other socialist countries, where the function of art was largely restricted to praising workers and the system that supported them. Arturo took advantage of that official tolerance while avoiding politics altogether. Copies of *Artforum* and *Art in America* magazines still circulated on campus and, in their pages, he discovered and was inspired by the work of Andy Warhol, Robert Rauschenberg, and Jackson Pollock.

As an artist in a Cuba largely closed off from the rest of the world, Arturo's best bet for a career after graduation was teaching art. He remained on campus to pursue a graduate degree, defending his portfolio in front of Antonio Vidal, a well-known Cuban artist, who nominated him for a scholarship at the prestigious V. I. Surikov Moscow State Academic Art Institute. But before he left for the Soviet Union in 1978, Arturo was dragged into a confrontation that disillusioned him about the Cuba that the revolution had created.

He had joined the Young Communist League when he was just thirteen, motivated not by any sympathy with communism, but by a country boy's innate pragmatism. Belonging to the group brought privileges and opened doors. One day, the head of the Young Communist League at the art school, a student named Lorenzo, called him into his office to tell him he'd heard of students who were engaging in counterrevolutionary activities.

"What are they doing?" Arturo asked.

They were involved in unauthorized mysticism that was leading them away from the socialist ideology of the revolution.

They were practicing yoga.

Lorenzo wanted Arturo to find out who they were and then to use the "*fusilamiento del dedo*" to denounce them publicly, leading to their expulsion from the school.

Arturo had been painted into a corner. Doing what Lorenzo wanted would put him in good standing with the league, but it violated his sense of fairness. If he refused, he could lose his scholarship to Moscow. To complicate things, he was sure he already knew some of the offending students. Not long before, he'd run into his good friend Alejandro, with whom he often shared books and discussed the ideas in them. Alejandro had tried to hide a book he was carrying behind his back. Arturo asked him what was going on.

"I'll level with you," Alejandro had said. "It's a book that you can't read."

You can't even see it. They can punish me if they catch me with it, but it would be far worse for you because you're in the young communists and I'm not."

Arturo figured the book had to have been a yoga manual and that Alejandro had tried to shield him by hiding it. There was no way Arturo would turn him in. He went back to Lorenzo to try to reason with him but got nowhere. Lorenzo accused him of attempting to protect the offending students and swore he'd have Arturo thrown out of the Young Communist League, which would cost him his Moscow scholarship.

Arturo didn't know much about yoga, but he was quickly learning about the ways a communist system could set its hooks into people who strayed from a strict ideological line, or who simply were different. He stormed into Lorenzo's office and warned him to back off. Whatever he threatened to do to Lorenzo if he didn't drop the issue seemed to have worked. A short while later, Arturo was summoned to a regional meeting of young communists, fully expecting to be tossed out of the league and blocked from going to Moscow. But the meeting adjourned without reaching a decision. No one told him what had been discussed inside, but it didn't matter to Arturo. He already knew enough about Cuban-style communism to be determined to keep it at arm's length, though he wasn't against taking advantage of the opportunities it offered.

CHAPTER 3

UKRAINE, U.S.S.R.
1976

Kiev was a long way from Tacajó, and despite what Cary had told herself about her own strengths and ambitions, the strange new sights, sounds, and smells of a foreign land took a toll on her. She was lonely, and she wondered if she had made the right decision. When Zenaida wrote to her, she warned her that she risked forgetting what it meant to be Cuban if she stayed away too long. She kept her up to date about Esperanza's classes and the young men she was seeing. She also reminded Cary that her boyfriend, Miguel, was waiting for her back home.

Cary's upbeat spirit came close to failing her. Some days, only the words to "Pregúntale a las estrellas" kept her from spinning out of control. Then, about three months after she arrived in Kiev, her friend Alina came to her room with some exciting news: she'd run into a guy Cary had been looking for since she'd landed in the U.S.S.R.

That first day in the land of Lenin had been a real letdown. After twenty-two stomach-turning days at sea, Cary stood on the deck of the *Kazakhstan* and looked out over the city of Odessa, where she was supposed to switch to a small plane bound for Kiev. The day was bleak and damp. For as far as she could see, the waterfront was stacked with ugly rows of shipping containers and nothing but warehouses, factories, and industrial cranes. She was so disappointed. Maybe she'd made a gigantic mistake leaving Cuba.

Then she heard something weird but familiar coming from the Odessa docks. It was a few young voices singing "Guantanamera." Cary refocused her eyes after the long sea voyage and saw where the strange sound was coming from. A group of Cuban students stood on the dock singing. They looked and sounded happy, despite the grayness. Who knows, she thought, maybe they also had been disappointed at first, and if they eventually got used to the cold and gray, maybe she could too. But first she had something important to take care of. Almost every day during the three-week crossing she had written a letter to Miguel, and now she needed envelopes to mail them to him in Havana. Her eyes settled on a skinny, light-skinned young man who seemed to be in charge. "I need a favor," she told him.

"Don't worry," the skinny guy said, and before she could object, he rushed off to buy the envelopes with his own money. She sealed her love letters and sent them back to Cuba. But, she admitted to Alina, the skinny guy was cute.

She had to put him out of her mind and focus on getting to the university in Kiev. She and three other Cuban students grabbed their cardboard suitcases, which were identical but for the color—blue for Cary and Marisela, beige for José and Alberto. Their sameness was a reassuring sign of what Fidel had promised when he said, "Revolution is equality and full liberty." They boarded a small plane to Kiev.

It was months later when Alina told Cary she'd seen the skinny guy at a dorm party. She had found out that he was from Cárdenas and was studying in the school of mechanical engineering, right there in Kiev. Cary decided to go to the next party, and when she knocked on the dorm-room door, the skinny guy opened it and introduced himself. "My name is Jesús Fidel Matienzo. Fidel," he boasted, "same as el comandante!"

Jesús Fidel had begun his studies in Kiev a year before Cary arrived, making the voyage across the ocean in an aging Rossiya-class Soviet cruise ship. He had been in Odessa on vacation during the summer when her ship tied up, and he had helped organize the impromptu welcoming ceremony. He too felt that their brief meeting had stirred up something, but like her, he hadn't expected their paths to cross again.

Cary fell for Jesús Fidel, and once she got to know him, he confessed that he had deceived her about his name. He had been given the second name Fidel not to honor the rebel leader but because he had been born on April 24, the feast day of Saint Fidelis. Anyway, nobody in Cárdenas called him Jesús or Fidel. Everyone knew him as Pipo, a popular Cuban nickname. He may have fibbed about his links to Castro, but he believed with all his heart in the revolution that had transformed his life. Before 1959, his father sold fruits and vegetables at the Plaza Malakoff in the center of Cárdenas, and his mother stayed at home with their growing family. After 1959, she enrolled in university and became an elementary school teacher. His father was given a job as a lineman with the railroad, and when he moved into a leadership position he won the right to a big apartment attached to the train terminal in Cárdenas. Pipo and his four brothers and sisters grew up there, and when he was fourteen, he joined the Young Communist League.

Cary had been disappointed when Pipo didn't ask her to dance at the dorm party, but she was delighted when she found out that he was a whiz with numbers. Besides struggling with Russian spelling and grammar, she was having trouble with the advanced math in her economics classes. They started studying together, and when she finally ended her long-distance romance with Miguel, her relationship with Pipo blossomed.

Cary entered the program for economic engineering and focused on light industry, specializing in textiles and clothing manufacturing. She initially moved into a suite with other Cubans, but soon realized that if she stayed there, she'd never learn to dominate Lenin's language. She switched rooms, joining women who were native Russian speakers. Marxism notwithstanding, Cary soon found out that they were more different than alike. One day early in her stay, one of her Russian roommates was visited by her friend Tanya, who was from the Soviet Republic of Azerbaijan. After Cary introduced herself, Tanya peppered her with questions, curious about life in exotic Cuba. Cary described the Cuba she had left behind, and the new socialist world that she was going to help construct when she returned.

That was great, but what Tanya really wanted to know was whether, in the blue cardboard suitcase she had carried from Cuba, Cary had brought a pair of "American *jeanskis*."

"Come again?"

"You must have a pair of American jeans with you, don't you?"

This was at the height of Fidel's intolerance of bourgeois Western culture and anything that seemed to glorify American values. Cary was surprised that her new friend envied American blue jeans and was even more shocked that she expected a Cuban communist like her to own something so closely linked to capitalist culture. When she got together later with her Cuban classmates, she told them what Tanya had asked her, and they all had their own stories of the Russians' "peculiar ideology."

"These Russians don't think the way we do," she told her friends.

She got another surprise on her first May Day in Kiev when she and a few Cuban friends headed to the main plaza for the International Workers' Day parade. The May 1 celebration of workers' rights had always been a huge day in Cuba. Cary'd take a bus to the Plaza de la Revolución in Havana and stand there until the sun came up, waiting for Fidel to speak. He would go on for three or four hours, and when he finished, she and her friends stayed to drink rum and dance. In Kiev, her Russian roommates mocked the Cubans for wanting to waste their time going to the local parade. When Cary came back from the plaza, she turned on the TV to watch Soviet leader Leonid Brezhnev's speech. One of her Russian roommates got up and turned off the television.

"Why'd you do that?" Cary was confused.

"Who wants to listen to that old man?" the girl answered in Russian.

Brezhnev then was secretary general of the Communist Party, and a Ukrainian to boot. In Cary's mind, he was the U.S.S.R.'s Fidel, and she felt they were obliged to watch him on TV.

"Don't come to our country and tell us what to do," the Russian snapped at her.

Cary later wrote to tell her mother she didn't know what kind of communists her roommates were, but she knew they certainly were not like Cuban communists.

In the spring of 1979, the year before he received his degree in electromechanical engineering, Pipo organized a school trip to Moscow. While the other students toured Red Square, he and Cary walked to the Cuban embassy, where they were married in a binding civil ceremony. Zenaida had demanded that they be formally married. It was an old-fashioned attitude for revolutionary Cuba, but she knew from experience with Aristede that a common law marriage could be dissolved with nothing more than too much rum or a flirty smile. Despite the thousands of miles separating them, Cary dared not disobey her mother's command. Besides, she had already decided that Pipo was the man for her. He was smart and kind, filled with kinetic energy and good humor. She also knew that his parents had been together for decades. She was determined to have a different kind of married life than her mother or her grandmother, who had raised their children on their own. Their friends arranged for them to have a private berth on the train back to Kiev, and once there, the couple threw a big wedding party. They even hired a local photographer, and when he put one of their photos in his studio window, local people who'd rarely seen black faces gawked at it.

Cary's roommates moved out so that she and Pipo could live together in the dorm. She finished her studies a year after he did and returned to Cuba a married woman with an advanced degree in economics and the promise of a job. The five years she'd spent in the land of Lenin had opened her eyes to a world far larger than she had imagined. Her time there also helped her realize that communism had ideological variations. She learned about the extent of political commitment, and the power and privilege that went with party loyalty. Pipo was intent on advancing up the ranks of the Communist Party, and he pressured her to get her own red card because, as he often asked, how would it look if the wife of a party loyalist didn't belong to the party?

During her time in Kiev, Cary also discovered some important things about herself. In 1978 she had become pregnant, but when she was just twelve weeks along, she had to be rushed to the hospital. When a nurse checked on her after the miscarriage, Cary asked if the baby had been a boy or a girl. It was too early to tell, the nurse told her. Then she mentioned a word in Russian that Cary did not understand.

Bliznets.

She found out later what the nurse was saying.

Bliznets.

Twins.

CHAPTER 4

MOSCOW, U.S.S.R.
1978

Arturo Montoto spent six years in Moscow, painting, studying Russian, and sitting through endless classes in Marxist theory. He came to understand that Cuba had somehow invented its own form of communism, one that was different from the Soviet system in both substance and spirit. It wasn't simply that Cuba was considered part of the nonaligned movement, or that Fidel had just assumed leadership of that group. The two countries operated in fundamentally different ways. Although the Communist Party of Cuba held supreme power, Cuba was being run according to the personal ideology of Fidel Castro and his family. Some called it *castrismo*, and others just got used to saying, "this thing." It was a mash-up of socialist concepts shaped by Fidel's obstinate will. Havana took money from Moscow, lots of it, but Fidel rarely took orders from the Kremlin.

His first few months in Moscow were so depressing and stressful that Arturo was nearly hospitalized. Things turned around for him when he fell in love with a fellow art student, a Russian woman whose name was Elena, just like his mother. Before he finished his first full year at Surikov, his girlfriend gave birth to their daughter, who they also named Elena. He turned thirty while in Moscow and was expected to move up from the Young Communist League that he had belonged to for seventeen years to the Communist Party of Cuba. Just as he'd understood the benefits of belonging to the party when he was thirteen, he knew that membership would help make his career as an artist more secure. Few options were available for a young Cuban artist at that time. The Cuban art market barely existed, and the only painters whose work sold had made their reputations long before the revolution—and even they weren't earning much. "We didn't have any pretensions about being famous artists or making a lot of money," he recalled. "We just focused on learning as much as we could about art. We wanted to get better at what we were doing." The only practical career path was teaching, and belonging to the Communist Party would give him a head start on a position with prestige to equal his training and expertise. But he'd seen too much, from the attempt to entrap the art students who practiced yoga to the constant surveillance he'd lived under in Moscow, to remain loyal to an ideology he found abhorrent. When Cuban officials asked him to explain why he wanted to leave the party after it had done so much for him, he told them that, frankly, joining the Young Communist League had been a mistake, one he sincerely regretted.

He returned to Cuba in 1984 without his Russian girlfriend, his Russian daughter, or his Communist Party membership card. He also had no clear expectation of what lay in his future. Like other students who came back to Cuba with their foreign degrees, he had to wait for the government to give him a job. When he heard from the state, he was given a choice of teaching art to elementary school children in the province of Camagüey, in the center of the country, or on the Isle of Pines, off the southern coast, which the government had renamed Isle of Youth. Acting with the kind of presumptuousness typical of Cubans, he refused to take either position. "I don't want you to think that I am vain or thinking too much of myself," he told his superiors. In Moscow he'd been awarded the official title of muralist, the only Cuban so honored, and he felt he was overqualified to teach art to young children. He agreed wholeheartedly that it was important for them to learn to appreciate art, but plenty of others who hadn't spent six years at Surikov could help them do that.

Because of special indulgences that Cuba afforded some artists, he won that battle, but he did not get the prestigious position he thought he deserved. He was sent to work taking photographs for a school in Havana where he also was expected to teach photography to the children. It was far from the painting that was his passion, but having turned down the other positions, he had little choice but to accept this one and get on with his life. But first he needed to find a place to live.

He had no desire to go back to Pinar del Río, and he couldn't get into student housing at the art school. The heart of Havana was already so overcrowded with people pouring in from the provinces that it was impossible to find a decent place to live and work. He decided to join his younger brother, Juan, who was living opposite Old Havana in a curiosity shop of a town called Guanabacoa that reminded him of the Fenix neighborhood in Pinar del Río, where the city and the countryside met. In Guanabacoa, one of Havana's fifteen boroughs, he found colonial churches, formal town squares, and, on the outskirts, acres of subsistence farms. And yet he was close enough to get to Havana, where he worked, even if it took a long time.

Guanabacoa had been absorbed bureaucratically into the capital decades earlier, but it very much remained apart from what Havana represented. Nestled among modest hills so rich in minerals that, in the early nineteenth century, they caught the attention of Alexander von Humboldt as he explored Cuba, the town was almost as old as Havana itself. Throughout its history, Guanabacoa had been overshadowed by its world-famous neighbor, but being second didn't mean it was without pretension. In the early sixteenth century, it was known as "*el pueblo de Indios de Guanabacoa*" (the indigenous community of Guanabacoa). Historians believe it consisted of a small group of native Taino who had survived the cruelty and diseases of the Spanish conquistadors, along with stragglers from other tribes from the Yucatan peninsula and Florida. In 1555, when Havana was attacked by the French pirate Jacques de Sores, the seat of government in Cuba was briefly moved to Guanabacoa, giving rise to the saying, "Like putting Havana in Guanabacoa," which Cubans use when someone tries to stuff something too big into a space too small. The town liked to brag about its role in major events in Cuban history, ranging from the 1762 invasion of Cuba by the British—when its mayor, known as Pepe Antonio, led local residents to block the advancing British troops—to the vicious street fighting in the uprising against Batista. Its streets inspired Rita Montaner, one of Cuba's most popular singers, and Ernesto Lecuona, a classical composer. The popular entertainer known as Bola de Nieve grew up not far from the center of town. Despite its colorful history, few tourists or national politicians ventured there, and its eccentric mix of African secret societies and Christian religions, along with two Jewish cemeteries, made it a symbol of the complexity of Cuban culture. Even after it lost its seacoast in a 1976 restructuring, and its ancient urban core became sadly neglected, it was officially designated part of Cuba's historic patrimony.

Arturo settled into a small shack he built in a rough section of town where the streets were not paved, roosters greeted the dawn, and rum flowed more reliably than the municipal water supply. He was an outsider to his neighbors, most of whom hadn't gone to school past the ninth grade. But he appreciated the simplicity of their lives, and they respected him. When, after a few years, he took a position teaching painting at the Superior Institute of Art he once attended, his neighbors started calling him "El Profe," the professor.

He taught and painted, and they left him alone. Then one evening, on his way back from class, he passed an outdoor gathering and heard someone calling him. "Profe, come here." He had stumbled into a nominating session for a local election. Cuba had recently revamped its contrived electoral system so that, at the local level where there was very little power, candidates for the largely ceremonial post of ward leader were nominated in neighborhood meetings.

We think you should run, they told him. He shook his head no, his long, uncombed hair twisting from side to side. "Look at me," he said. He was the model of a bohemian artist, just slightly better dressed than the legendary Gentleman of Paris who roamed downtown Havana in a cape and rags until he died in 1985. Arturo's pants were baggy, his shoes scuffed and worn, and his attitude toward the Castro government anything but loyal. "You don't want me," he said.

But they insisted. One of his neighbors raised his hand and asked for permission to speak. "I propose El Profe." The man described Arturo in vague terms that offended no one and were only partially true, calling him a fine artist who had graduated from a fancy foreign art school, a patriot, and a true revolutionary. Not a word was mentioned about his actual political views, which were anything but aligned with Castro's regime. With a unanimous show of hands, it was settled. Arturo Montoto became a candidate for delegate in the municipality of Guanabacoa. He had his photograph taken, and he provided facts for the single-page biography that was the only campaign literature any candidate was allowed to prepare. He could not hold any campaign rallies. He was prohibited from running ads in the newspaper, and he was not given any opportunity to appear on TV to outline any program. In this version of Cuban elections, voters had to make their decision solely on the biographies posted at the voting places.

People on the committee who tallied the votes told Arturo that actually he had gotten the most votes. But you have to understand, they told him, that it was important for the sitting delegate to stay in office.

Arturo was relieved. He would have made a terrible delegate; he knew that. He never thought of himself as qualified to represent his neighbors, but he felt accepted by the town's residents and was impressed by its culture and history. When he was approached by the Guanabacoa Municipal Museum to take photographs for an architectural history project, he jumped at the chance. Even as Guanabacoa was transformed into a center of light industry in the twentieth century, it retained many of its historic buildings and long-standing traditions. From the municipal building, facing the Central Park, up to where it meets the Vía Blanca, José Martí Avenue—the most important street in town—was lined with historic buildings, many with architecturally significant facades. María Eugenia López Rossitch, a local architect whose family had owned a factory in Guanabacoa before the revolution, had been hired to survey building styles along Martí. Her work would serve as a blueprint for preserving Guanabacoa's heritage, at one time considered to be as rich as that of Trinidad, a colonial gem in Cuba's south that was designated a UNESCO world heritage site in 1988. Arturo took photographs of the buildings to accompany her architectural assessments. Working together so closely, they struck up a personal relationship that led to marriage. They settled not quite in the city, and not quite in the countryside.

In Guanabacoa.

CHAPTER 5

GUANABACOA

1979

For as long as María del Carmen López Álvarez could remember, the past had remained alive inside her old house near the center of Guanabacoa, and traditions were ever present around her. She and her parents lived there with her great-aunt María del Carmen, after whom she had been named, and who was the living representation of a lost past. The old woman called her "Mari," and she called her "Great-aunt Tata." They shared the same name and—despite the great difference in age—many of the same passions. When she was just a girl, she listened, wide-eyed, to Tata's tales of imperial Spain, the wars of the monarchs of Castile and Aragon, and sometimes the stories of their own family as they carved out a new life in Cuba before Tata's father, Mari's great-grandfather, died of what they called apoplexy. Then one day when Mari was a young adult, Tata told her the scandalous truth.

"Swear that you will never tell anyone what I tell you," Tata said, her voice light as the wind from a butterfly's wings. "What I said about my father's apoplexy? That was not real. What is true is that after he lost everything, Papi was so ashamed that he killed himself."

For a Catholic family in Cuba, suicide once was an unmentionable event, a stain to be kept hidden. But the shame that led Mari's great-grandfather to kill himself so many years before was misplaced. The loss of the family fortune was a temporary setback. His real legacy was the little house on Corralfalso

Street that became a polestar for generations of his descendants. It was not the oldest house in Guanabacoa, and it was far from the grandest. But it had a good chance of being the house that has remained in the hands of the same family the longest—no small feat considering how property rights had been scrambled since 1959. When the government nationalized everything, from the largest office building to the smallest corner store, private houses were spared only if their owners lived in them.

From the outside, the old house seemed to be holding a vigil against time, gallantly defying the mounds of trash on Corralfalso and the general decay of everything around it. The heavy wooden front door, preserved under myriad coats of red paint, stood seven steps above the level of the street, insulating the cool, dark interior from the chaos outside. Still, when horses pulling decrepit wagons clip-clopped by, the sound streamed in through the glassless windows just as it must have a century and more before. The tile floor, shades of rose swirling with beige and a hint of pale green, were the same tiles that Mari's great-grandmother Eustoquia walked on as she tried to reconcile herself to a future she had neither dreamed of nor wanted. The tall glass chandelier, the same one that Eustoquia sat under pondering the well-being of her family after Cuban rebels vanquished the Spaniards to win Cuba's imperfect independence, still lit the front parlor when Mari had visitors. On one wall there was still a framed portrait of Mari as a young woman, dressed in the formal ruffles and collars of a Spanish dancer, a lacy *peineta* adorning her blond curls. Below the picture, on a marble pedestal, a graphite bust of a young Julius Caesar stared across the room at a plaster bust of Raphael, both sculptures created by Mari's mother when she was an art student. Mari's traditional wooden rocker faced another rocker just as it might have in Eustoquia's time, the two of them often enveloped by the aroma of freshly brewed Cuban coffee, insanely sweet, served in tiny cups any time of the day or night.

In the dining room, a small jug the color of an aging rind of cheese sat in plain view. Tata told Mari many tales about that jar while waiting for sleep to come to them both. It was in the second half of the nineteenth century that Eustoquia, her mother, had departed from the Asturian port of Gijón, in the north of Spain, on a harrowing monthlong journey in a flimsy wooden barque to meet her betrothed husband in the colony of Cuba, Spain's fabled New World jewel. An arduous passage under the best of circumstances, the bobbing and rocking were so violent that when she disembarked in Havana, Eustoquia vowed never to board another ship. Most of her dowry was lost in the storm, all but the orange jar that originally had been filled with date preserves.

Eustoquia was brought to the house of relatives in Guanabacoa, where they prepared her for the wedding. She was to marry a Spanish tailor who had a thriving workshop in the city. Most of Spain's New World colonies had already won their independence, but Cuba was too precious for Madrid to give up without a fight. Besides, many wealthy Cubans, most with European roots, still worried that, with the island's teeming black population, independence would turn Cuba into another Haiti.

The wedding was held at the Church of the Holy Spirit, the oldest in the city. Throughout the ceremony the uneasy groom's face was contorted with fever. Doctors had to be called. They diagnosed smallpox, and three days later, Eustoquia became a widow, the name of her husband lost to history.

The young widow quickly drew the attention of another Asturian who was in Cuba without a wife. Juan Manuel Álvarez y Álvarez lived on his coffee plantation in Colón, about 120 miles east of Havana. On his way to the capital for supplies, he passed through Guanabacoa and soon was attracted to Eustoquia's charms. A disciplined Catholic, she waited three years before returning to the altar. In no time, she sold her unlucky first husband's workshop in Havana and moved with Juan Manuel to his coffee plantation in Colón.

By April of the following year, Cuban rebels were closing in on Colón. One day, the quiet of the plantation was shattered when rebels galloped up to the main house and shouted for the family to surrender their horses. Juan Manuel refused to hand them over, telling the rebels that his horses had not been involved in any conflict with Cubans and neither would he, a Spaniard, allow them to be used against the monarchy. He drew his pistol and shot the horses dead. The rebels threatened to kill him, but his thirteen-year-old daughter—Mari's great-aunt Tata—stood between them and her father.

I may be the daughter of Spaniards, she declared, but I was born here, and I am just as Cuban as you.

The rebels turned their horses and left, but not before setting the family's house and fields on fire. Ruined financially and facing an uncertain future filled with war and retribution, Juan Manuel took his own life, leaving Eustoquia a widow for a second time.

Whenever Mari retold this majestic Cuban saga, she had to admit she didn't know how much of it was true. But she kept a yellowed document in a breakfront that confirmed at least some of it. With money that Juan Manuel had hidden from the rebels, his widow bought a house in Guanabacoa, where she had family and where support for the Spanish crown remained strong. The old deed shows that on April 28, 1897, when Eustoquia was forty-two years old, she paid the previous owner, Ángel Rigil y Peral, five hundred Spanish gold pesos and took possession of the house on Corralfalso, across from the religious compound of the Escolapios priests. Eustoquia made the move from Colón in two horse-drawn carriages, carrying the small orange jar that had survived the trip from Spain and whatever else she was able to salvage from the fire, including a large clay *tinajón*.

WHEN MARI WAS GROWING UP, that *tinajón* stood in the patio next to her doll house. She was not yet four, and Fidel was still a year away from victory, when her parents brought her to La Milagrosa, a Catholic school for girls a few blocks away. She was too young for regular classes, but she was old enough to try something they thought could keep her busy, as well as steep her in the lore of her ancestors—traditional Spanish dance.

Her parents kept her at La Milagrosa when she started regular classes. Castro was just consolidating his power then, and for a while the revolution was remote from her life. She was taught by the Daughters of Charity of St. Vincent de Paul, whose white linen cornettes were said to resemble a swallow's wings. It was when Mari was in the third grade that the revolution became real for her. That's when the Castro government seized all private schools and prohibited the teaching of religion. The sisters were sent away, and La Milagrosa was turned into a public high school. Mari was sent across Corralfalso to Los Escolapios, where a prestigious Catholic school for boys had become a coed public elementary school. The school buildings and convent dating back to the early eighteenth century became property of the Cuban government. But the church connected to them remained under control of the clergy.

On her first day at Los Escolapios, renamed Jesús Garay for a militiaman who died at the Bay of Pigs, Mari was one of only four girls in a class with more than twenty-five boys. She was as slender as she was spoiled, a timid girl with doting parents. Her only comfort in the new school was her familiarity with Los Escolapios. Every year, her parents had brought her across the street to the central courtyard, with its life-size statue of Jesus, to congratulate the pastor on his birthday.

When she was in the sixth grade, her mother surprised her with a light jacket she had designed and sewn herself. It was a gorgeous red, with tufts of white rabbit fur around the collar and the pockets. Any time before 1959, it would have been a stylish coat that a middle-class girl in Guanabacoa would have been thrilled to own. But when she got to school wearing the red jacket with the rabbit collar, her classmates mocked her, calling her *niña bitonga*, spoiled brat. She never wore that jacket to school again.

But she had a direct link to her own past that gave her the courage to stand up to the taunting. When Mari had turned seven years old, Tata—who never married or had children of her own—had given her a simple gold ring. Tata had received the ring as a gift from her mother on her seventh birthday, just as her mother, Eustoquia, had received it on her seventh birthday. It was a thin band with black enameling and small stones set in the images of a cross, a heart, and an anchor that represented faith, hope, and charity. Every day, when she went to the new government school where the other students sometimes made fun of her, Mari wore that ring.

MARI FACED ONE OF THE TOUGHEST decisions of her young life when she was ready to go to university, a test of both courage and faith. Cuban universities did not charge tuition, but they required a personal evaluation for admission, a test of scholastic aptitude and revolutionary attitude. On the day she was

interviewed, she was brought into a classroom where five questions were written on the blackboard. They were no surprise to her. She had been asked the
same questions since the ninth grade. Grades and personal discipline were no
problem, not for her. Activities? Spanish dance, of course. But question number five, at the bottom of the list, was the one that had made her lose sleep. She
knew that the way she responded to that question would affect her for the rest
of her life.

No. 5: Do you believe in God?

If she answered no, she became a strong candidate for membership in the
Young Communist League. Belonging would open many doors, just as Pipo
Matienzo and Arturo Montoto had discovered, and eventually it could pave
the way to membership in the Communist Party. Being admitted to a select
university in Cuba or in some other socialist country, being picked for a plum
job, moving up the wait list for a new apartment—all would be easier if she
just said no, even if it went against all that she stood for.

But saying yes would mark her as someone out of step with the revolution,
and there would be consequences, perhaps for life.

When it was her turn to be evaluated, Mari thought about her first communion in the chapel at La Milagrosa, and about the masses she had attended
at Los Escolapios, where she knew that Eustoquia, when she was alive, had
habitually attended the 6:15 A.M. mass. She thought about how her father had
never joined the Communist Party and when asked would say, "Only my pil-
low knows for sure what I think." When she answered the question about religious belief, she did it in a way that a few of her more politically attuned
friends had coached her.

"I do not think I have the qualifications to join the young communists,"
she said.

She had tried to lessen the impact of her refusal to renounce her religion,
but in the decades ahead she would come to realize that her life in Cuba had
been derailed at that moment. By rejecting the official ideology of Castro's
communism, and contradicting his dictate prohibiting belief in God, Mari
had challenged his entire system, and she paid a dear price for it. She was
denied the kind of education she desired, the career she longed for, and the

promotions that would have recognized her skills. She became an exile in her own country.

In her preuniversity classes, Mari had excelled in chemistry and she was keenly interested in microbiology. But instead of the top research center where she hoped to study, the only place that would admit her was a veterinary school. When she graduated, the Young Communist League evaluated her again, this time examining her aptitude for work to determine what kind of a job she'd get. They gave her high marks for academic achievement, but denigrated her revolutionary demeanor. Her review came down to a single word: apathy.

She wasn't a good communist.

She knew it was true. Even setting aside her unshakable religious convictions, her own personal nature rebelled against communist ideology and the public demonstrations of zealotry it seemed to demand. She hadn't been through the indoctrination that later became standard for Cuban schoolchildren. Dressed in white shirts with red or blue neckerchiefs, they recited the group's motto: "Pioneers for communism. Let us be like Che!" She never felt comfortable with the marching, shouting, and saluting that were expected at rallies. At the start of the Castro era, her parents believed that there were advantages to supporting the new regime, but as the government intruded more in their lives, their tolerance was stretched thin. When his family's small garage at the rear of his house on Corralfalso was seized, it was the last straw for her father. He had never openly criticized what was going on, but from then on, he refused to be a part of it. That was the way many Cubans reconciled themselves to what was happening all around them. They had cheered Fidel and his rebels as they fought Batista, but the real revolution came later with his turn toward communism. Mari's father did not allow politics to be discussed at the dinner table, and though he considered it a waste of time for his wife to belong to the Federation of Cuban Women, he kept his criticism to himself. Most of his energy he funneled into the one true passion of his otherwise buttoned-up life. Cars.

Before the revolution, Cuba had one of the highest per capita car ownership rates in the world. After 1959, it became much harder to import cars because of the U.S. embargo, but Cuba's car fever did not abate. Guanabacoa remained thick with cars. All types of cars: Cadillacs, Chevrolets, Dodges, and Oldsmobiles. Whale-tailed Plymouths. Buicks studded with artificial portholes, along with Fords, a few Studebakers, and some boxy British makes like Singers and Vauxhalls. Mari's father, Pedro José López, adored his family and treasured the old house that sheltered them. But nothing topped his infatuation with their prewar Ford. He fussed over the dark sedan obsessively and established a set of strict rules for its use. Whenever he drove, his wife sat beside him in the front seat and Mari, their only child, sat in back. No more than one other person could be allowed in the back seat with her, and whoever that was had to meet the weight requirements he set so as not to overburden the Ford's suspension. Mari grew up suspecting that although she was the shining light of her father's life, there probably were times when he loved his Ford more.

Mari loved the Ford because her father loved the Ford, but sometimes she was jealous of it. When she was coming of age, she begged him to teach her how to drive. Pedro was patient, but he wasn't comfortable with his Ford in the hands of anyone else, not even his only child. When a driving session ended, he would slide over to the driver's seat and wipe her sweat off the huge steering wheel. He wiped down the transmission lever too.

Eventually, getting spare parts turned into an ordeal, and it was inconceivable to Pedro to do what other Cubans routinely did—disgrace the original design of an American classic by stuffing in the gearbox of a Russian Lada or switching a Detroit V-8 for a tinny four cylinder made in Japan. He sold his Ford and never drove again.

The deeply conservative Catholic values that he passed along, combined with the legacy of Eustoquia, anchored Mari to the house on Corralfalso. When thousands of disaffected Cubans stormed the Peruvian embassy in Havana in 1980, prompting Castro to open Mariel Harbor to anyone who wanted to leave, she passed up a place that had been saved for her on a relative's boat. For the girl who once wore a rabbit-fur collar to a socialist school, remaining in Guanabacoa was uncomfortable, but leaving the house where she had always lived was unthinkable. Eustoquia's ceramic jar reminded her that although the Cuban government often dated history from 1959 forward, her roots ran far deeper. She often felt she was in the wrong place at the wrong time. And few pursuits could have left her more out of step with the revolution than celebrating the culture of the colonialists who had dominated Cuba for almost half a millennium.

But for Mari, classical Spanish dance became her world. The passion of her life. Her Ford.

INSTEAD OF CONTINUING IN MICROBIOLOGY, Mari was assigned in 1978 to the ministry in charge of Cuba's tuna fishing fleet, overseeing mundane yet necessary inspections for food safety. The humdrum work was a pale version of the sophisticated science she had dreamed of doing, but there was a silver lining. The tuna fleet docked on the Havana waterfront, a bus ride away from Guanabacoa. That meant she could continue living in the old house on Corralfalso. Every morning, she took the pokey 95 bus from Guanabacoa, getting off in Old Havana in front of the Egido market, a short walk from the waterfront. She soon discovered that half a block from the bus stop in the other direction, nestled between the market and an apartment building, was the chapel of Santo Cristo de Limpias, which was dedicated to a twentieth-century miracle. In 1919, crowds of devout Catholics had jammed the church of St. Peter in the village of Limpias, Spain, to witness the statue of the crucified Christ that was said to move its eyes and shed drops of blood. Capuchin monks had built the chapel in Havana in the 1940s and kept it open during the darkest years of religious persecution under Castro.

Mari usually finished work at 5:15 P.M. Sometimes she kept walking past the bus stop to the chapel so she could chat with Padre Jacinto, the resident monk, before six o'clock mass started. She'd try to slip into and out of the chapel without anyone seeing her. She didn't need another negative mark on her record. Then one day when she was heading to see Padre Jacinto, she spotted him speaking with someone else. Her first impulse was to run away, but when the priest heard the click of her heels, he turned around and saw her. So did the person to whom he was speaking. Mari recognized him. She had seen his wavy hair and rugged features on one of the tuna boats. He seemed just as surprised to see her there as she was to see him. Their eyes met, and when both realized that they had come to the same forbidden place for the same reason, an understanding arose between them.

After that day, whenever they saw each other at work, they exchanged the smiles of people complicit in a shared secret. Román Calvo was Catholic like her, born in Guanabacoa as she had been, and he too had begun his education in a Catholic school. He and Mari hadn't known each other before, but now they recognized that not only were they working together, they shared the same willingness to risk punishment for their faith. He had planned to study mathematics in the university, but instead he fell in love with the sea. He never rose higher in rank than captain because he refused to join the Communist Party, a consequence of personal integrity that Mari recognized immediately.

CHAPTER 6

OLD HAVANA

1981

S oon after Cary returned from Kiev with a husband, a degree in economic engineering, and an understanding of the differences between Soviet communism and the Cuban system she believed in, she was given her first job. A telegram directed her to show up at the offices of the textile industry in Old Havana and report to the chief of personnel in the children's clothing division.

"Who are you?" the chief asked when she walked into the office on O'Reilly Street in what, decades later, would become the heart of Old Havana's tourist district.

"An engineer," Cary said.

"Engineer?" He stared at the young black woman. "What kind of engineer are you?"

When she explained that she had graduated from the University of Kiev with a degree in economic engineering, the personnel chief looked puzzled.

"What's that?" he asked, repeating the question that Cary's mother had raised five years earlier. "Either you are an economist or you're an engineer."

She told him she had been trained in the most modern methods of organizing production and maximizing the efficiency of work.

He looked puzzled. If she was an economist, he'd know where to place her. The same if she was an engineer. But this strange new category, imported from overseas, had him temporarily stumped. "All right," he said at last, just to move on. "We'll find something."

She was put to work on salaries and workflow, figuring out such things as how many blouses or sheets a seamstress was expected to sew in a day, and what the material and salary requirements would be for that worker. Her training in Kiev enabled her to handle the work so proficiently that she was quickly promoted. And as she rose in the ranks of the ministry, she was pressured to get more involved in the Communist Party. Cary was twenty-eight, a dedicated worker and a true believer in what Cuba had become, but she wasn't sure she wanted to get involved in the political side of communist life. Pipo had been encouraging her to join the Communist Party since they were in Kiev, but when she had asked her mother what she should do, Zenaida insisted that she'd already given enough to the state. Cary told her she wanted to do all she could to help Cuba, but her mother said she was being foolish, that she didn't really understand what Cuba was truly becoming.

While Cary had been out of the country Cuba had changed, and many people—not just the well-to-do families that had gone into exile right after Fidel took over—had grown weary of waiting for the revolution to fulfill its promises. She was still in Kiev during the long, ugly standoff at the Peruvian embassy that triggered the Mariel crisis. She hadn't seen the surly criminals being let out of their prison cells or the bewildered mentally ill patients who were pushed out of their asylums and forced, on Fidel's orders, to board the boats that had come from Miami to collect the antisocial scum that he was only too glad to be rid of. Zenaida admitted that she too had grown tired of the revolution and had been tempted to leave with all the others. But she didn't want to go while Cary was so far away. And there was another reason: the discrimination she had experienced working with Americans at the Guantanamo base had made her wary of the United States.

The bottom line, she told Cary, is beware: Cuba isn't the place you think it is. Then one day she did something that confused and disturbed Cary. She waddled over to her dresser and came back with something in her hand. "You see this?" Zenaida held up a battered blue Jamaican passport that her own mother, Sarah Ann Ewen, had presented when she landed in Cuba in 1922. In it was the photo of a young black woman staring into a future she both craved and feared. "Someday, if you decide to look for a way to get out of Cuba, you have this," she said. Her message was clear. Your grandmother left home to search for opportunity, and someday you may need to do the same.

Cary was deeply offended. It was inconceivable that she'd ever consider herself anything but Cuban, and leaving her beloved homeland was beyond unthinkable. Disregarding her mother's cautions and complaints, she simultaneously joined the Young Communist League and the Communist Party. She also became active in the Federation of Cuban Women after helping Raúl Castro's wife, Vilma Espín, set up a project in Old Havana called Quitrín. It provided job opportunities for women sewing traditional Cuban clothing, mostly billowy white dresses and men's crisp white guayabera shirts. Cary greatly admired Espín, who had fought in the Sierra with Fidel and Raúl, and who had become an outspoken advocate for women in the new Cuban society.

By immersing herself in the system so thoroughly, Cary hoped to avoid some of the obstacles her mother had encountered in her life. Zenaida had never joined the Communist Party, and when she needed help she had no one to advocate for her. And nowhere had she suffered more, and needed more help, than in her perpetual search for a place to live.

Housing was a long-standing problem in Cuba. As early as 1953, after his attack on the Moncada barracks failed and he was thrown into prison, Fidel had promised that once he succeeded he would wipe out the "infernal *cuarterías*" and overcrowded tenements and replace them with so many houses and modern apartment buildings that Cuba's severe housing shortage would be just a bad memory. For a brief time after 1959 it looked like he might be able to keep that promise. The new government confiscated private houses and apartment buildings from owners who had gone into exile, properties like the houses where Arturo Montoto and other art students lived after Batista fled. All investment properties were taken over, even if their owners remained in Cuba, which was what happened to María del Carmen's family when her uncle Virgilio's garage and the property adjacent to the house on Corralfalso were seized. Without paying the owners anything, the regime redistributed their properties, often splitting a single house into multiple dwellings without regard to building codes or safety. The exodus of more than 750,000 exiles in those early years had freed up valuable living space and made Castro popular with all those who moved into the vacant houses and apartments. But the need for housing remained enormous, especially in Havana, where families like Cary's from the eastern end of the country flooded in despite government attempts to keep them in the provinces.

Castro focused his most ambitious building efforts on the outskirts of Havana, putting up countless Soviet-style five-story apartment blocks. He seemed to turn his back on the old capital and the colonial past it represented, allowing the dignified buildings in Old Havana and the newer ones in the Vedado neighborhood to fall into ruin. At the same time, he eagerly confiscated monumental works of his predecessors and claimed them as his own. The Plaza de la Revolución, one of the most visible images of the communist government, had actually been completed by Batista's government in 1958 and was originally known as the Plaza Cívica. Fidel renamed it and tacked the iconic profiles of Che and Camilo Cienfuegos, a popular rebel commander, on the facades of the bland office buildings surrounding the monumental space. Elsewhere around Havana, Fidel converted the massive legislative building that resembled the U.S. Capitol into a science academy and technical library. And he took over the elegant brick tower just off the Malecón in Central Havana that Batista's administration had started building to house Cuba's Central Bank, and made it into the revolutionary government's premier hospital.

The government had called Havana "the Capital of all Cubans," to emphasize its central role in the country's economic, political, and cultural fields. And at times after the revolution it seemed that every Cuban was intent on living there. The city was a powerful magnet that pulled in people from every other province. No matter what the government tried, no enticement was strong enough to keep people from both ends of the island from swarming into Havana to find work, to find food, to find a way to survive. Two and sometimes three generations of the same family stuffed themselves into tiny apartments in Old Havana's ancient buildings, straining the electric grid and overworking the water supply.

In the 1980s, the government tried to ease the crunch by helping people build their own housing, a nontraditional approach to the problem. Volunteers were organized into microbrigades according to where they worked and were given time off from their regular jobs to build multifamily housing on public land with construction material and some assistance provided by the state. In return, they were promised a chance to get a decent place to live.

Zenaida had spent much of her life searching for decent housing. From the moment her mother died through her troubles with Aristede in Guantánamo, and then when she moved back to Tacajó, she rarely had a place of her own for very long. Things didn't improve much after she arrived in Havana. She found a place to live when she took an off-the-books job taking care of an elderly man who was in poor health. When Cary and Esperanza joined her in Havana, they lived in a school dormitory, but Zenaida was desperate for something stable, and she thought the only sure way to find that was to join a microbrigade that the hospital was forming to erect several multifamily buildings in San Agustín, a neighborhood on the outskirts of Havana.

At first, she worked as a nurse at the construction site, taking care of the volunteers' cuts and bruises. A makeshift clinic was built of wooden planks and an asbestos-fiber-panel roof. It wasn't much bigger than a closet, but there was enough room inside for her to bring in a cot so she could sleep there. Although she knew nothing about masonry or plumbing, she volunteered to carry concrete blocks and sift sand for making cement. When construction ended, she was disappointed to learn that party officials and veterans of Castro's military adventures in Africa had been given apartments, but not her.

She was not deterred and volunteered for a second microbrigade in San Agustín. During the project, she lived in a construction shack without a kitchen or a bathroom. Esperanza also lived in the shack while she attended classes at the School of Architecture and Cary was in Kiev. One night, a drunken Russian worker forced his way into the shack. Zenaida punched him so hard he stumbled out.

After working on two separate housing projects over four years, Zenaida finally got what she had been promised: a two-bedroom unit with living room, dining room, kitchen, and bath. She wrote Cary in Kiev, telling her that she and Esperanza already had decorated their new home, putting up curtains and painting the bathroom blue. When Cary came back to Cuba on vacation after her first two years in Ukraine, she brought sheets, towels, pots and pans, and a small refrigerator that she'd purchased in Kiev for the new apartment. But by the time she got off the ship in Havana, the government housing agency had kicked out her mother and sister after they had been in the apartment for only three months. It was an arbitrary move, but not an uncommon one in a tight housing market controlled by the state. An army veteran who lived with his family in an overcrowded apartment in Regla, the small waterfront town bordering Guanabacoa, had been given Zenaida's apartment. She was promised another, but nothing was certain.

Disappointed, Zenaida and Esperanza had moved in with relatives in Old Havana. But it was tight, and they ended up arguing constantly about sleeping arrangements and using the stove. Odors from a broken sewer pipe made the apartment so rank that some nights they preferred to find a spot on the five-mile-long Malecón seawall, which Cubans call the longest sofa in the world, and sleep there.

Soon after she had arrived on vacation, Cary pulled her sister aside and told her they had to do something. They caught the ferry and crossed Havana Harbor to Regla and found the officer's apartment at the far end of a long, dark corridor that reminded them of their *cuartería* in Tacajó. Cary explained their situation to the officer's surprised wife and asked if there was any way she could speed up their move to the new apartment so her mother could take over theirs. The officer's wife looked suspiciously at the twin sisters pleading on their mother's behalf, but then agreed to help.

Finally, after so many years of wandering, Zenaida and her girls had their own home. They hadn't been in the Regla apartment for more than a few months when Zenaida was given a larger apartment in Building 6A of a new microbrigade complex in the Bahía neighborhood, just outside Guanabacoa. She and Esperanza moved into apartment 21, and when Esperanza married a tall, deep-voiced man named Miguel Mitchell Palacios, an accountant who lived in the same complex with his mother, he moved in with them. After Cary returned from Kiev, Zenaida made room there for her and Pipo too.

—✦—

By the time Cary was promoted to the national workforce office of the Ministry of Light Industry in 1983, she was a card-carrying member of the Communist Party and had proven that her degree in economic engineering was not just a fancy play on words. She was in a good place at the right time. The Third Congress of the Communist Party in 1985–86 launched a concerted effort to bring more blacks and women into positions of authority. Race was still a sensitive issue in Cuba. Many white families had pulled out and left after Fidel embraced communism, and centuries of intermarriage had resulted in a large mestizo population. But despite the government's efforts, there remained advantages—both real and imagined—to being white, or claiming to be. Recent census figures indicating that more than 60 percent of Cubans consider themselves white are based on self-reporting, and an afternoon spent on any street in Cuba raises questions about the accuracy of that number.

As a young black woman at a time when the government's affirmative action policies were vigorously enforced—at least within state enterprises—Cary kept moving up at the ministry and within the party. Pipo did well too, at the construction-standards institute where he worked. With their combined salaries, they had enough money to slip away for occasional weekends at the Riviera Hotel on the Malecón and for a yearly vacation at the beach in Varadero.

Cary's revolutionary fervor continued to intensify even as her mother became increasingly embittered. Zenaida had started to listen clandestinely to Radio Martí broadcasts from Miami and, within the walls of her overcrowded apartment, she dared to criticize Fidel. It was different for Cary. As she made her way to work in Old Havana every morning, she saw signs that the revolution was fulfilling many of Fidel's promises. Children were going to school. The clinics and hospitals were taking care of everyone. And Cuba's friends in the socialist camp were helping Fidel withstand the pressures of the U.S. embargo. They were crowded in Zenaida's apartment, but every Cuban Cary knew basically lived the same way. Nobody had a lot, but everybody had something.

The biggest challenge she and Pipo faced at this time was starting their own family. After the miscarriage in Kiev, Cary lost several other pregnancies. Once, she was already three months pregnant when she attended a work meeting wearing a yellow maternity dress. She rose to speak, and while she was making her presentation, the front of her yellow dress turned red. That was her third miscarriage. There would be several more. Esperanza did not have the same kind of problems, and her son, Leonardo, was born while they all were living in Zenaida's apartment. Cary celebrated the arrival of the family's next generation, but she told Pipo there simply wasn't room there for all of them. They needed their own home.

Cary volunteered for a microbrigade several times without being accepted. She wasn't strong enough to do the work. But Pipo was. His engineering degree and background in construction standards made him an ideal *brigadista*. Cary pushed him to join, telling him that continuing to work at the institute was unlikely to bring him recognition no matter how good a job he did there. Applying his skills as an engineer to a microbrigade, a project that the comandante himself had initiated, was far more likely to get him noticed by the people who counted. And she assumed they had risen far enough within the system to ensure that, if he did the work, they would not be passed over for their own apartment the way Zenaida had been not once but twice.

In 1987, Pipo volunteered for a joint microbrigade that his workplace and another institute were forming. Of the thirty-three people in the brigade, fourteen were assigned community projects like building day-care centers and medical offices. The remaining nineteen were left to construct, with some help from the state, a thirty-unit apartment building on the slope of one of the many hills in Regla. When Pipo first looked over the building site, nothing about it seemed promising. Regla was known as the "Little Maestra" both because of the revolutionary fervor of its inhabitants and for its physical location on a series of steep hills that mimicked the majestic Sierra Maestra, where Fidel had fought. All he saw was a giant mound of dirt, overgrown with weeds and garbage, that sloped down toward a waterfront tank farm that stored jet fuel shipped in from the Soviet Union. There was nothing majestic about it.

Regla was an industrial town, but this construction site was an urban wasteland so bleak that only the extreme shortage of housing could make it seem like a decent place to live. The job ahead of the brigade was enormous. The state sent in bulldozers and backhoes to dig out the building's footprint and pour a concrete foundation, but most of the rest of the project was left to the crew of nineteen—fifteen men and four women. Their first task was to figure out what they knew and what they needed to learn. And fast. Workers had plenty of incentives to do the job right, but desire alone couldn't ensure that measurements were correct, or cuts straight. They needed a construction manager. They turned to Pipo.

He was given the blueprints for Model SP79, a long, narrow rectangle without color or adornment. It was a utilitarian-style Soviet model that was being used all over the island. SP79 rose five stories, with six apartments per floor ranging in size from one to three bedrooms. After the foundation was laid, the brigade broke down the project into a series of individual jobs that could be handled by volunteers with minimal construction skills. They learned as they went, experimenting on the bottom level and developing masonry, plumbing, and electrical expertise as they proceeded to the upper floors. The four women in the brigade learned how to cut and lay tile in the ground-floor kitchens and bathrooms. By the time they reached the top floor, their work looked professional.

Pipo made sure the crews followed the blueprints carefully, but he used his own judgment to enhance the building they all hoped to live in. He applied extra cement where the beams were joined to make the floors sturdier and more soundproof. He put additional steel plates in the stairs and increased the number of connection points for railings from the three indicated in the blueprints to five. Taking a lesson from what he learned in Kiev, he instructed the crew to vibrate the forms to eliminate any *cucarachas*, air pockets, that could weaken the concrete.

The microbrigade finished SP79 with few delays. It was opened ahead of schedule in 1989, two years after ground was broken. It was an achievement that—as Cary had predicted—was recognized by higher-ups, including Fidel. The huge Karl Marx Theatre in Havana was reserved for a special ceremony honoring the microbrigades. Fidel personally acknowledged Pipo's hard work and awarded him a white construction helmet that, decades later, Pipo still treasured.

Cary stayed at home with her mother on the night Pipo went before the housing commission that would distribute the new apartments. He thought they had only a slim chance of getting one because his workplace was entitled to just half of the thirty units, and some of the apartments surely would be held back for veterans and Communist Party officials. They also were at a disadvantage because they had no children, and families with kids were given special consideration. But a Bulgarian engineer on the commission spoke up in his defense, describing how hard he had worked on the building. Give them a big apartment and they'll have children, the Bulgarian told the other commissioners.

As the hours passed without any word from Pipo, Cary worried that their application had been denied. "Do you think we'll get it?" she asked her mother. "It's hard to say." Zenaida sighed, clutching a set of rosary beads.

It was after 10:00 P.M. when Pipo finally returned. He bounced out of an old American car that worked as a taxi and shouted, "Twenty-four four, twenty-four four!"

"What's he talking about?" Zenaida was watching from her window. Cary wasn't sure. "Twenty-four four" could refer to his birthday, April 24, but what did that have to do with anything? When he burst into the apartment smiling ear to ear, Pipo explained. Yes, twenty-four four was his birthday, which was meaningful because their new home was apartment 24 on the fourth floor of SP79. And who could believe it? Twenty-four was an end unit, one with three bedrooms.

They moved into their big new apartment in October 1989. It took many trips on the bus to move all the dishes, glasses, sheets, towels, and other household items Cary had purchased in the Soviet Union. When her neighbors dropped in, they were impressed. Not only had she decorated her home with things that were unavailable in Cuba, Cary and Pipo had the large apartment to themselves. And they were only in their early thirties.

A few weeks after moving in, she heard the news that the Berlin Wall had fallen. But they were too busy to think much about it or what it might come to mean for Cuba. She tried to keep politics out of their new home, but she couldn't block it completely—nor could she forget how just a few months earlier she had added her name to a petition to execute a man whose most serious offense may have been that he was too popular.

General Arnaldo Ochoa was a highly decorated veteran of Cuban military campaigns in Africa, an able commander to whom Fidel had awarded the nation's top military honor, Hero of the Revolution. The specifics of the case against him were murky. Ochoa had been convicted in a show trial of drug smuggling and treason and had been sentenced to death. Many Cubans believed that Fidel was simply trying to get rid of a potential rival and pleaded for him to be pardoned. As a member of the Communist Party, Cary was expected to sign a statement of support for Ochoa's execution. Ochoa's trial had been televised, and the official news media took every opportunity to lay out his alleged crimes, without giving him much chance to defend himself. Cary felt uneasy about condemning a hero of Cuba's foreign wars to death when, to her, the evidence seemed inconclusive. She confided in an old friend in the party and asked what she should do.

"*Negrita*," he told her, "these guys are going to kill Ochoa whether you sign the petition or not. Listen to me. Sign it, and don't look for problems for yourself in the future."

She signed. She wanted the party to see that she had been loyal, but there was nothing about the execution that made sense to her.

That same confusion enveloped her that summer when Cuban television was filled with images of the caskets of Cuban soldiers who'd been killed in the African campaigns. Young men sent so far away to die, and for what? The images, night after night, seared into her memory, and she couldn't help but notice that many of the mothers waiting to receive the remains of their sons were black. *Did we have a revolution for this?* Cary wondered.

But then her thoughts turned inward, and she put those doubts aside.

Within a year of setting up house in SP79, she was pregnant for the eighth time. After all they'd been through, she and Pipo tried not to be too optimistic. They decided that if this pregnancy went to term, and if the baby was a girl, they would name her Milagrita, their little miracle. An aunt, her father's sister who was deeply into Santería, the Afro-Cuban religion that mixes Catholic saints with African deities, offered to say prayers over her in a special ceremony. Although Cary was named after the Catholic patron saint of Cuba, she also had been initiated into Santería, and had allowed her aunt to perform the same ceremony during her earlier pregnancies, which all ended in miscarriages.

This time, she thanked her aunt for offering to help but told her she preferred not to invoke the Santería gods again.

In January 1991, her contractions began, and Pipo rushed her to the hospital. She needed a cesarean section, but thirteen years after the first miscarriage in Kiev, she held her baby, a healthy boy they named after the doctor who delivered him, Oscar de la Concepción de la Pedraja, a friend from Tacajó whose brother, Octavio, had fought with and died alongside Che Guevara.

Their family was delighted, and no one was happier than Pipo's mother. She hadn't been thrilled with the ambitious young engineer whose skin was so much darker than Pipo's. The long-held notion of trying to *mejorar la raza*, literally to improve the race, by having lighter-skinned children, was still widely accepted in Cárdenas. Pipo's younger brother had married a blonde woman from East Germany while he studied there, and his mother had hoped Pipo would follow his example. Then, for many years, the color issue was moot because of Cary's many miscarriages.

Now that Cary had borne a child with caramel-colored skin much lighter than her own, all was forgiven.

RACIAL SENSITIVITIES HAD DEEP ROOTS in Cuban culture, and María del Carmen discovered that no laws or party congresses could correct all of them. After her chance encounter with Román Calvo at the chapel, they had continued to meet as friends whenever he was on home leave. He was not one for small talk, but they did have their work in common, and when they got together, usually over coffee, he smoked several H. Upmann brand cigarettes and told her about his adventures on the open seas. She confided details about her quiet life in Guanabacoa, her worries for her aging parents, and how out of sync she felt she was with what was happening in Cuba. She even asked him for advice about a romantic relationship with someone she had started seeing, a local man whom her family did not approve of because of the color of his skin. Despite her parents' strong opposition, she continued seeing the man, and they had a child together. But the relationship didn't last, and like her great-grandmother Eustoquia with her first husband, Mari let his name be lost to history.

After he found out that her relationship with that man had dissolved, Román—who shared Mari's European ancestry—told her bluntly that she had simply picked the wrong man. He and Mari both were quite shy, and their romance could hardly be described as whirlwind. In 1990, more than a decade after they'd met in the chapel, they finally were married in a ceremony there. He formally adopted her son, Virgilio, and moved his few belongings into the house on Corralfalso. Theirs was not a typical marriage. When Román left on a sea voyage lasting months, they'd stay in touch by ship-to-shore radiograms. But because they were not authorized to send personal messages, they kept their conversations brief and eventually developed a language of their own. "How are things in your department?" he'd ask. It was their code for news about home.

The bits of information she received let her know where in the world he was. She kept busy caring for her son and her parents, putting in her time at work inspecting tuna, and visiting the Capuchins' chapel. He dealt with the loneliness of so many nights at sea by working on mathematical puzzles, smoking one H. Upmann cigarette after another, and sometimes gazing at the vast night sky, imagining that she was looking up and seeing the same stars.

CHAPTER 7

REGLA

1990

Whenever Cary walked through apartment 24, past the neat bathroom and the tidy kitchen, the room where little Oscar slept, and the balcony where she could peer at the waters of Havana Bay, she marveled at what surely was a miracle, one almost as awesome as her son's birth. How could two people who had started life under such unpromising conditions—she in Tacajó's hovels and he in the industrial dregs of Cárdenas—have achieved so much, so soon? They were college graduates with promising futures. Incredibly, they lived in a three-bedroom apartment that someday, after they had made monthly payments totaling about eight thousand pesos, would be forever theirs. She firmly believed that they owed most of their personal good fortune to the revolution, but she had no inkling that their perfect world was about to come undone. The fall of the Berlin Wall was just the beginning of a sickening catastrophe for Cuba. The Soviet Union, which provided $4 billion to $5 billion a year in subsidies, was disintegrating with stunning speed and taking with it the future that Cary and so many Cubans had dreamed of.

Exports to the U.S.S.R.—Cuba's principal market since the U.S. economic embargo began in 1962—dried up, leaving Havana chronically short of money to pay for necessities like oil to run electric generating stations. Soon, both exports and imports came to a virtual halt, and Cuba's economy imploded. What Cary and Pipo thought of as good times ended abruptly—replaced, it seemed, from one day to the next by shortages of food, gasoline, electricity, everything. During a speech in 1990 marking the thirtieth anniversary of the creation of the CDR, Fidel leveled with the Cuban people about the dire situation that Cuba was in. He warned them that Cuba was entering a "special period in time of peace" and called on Cubans across the nation to be prepared to sacrifice everything to sustain the revolution.

"I ask you . . . what are we going to do? Give up? Never. What are we going to do? Are we going to renounce the revolution? Renounce socialism? Renounce independence? Never. What we have to do is resist and fight. We must resist, fight, and, of course, win."

To each of Fidel's questions, the crowd shouted, "No!" But the Cuban people had no idea of the extent to which their leader would call on them to sacrifice.

As gasoline and diesel fuel became scarce, trucks, buses, and old American gas guzzlers were sidelined. The government imported fleets of Chinese bicycles with names like Flying Pigeon and Follow Me so people could get around. Cary had to pedal the long road from Regla around the waterfront to the Department of Human Resources at the Union of Textile Workers on Lamparilla Street in Old Havana. Regla and Guanabacoa sit at the southeastern end of the 3.3-square-mile harbor, but the numerous coves that serrate the water's edge, which proved so ideal for shipping, made the ride a chore. At the end of each day she had to bike back to Regla, often in the dark, along with other workers who found it safer to travel in packs. They rode through pitch-black streets, with only a pinprick of light from a small generator lamp on each bicycle piercing the night.

Daily life in the socialist paradise that Cuba had hoped to become was reduced to three basic challenges: finding breakfast, lunch, and dinner, and there were days when even that was cut to two meals or sometimes just one.

As they had since the early 1960s, Cubans presented their *libreta*, their little ration book, every month to buy rice, beans, sugar, cooking oil, and other basic products, along with a daily allotment of bread, at state-run stores and bakeries. Rationing was supposed to have been temporary, but it evolved into an integral and long-lasting part of Cuban life. During the special period, even the *libreta*'s modest rations were cut back drastically. Beef practically disappeared, and chicken and pork became so scarce that Cubans were forced to look for substitutes. They flattened and tenderized grapefruit rinds and fried them as if they were steaks. Banana peels ground up and mixed with spices became another pale substitute for meat. Eggs were strictly limited. Cary received a total of nine eggs a month for herself, Pipo, and Oscar. She hard boiled them and gave half an egg to Oscar with his breakfast, and the other half at dinner to make sure he had real protein in his diet. Months went by when she and Pipo didn't taste a single egg.

It got worse. The Soviet collapse cut Cuban sugar exports by 80 percent, setting off a tsunami of shortages. Cuba scrambled to convert cane fields to food production, but without fertilizers or fuel for tractors, fresh vegetables ended up being as scarce as meat. It was a dramatic comedown for a country that, before the revolution, had produced 80 percent of its food. With the shortages of the special period, Cuban agriculture was transformed into organic farming overnight, which helped the environment but not hungry Cubans. Eventually, Cuba had no choice but to import 80 percent of the food it consumed, and Cubans ate a lot less than they had before the crisis.

Weeks went by when city residents had little more than dried peas to eat. That's when Pipo would leave SP79 at around two in the morning and pedal his Chinese bike forty miles to the farms of Güira de Melena to barter a pair of old shoes or a ripped shirt for a few plantains and some root vegetables. He pedaled back with his treasures, hoping not to be stopped by police.

As the shortages continued, even rum—a liquor synonymous with Cuba and so much a part of life that Cubans routinely referred to it as vitamin R— became scarce. To stave off despair, the families of SP79 organized *sábado corto* parties where everyone brought whatever they had, including any Cuban rum left in a bottle. They didn't end up with very much booze or food, but because they were so hungry it didn't take a lot of alcohol to make them happy enough to start dancing and forget for a while how bad things really were.

One of the biggest feast days of the year in Cuba had always been Nochebuena, when the centerpiece of the traditional Christmas Eve feast was a piglet or a pork loin, slow roasted with garlic and bitter orange. The tradition continued even after Fidel outlawed Christmas. No matter how they were prepared, grapefruit skins and banana peels could never substitute for the roast pork, so inventive Cubans searched for alternative ways of getting what they wanted. In SP79, families discovered that the rear balcony of every apartment, with its small sink, running water, and a floor drain, made a suitable place to raise a pig. Families bought piglets when they weighed just a few pounds and carried them up to their balconies where they were fed scraps and grew reasonably fat. One of Cary's neighbors had a pig so well behaved it could be walked down the stairs to graze outside. Most never enjoyed such freedom and spent their entire lives crammed into their balcony pens. Cary and Pipo had their own pig that Oscar, still a toddler, named Ponka. When the time came for Ponka to fulfill its destiny, Cary concocted a pleasant tale for Oscar, telling him that a farmer had brought them a Nochebuena dinner, and in exchange, he took Ponka to his big farm in the countryside and let him run free.

MARÍA DEL CARMEN ALSO STRUGGLED to put on Nochebuena dinners during the special period, but there wasn't room to raise a pig in her little house. One year her husband sent her a secret ingredient for dinner that she was sure would make the night feel as special as it used to. Román sometimes came home with gifts from the exotic places he'd been to with the tuna fleet. Once he brought back a stereo system. Another time it was a TV. As captain, Román also could arrange for things to be sent home on other boats before he returned.

As soon as Mari received a message that a boat had docked in Havana with a package from Román, she ran down to the docks to get it. She couldn't read the labels—they were written in some foreign language—but the two large cans about the size of soccer balls each bore a drawing of what she thought was a pig. She was delighted, believing that Román had sent them a special Nochebuena treat that was impossible to get in Cuba. A canned ham wouldn't be as good as a traditional roast pork, but in those extraordinary times it surely was better than grapefruit rind.

Mari decided to share her good fortune with a friend and her children, who also were willing to attend Christmas Eve mass at Los Escolapios church despite the danger of reprisals. She invited them to join her and Virgilio for dinner after mass. She spent much of the day getting ready. It took time to prepare the black beans, white rice, and root vegetables that traditionally accompanied the roast pork. But when she opened the cans that Román had sent, she found not the luscious ham she expected, but pasty coils of what looked like thin sausage. She didn't know what they were exactly, and she wasn't willing to experiment with them in front of her friend.

They had chicken instead.

The next time she communicated with Román she told him about the ruined dinner. He confessed that he hadn't been able to read the labels either. They had a good laugh, but as the shortages grew and conditions continued to deteriorate, they couldn't ignore how desperate Cuba had become. "I left one country and I came back to a different country that didn't even have toothbrushes or shoelaces," Román told Mari when he finally returned home after a long voyage. The tuna fleet continued to bring back fish, but that became increasingly difficult as the boats themselves aged, needing repairs and replacement parts that Cuba simply could not afford. One by one, the boats became unseaworthy and were abandoned or sold for scrap. At the end of 1993, however, their catch still was an important Cuban export. When the ships returned to Cuba, the tuna and shark in their holds were beheaded and eviscerated. As part of her job with the fleet, Mari had to prepare samples for food safety testing.

She was aware that as the special period's deprivations worsened, she was in a compromising position. Where no one had enough to eat, she had access to a fantastic bounty of fish. What would it take for her to divert a small sample to a friend willing to pay for it, or simply carry it home for herself and Virgilio? They certainly could use it, but that wasn't the way she had been raised. Desperate times did not change anything. Stealing was still stealing.

Security was tightened, and new guards started patrolling the offices and labs where she worked. One day, she received orders to prepare a sample that weighed as much as eighty pounds, enough to feed a whole block. As she was cutting up the large fish, one of the new guards stopped her.

"Where are you going with all that?" he demanded to know.

"To the lab," she said. She'd seen him only a few times around the office. "These are the samples I was told to prepare."

He looked at what, to him, must have seemed a monstrous specimen, and then looked at Mari. "That's impossible."

He arrested her on suspicion of stealing the fish and hauled her off to a detention center. Mari's coworkers were upset when they saw her being taken away. They knew about her religious views, but they also understood that in desperate times anyone could be tempted. Mari tried to assure them that it was all a misunderstanding.

"Just tell the director that they've taken me away," she said. She expected everything to be resolved as soon as calls were made. "I'm sure it'll be all right."

She had done nothing wrong and had written orders from her supervisors to prove it. Within an hour after arriving at the detention center and showing proof that what she had been doing was indeed part of her responsibilities as a safety inspector, she was back at her office. Mari was relieved that things had not spiraled out of control, but she was also worried. It was impossible to ignore what was happening around her. The prolonged blackouts, the empty store shelves, the clinics that had not even the simplest medicines and were forced to rinse and reuse latex gloves until the fingertips wore out, all were pushing the famous Cuban trait of putting up with anything to the limits of what a sane person could endure.

CHAPTER 8

GUANABACOA

1993

As the special period worsened, Cubans were tested in almost every way nearly every day. For some it was the lack of decent food and the scarcity of desperately needed medicines that pushed them toward the edge. Others raged against the ever-longer blackouts that left them sweat soaked and bored. On suffocating nights in Guanabacoa when the electricity was out and fans didn't work, Jorge García dragged mattresses onto the roof of his house on San Sebastián Street so his family could catch a breeze as they slept in the open air. He had learned how to bread the skin of plantains and fry them to have something to eat when there wasn't enough food. He kept inventing, out of necessity, and putting up with the shortages and the darkness.

But when he ran out of blank sheets of paper and could no longer print the pages of *Colmillos*, the magazine he wrote, printed, and distributed as president of the Doberman Club of Havana, it all became too much. Jorge adored the dogs and everything about them. He raised and trained them. When there was hardly enough food for himself, he looked for ways to keep his dogs fed—he haunted slaughterhouses for offal and scavenged fat and gristle when farmers' horses died. He'd loved dogs since he was a boy and kept a stray that followed him home from school. He was infatuated with the majesty of the Doberman's lineage. Most of all, he admired their strength and cunning, basic survival instincts that every Cuban needed.

Jorge enjoyed putting out *Colmillos* and discovered that he could string together words and sentences with grace and style that others admired. He wrote stories about training the dogs and about the Cubans who raised them. The typed stencils went into a hand-cranked mimeograph machine, and he personally distributed the finished magazine to the members of the Dober-man Club throughout the capital.

As shortages drained the spirit out of daily life, anxiety increased, and so did government repression. To maintain order, security agents reacted swiftly to any public expression of discontent. When groups of desperate people forced their way into the embassies of Belgium, Chile, and Germany, the gov-ernment cleared them out quickly to avoid a repeat of the Mariel debacle. Jorge was accustomed to the anxiety that such repression generated. He was old enough to remember what life had been like under Batista, and the special period revived those memories.

Like María del Carmen, Jorge and his family had a long and emotional connection to Guanabacoa. His ancestors had come from Spain and settled both in Guanabacoa and in what became the province of Artemisa, west of Havana. His grandfather, César Mas, was a printer and newspaperman who set down roots in the San Sebastián neighborhood of Guanabacoa in a tum-bledown wooden house on the corner with Aguacate, one block uphill from the Brazo Fuerte bakery that Cuban rebels burned in 1896, the same year Eustoquia's plantation in Colón went up in flames. Jorge was born in the house, and after his grandfather died and his father, Jorge Luis, abandoned the family, he grew up surrounded by women. He was enrolled at Los Esco-lapios when it was an all-boys school run by priests. His grandmother Victo-ria walked him there every day and made sure he received the Catholic sacraments.

Growing up in a house without any permanent male presence in 1950s Cuba left Jorge open to taunts from other youths in his neighborhood. They picked on some feminine mannerisms he had developed and called him a *maricón*, a faggot. In 1951, when he was seven, a neighbor invited him to the beach at Cojímar. He took the boy to a secluded spot and sexually assaulted him, forcing Jorge to touch his genitals while masturbating in front of him. When Jorge entered adolescence, he rebelled, leaving behind the Catholic church and its sacraments to make up for the time he felt he had lost being innocent.

In the hectic months following the triumph of the revolution, when he was just coming into his own as a young adult, Jorge finished school and took a job at a Guanabacoa company that produced fruit juices. He blew much of his salary in Havana's dingy waterfront bars and brothels, at last enjoying what it was like to be a single man at the dawn of revolutionary Cuba. Fidel and his bearded rebels were little more than images on TV, but his uncle Gustavo, who was tall, with a pencil-thin mustache, was for Jorge the dashing face of the insurrection. Gustavo roamed the streets of Havana at night, setting off bombs and harassing the dictatorship. By day, he disappeared.

Batista's men knew that Gustavo sometimes hid out at the house on San Sebastián, and they kept it under surveillance. Colonel Esteban Ventura Novo, chief enforcer of Batista's counterrevolutionary forces in Havana, stormed the house several times looking for him. As Jorge and his mother watched, they ripped open mattresses, knocked over lamps, and emptied out drawers searching for proof linking the family to Castro's 26th of July Movement.

By the time Jorge accompanied his family to the airport in Havana to welcome home his uncle from the Sierra Maestra in early 1959, Gustavo had a full beard like Fidel and the rank of captain of the Sierra. Jorge's entire family supported the rebels. His mother said Fidel was going to solve all the problems that plagued their lives. His aunt Nena placed a placard on her front door, a sign many homes in Guanabacoa were proud to display. It read, THIS IS YOUR HOUSE, FIDEL.

Gustavo received a hero's welcome at the airport, and the celebration continued at the house on San Sebastián Street. Later, the family traveled to Artemisa for a reunion with that side of the family. Gustavo had brought them together after many years apart. But in a short time, the revolution divided them again. One of Jorge's cousins in Artemisa was known as "Jalopy César" because he sold old clothes from the trunk of his beat-up American car.

During the years of fighting against Batista, he had used the car to transport firearms to the rebels. Then he, like many others, became disillusioned as Fidel made clear the red tint of his revolution. Replacing one dictator with another was not what they had fought for. They organized and armed counterrevolutionary cells in several parts of the country. The most serious threat to the communists in Havana arose in the Escambray Mountains that run along the spine of Cuba's middle provinces. Fidel called those resistance fighters *banditos* and pursued them relentlessly until the last insurgents were eliminated in 1965. Other anti-Castro movements flared up across Cuba, and they too were eventually snuffed out. Aligned with one of them, César was charged with counterrevolutionary activities and thrown into prison. Gustavo tried to intervene, hoping to use his stature to persuade the revolutionary authorities to release him. They didn't. A few months later, Jorge's family received word that César had suffered a heart attack in prison and died. He was thirty years old.

None of it made sense to Jorge, not his cousin's untimely death, or Fidel's embrace of communism, which the comandante had denounced before 1959. He was still a teenager when he joined a counterrevolutionary cell in Havana, volunteering to post anti-Castro stickers on buses and buildings in the capital. They were small acts of defiance, but they emboldened him. In 1961 he took time to celebrate his seventeenth birthday at the Taverna de los Ricos bar in Cojímar, where his cousin Andrés worked. Despite the chaos in the streets and the uncertainty he felt about the revolution, he was determined to enjoy himself, and at the bar he had more than his share of rum. As he remembers it, someone had put "Ebb Tide" on the jukebox when a local girl, on vacation from school, entered the room.

He fell under the spell of the girl, a petite beauty named Elisa Suárez. He couldn't take his eyes off her, except when he realized that the room was spinning so viciously that everything he'd put into his gut was about to come up. His cousin guided him back to his own room where he quickly fell asleep. When Jorge opened his eyes, Elisa was looking down on him with amused pity and an impish smile.

Six months later they were married. Like many other young Cubans, they had trouble finding a place to live. After a brief stay in Elisa's sister's house in La Coronela, a suburb of Havana, they dragged their belongings to the ramshackle wooden house in Guanabacoa where Jorge had grown up. His mother and grandmother were still living there, but they found a way to squeeze in the newlyweds, and more. In 1964 their first child, Jorge Félix, was born. A year later, they had a daughter, María Victoria.

Everything seemed to be going well for them, but during the delivery of the second baby, doctors detected a murmur in Elisa's heart. Tests confirmed a mitral valve stenosis and other problems. She lost so much weight that Jorge started calling her La Flaca, the skinny one. A year later, Elisa underwent cardiac surgery that took care of the immediate issue but left her with a weakened heart and a warning from the doctors not to get pregnant again.

The young family was uprooted in 1970 when nearly every able-bodied Cuban was forced to work on Fidel's quixotic 10-million-ton harvest. Jorge wasn't disappointed that just 8.5 million tons of sugar were cut. He was just glad to go back home. The futile nature of Fidel's sugar dream, the senseless months he had to spend away from his family, the dirt and insects and backbreaking, mind-numbing routine of cutting cane all left Jorge thoroughly disillusioned with Castro's Cuba. But he was trapped. At that time the only way out was by sea, and Elisa was in no condition to get into a homemade raft. For better or worse, Jorge recognized that his life was in Cuba. Whether he believed in Castro or felt that Cuba had been swindled by Castro's false promises, he'd have to find a way to survive there. After bouncing around a few jobs, he became an educational administrator and in 1973 was named director of the Jesús Garay school, the old Escolapios school that he had attended when he was a boy.

When Elisa became pregnant again, doctors initially favored terminating the pregnancy because of her poor health. They eventually decided that doing so might be more dangerous than letting her go to term. On November 14, 1973, when she was twenty-nine and not supposed to be having any more children, Elisa delivered a healthy baby boy that she and Jorge named Joel, combining the first two letters of his name with the first two letters of hers.

La Flaca needed more surgery in 1977, but Fidel interrupted their lives yet again. Her operation had to be put off because Jorge was sent to Angola, where more than twenty-five thousand Cuban troops were fighting along-side left-wing rebels. At thirty-three, he was considered too old to take up arms and fight, but during his three years in Africa, he was put to work as a kind of media trainer. When he returned to Cuba in the spring of 1980, just as the Mariel boatlift was beginning, La Flaca finally could be admitted to the National Institute of Cardiology and Cardiovascular Surgery. The surgery was successful, but doctors advised her not to return to her job as a first-grade teacher. She retired, and Jorge continued working, moving from one adminis-trative post to another. He felt confident enough about the future, despite his political misgivings, to borrow sixty thousand pesos from a friend to rebuild the old house on San Sebastián Street, doing much of the work himself with help from family and friends. He hired an electrician for some projects and left most of the plumbing to his wife's brother-in-law, Fidencio Ramel Prieto Hernández, the chief of operations at the Port of Havana, whom everyone knew as Ramel.

A dispute at one of the schools ended Jorge's administrative career. He had gone as far as someone who had refused to join the Communist Party could go. Years before, when he underwent the same kind of evaluation as María del Carmen, he answered the question about religious beliefs the same way she did, saying he was not qualified to become a member of the Young Communist League. She had given that answer to honor her faith. He did it so they'd leave him alone.

The sweeping prohibition on private businesses didn't stop him from using a cassette recorder that he had brought back from Angola to produce black-market recordings of popular artists like José Feliciano and the Beatles that were strictly prohibited but very popular. He also hosted local ceremo-nies and birthday parties, using his elegant voice to make introductions and pay elaborate tribute to those being honored. Soon he was earning enough to pay back the friend who had loaned him the money for his house. He worked with dogs and became well known as the guy who sold and trained Dober-mans. As affection turned into passion, he started *Colmillos* magazine and wrote a book on the breed that he sold to a publisher in Spain for two thousand dollars. With the money, he managed to buy an Olivetti desktop computer, making him one of the few individuals in Cuba privileged to own such an advanced piece of technology.

After the Berlin Wall came down and the Soviet Union dissolved, Jorge initially expected Cuba to respond the way Eastern European nations did, shedding communism and rousting their communist leaders. It was wishful thinking. Instead of collapsing, or opening space for people to let off steam, Castro's government clamped down on dissenting voices and ratcheted up anti-American propaganda. Criticize the government, and you could land in jail.

As the shortages intensified, milk—which Fidel had once promised would be plentiful—went missing from the stores. There was no beef at all, and the penalty for killing a cow without permission became as serious as it was for killing a man. Dried peas were ground up and mixed with coffee. Power outages became so routine and long lasting that lightless nights became the norm, and Cubans celebrated the brief periods when the lights came back on as fleeting phenomena that they excitedly called *alumbrones*. Most families in Guanabacoa contended with the same frustrations and tried to reconcile their lives to this new reality as best they could. For Jorge's family, the shortages, the prolonged darkness, and the accumulated weight of their deepening resentment of a revolution that had betrayed them led them to form a radical plan, a daring scheme that they hoped would lead them to freedom.

CHAPTER 9

REGLA

1993

They hadn't named him "little miracle," but to Cary and Pipo, Oscar surely was one. As daily life during the special period grew more trying, Cary was determined to keep her son at the center of her universe. But whenever she figured Cuba had hit bottom and the special period couldn't get any worse, some new challenge was thrown at her. It was taking her nearly an hour to bike to her office across the bay, and even longer at night when she returned on the ring road around the port with the streets pitch black. As her responsibilities at work grew, so did her time away from home. One night, after dealing with an emergency at the office, she didn't get back to the apartment until after eight o'clock, well past the baby's bedtime. Pipo, who had to bike five miles from his new job in Cojímar, also was late. By the time they both finally got home, they found out that one of their neighbors had already fed Oscar, bathed him, and put him to bed. Pipo carried him back to their apartment and gently laid him in his own bed. That's when he and Cary looked at each other and asked: Is this why we went through all those miscarriages, all that fear, all that disappointment and longing, just so that someone else has to put our son to sleep? Maybe Zenaida had been right when she told Cary she was giving too much of herself to the revolution.

Something had to change. Cary screwed up her courage and confronted her supervisors. She reminded them she had a two-year-old to take care of and told them that she was spending way too much time going back and forth to her job. She wanted to continue working, but she needed something closer to home. It was a bold demand, and the ploy might not have worked for other Cubans. But Cary was a rising star, a trusted member of the Communist Party whose husband had been dedicated to the party since he was a teenager. Cuba had already invested in them by sending them to Ukraine to study, then guiding their careers so that now they were ready for advancement. She'd handled every responsibility well, showing herself to be a leader. And the Communist Party's goals for advancing women and minorities into leadership positions still hadn't fully been met.

Cary was given what she had asked for—sort of. In May 1993, she was made the first female plant manager at the former Bolinaga aluminum company, which was renamed Novalum after it was nationalized in the 1960s. The location was ideal for her, about a mile up the hill from SP79 on the border of Regla and Guanabacoa. It was close to home, but her responsibilities as plant manager terrified her. Her degree in economic engineering and her years of experience in textiles had not prepared her for dealing with stamping aluminum sheets to make pots, pans, and other household utensils. That was just one challenge. There was another that would prove even more difficult. At her previous jobs, she had worked mostly with women. Novalum had a handful of women secretaries and security guards. The rest of the plant's employees—more than one hundred—were men, Cuban men who were not used to taking orders from any woman, let alone one who was just thirty-six years old, and black.

Novalum was typical of the kind of industry that had flourished all over Guanabacoa in the decades leading up to 1959. In several separate buildings strung along Vía Blanca—a major road that runs from the seacoast through Guanabacoa to the center of Havana—aluminum was cut, shaped, prepped, and painted. A cavernous warehouse stored bulk aluminum that came in large rolls or flattened discs from foundries in Germany, Russia, Spain, or Mexico. A few days into the job, Cary took aside one of the men who had worked there since before the revolution and leveled with him: "Look, Francisco," she confessed, "I don't know anything about aluminum. But I do know how to organize." She asked him to show her how things got done, starting with the warehouse. Cary stood at the entrance of the huge building and stared. Gigantic spools of aluminum stood before her in long rows. All she could think was, *What have I gotten myself into?* Managing women who sewed together pieces of cloth to make blouses and shirts was one thing. But managing men working on greasy equipment that smelled of oil and sounded like beasts as they hammered out pots and pans was something else entirely.

She stared at the aluminum spools for a while, uncertain what to say or do. Then it came to her. If she looked at the spools in a certain way, they were just like bolts of cloth. Any fabric, she knew, first had to be unrolled from the bolt, laid on a table, and cut according to a pattern. The way that Francisco described working with aluminum was basically the same. They unspooled the aluminum and then used a guillotine to cut it into sheets. The sheets were brought over to the stamping machines that pressed them over a mold.

The organization of the work was the essence of the economic engineering she had learned in Kiev, simply applied to metal instead of cloth.

She could do this.

She started with a top-to-bottom cleanup. Three decades after it was taken over by the state, the plant was a mess. Windows were cracked. The roof leaked. Trash and discarded aluminum were everywhere. She applied one of her mother's lessons about stretching a peso. Zenaida kept everything—buttons from old shirts, zippers from jackets—and reused them. The aluminum stamping process was far from foolproof, and Novalum's aging equipment guaranteed lots of mistakes. Defective pots and pans were removed from the production line, and the workers had gotten into the habit of taking them home either to use or, more likely during the special period, to sell. In backroom crucibles all over Havana, lopsided jugs were melted down and made into trim pieces for old American cars or other hard-to-come-by items like TV antennae. Cary put a stop to all that, instructing the workers to collect the defective pieces in one place. She then sold the batches of aluminum to a state enterprise that exported the scrap. She used the proceeds to fix Novalum's roof, replace broken windows, and repair aging machinery. Workers resented the move because it deprived them of desperately needed income. But officials took note of what she was doing, and, as was usually the case, working with the system had its rewards.

Early one morning, when the shadows were long and the corners of the sprawling central workshop dark, the minister of light industry showed up at the aluminum factory and called the workers to a meeting. Cary strode in wearing one of her favorite outfits, a blue skirt adorned with white flowers that once had been Zenaida's and a gray T-shirt with the Novalum logo—an aluminum jug—over the pocket. The minister said he was there to make an important announcement. After a year as manager, in which she had put the plant back on track, Cary was going to direct the entire Novalum enterprise, which included other plants in different locations and a total workforce of four hundred, nearly all men.

More than one hundred workers had shown up for the meeting that morning. Most applauded Cary's promotion, whether they liked it or not. But from back in the shadows one man let out a crude phrase in Spanish. "Damn," the man shouted, "who the hell would believe this?"

"*Compañero*," the minister responded to the man's remark, "what kind of a thing is that to say? If you have a problem, stop by the office later and we'll discuss it."

"No," Cary told the minister. "He doesn't have to stop by the office." She knew that most of the workers were not comfortable with her age, her sex, or her color and had resented her from the moment she arrived. Ending the free-for-all on scrap and cracking down on theft had only increased their resentment. She walked over to where the disgruntled man was standing and got into his face. "Understand this," she told him, loud enough for the others to hear. "I can't put myself in a tank of bleach and make myself white. Nor can I turn myself into a man. I'm a woman. And I am black. Is everybody else okay with that?"

"Yes," the workers shouted.

She stared right at the man who had complained. "I guess you'll have to get used to it too," she told him. "If not, then you need to get out."

One of her first moves as director was to revive a defunct assembly line that made the aluminum tubes for packaging premium Cuban cigars. Production had ground to a halt years before when the machinery broke down. Tubes then had to be imported from Europe, but they cost more to make and ship across the Atlantic. Cary had the Novalum mechanics figure out what it would take to get the line up and running. Then she used money from selling scrap aluminum to buy replacement parts. Soon she was receiving accolades for producing cigar tubes that were just as good as the imported ones but cost substantially less.

In the summer of 1994, Cary felt confident about her new position and what she had already accomplished when she set off for her yearly vacation at Varadero Beach. It had become a family tradition, thanks to Pipo's father. He arranged trips as bonuses for railroad workers and pulled strings to make sure something was always available for his son's family. Cary knew that she and Pipo were living better than other Cubans during this difficult time, but she reasoned that it was only because they had worked so hard and sacrificed so much for Cuba, going back to their years in Kiev. They deserved a week at the beach.

THAT SAME SUMMER, JORGE GARCÍA's son Joel worked as a disc jockey in local clubs and bars. One of his most popular gigs was near the big Ñico López refinery in Regla, where he ran a dance he called *discopetroleo*. As his reputation grew and his dreams got bigger, the limitations of the special period bore on him more heavily. He was a restless and ambitious twenty-year-old who desperately wanted out of Cuba. Joel found out that one of his father's friends, an amiable guy from Guanabacoa nicknamed Spike, who ran *quinceañera* celebrations and was only a few years younger than Jorge, also had decided there was no future for him in Cuba. He and Joel started working on a crude raft that they planned to launch from the shoreline at Cojímar, on what had until the mid-1970s been a part of Guanabacoa's coastline, praying that the waves would take them the ninety miles to Key West.

When Jorge found out what they were up to, he wasn't happy.

"Listen, Spike, I'm not going to get involved in this directly, but if you go ahead with this plan, you're going to end up dead," he told his friend. "I beg you not to do it." But Spike and Joel were determined to leave, one way or another. Jorge knew he couldn't stop them. Nor, in truth, did he want to. Life in Cuba was becoming impossible, and if he—already fifty years old—felt it, an enterprising young man like his son wouldn't stop until he found a way out. The only way to protect him was to come up with a better plan than escaping on a rickety homemade raft. But what did he know? Except for his stint with the army in Africa, he had never been outside Cuba. He had no experience navigating on the open sea. But he knew someone who did, someone who had tons of experience on the water, who in fact had access to vessels that could easily reach Key West and beyond. A real sailor, and a man of responsibility, who also happened to be a member of his family.

Jorge was ready to pin his hopes on his brother-in-law, Ramel, the same Ramel who, in his time off, had helped with the plumbing of the house on San Sebastián. Ramel had married La Flaca's sister, Ester, at almost the same time that Jorge and La Flaca tied the knot. Ramel was like the brother he never had, a simple country boy who had advanced through perseverance and a willingness to work. He had moved up steadily at the harbor, and in 1987 he was sent to Europe to oversee the purchase and transfer of a fleet of new work vessels, including several large modern tugboats called Polargos that also carried powerful water cannons for fighting fires. He was generous to a fault. Whenever he traveled to another country, he skimped on his per diem and used the money to buy gifts for his extended family. Once, when all the Cuban stores were practically empty, he surprised Jorge with a fine pair of dress pants from overseas. Jorge couldn't thank him enough.

Ramel was the ideal man to lead an expedition, but Jorge was worried that his loyalty to the party might stand in the way. Ramel had joined the Young Communist League when he was a teenager and advanced to the party when he turned thirty. Jorge knew that to recruit him he'd need someone who was just as involved in the party. He turned to another member of the family, La Flaca's brother Eddy, a party member who was a director at the Ministry of Agriculture.

Jorge put it to Eddy directly.

"You have to talk with Ramel and get into his head," he told Eddy. "He won't listen to me, but he will to you because you both think the same way."

Despite his party membership and high-ranking position with the government, Eddy had no illusions about life in Cuba. He had already tried several times to escape, without success. Once he started talking with Ramel, Eddy quickly realized that his brother-in-law was just as frustrated with life as he was. Ramel also had many regrets about having devoted so much of his energy to the party, and he saw nothing ahead but more disappointment. On top of it all, he was struggling with diabetes that he feared would only get worse if he remained in Cuba.

Together they designed an escape plan they thought was foolproof. Ramel knew the ins and outs of the entire port and was an expert in marine maintenance and construction. The ideal vessel for such a trip would have been one of the new tugboats, but they were kept under strict surveillance. Ramel had his eyes set on an old tug called the *13 de Marzo*, for the date in 1957 when a group of university students had tried—and failed—to assassinate Batista in the Presidential Palace. The date of the attack, like the 26th of July, had become a hallowed road marker of the revolution. At the beginning of 1994, the *13* had been completely overhauled. The huge motor was replaced with a newer and stronger five-hundred-horsepower engine, and the wooden hull was repaired and repainted. After it was used to haul tons of marine paint to the port of Cabanas, about fifty miles away, and then returned, he believed the *13 de Marzo* could make the ninety miles to Key West effortlessly.

Ramel planned to leave his wife behind in Cuba along with his granddaughter, but his two adult sons, Iván and Dariel, were determined to leave with him. Ramel recruited Raúl Muñoz, a tugboat skipper, to join them, along with Muñoz's girlfriend and a few relatives. He made sure there was room for Joel, Spike, his brother-in-law Eddy Suárez, and other members of their extended family, as well as Jorge's daughter, María Victoria, and her family, and his older son, Jorge Félix, along with his wife and sons. Jorge turned down a chance to join them, feeling that it was more important for the younger ones to have a shot at starting over. Besides, La Flaca was too weak to undertake such a journey.

They were ready to leave by the beginning of July, the hottest part of a sweltering summer that was made even more intolerable by the deprivations of the special period. All those who were involved were in their assigned places on the morning of the planned departure, but at the last moment Ramel called it off. Security on the waterfront had been heightened when a ship entered the port with supplies for the U.S. Interests Section, the only official American presence in Havana after diplomatic relations were severed and the embassy closed in

1961. Ramel felt that launching the expedition then was too risky, and he preferred to wait a week. He then picked a new date: Wednesday, July 13.

Ramel was on duty at the port that night. At home, his wife was holding a birthday party for Sun, their pet Doberman. After midnight, several groups of men, women, and children reported to their designated pickup locations in and around Guanabacoa. At Jorge's house on San Sebastián Street, more than a dozen waited for a small tourist bus that was driven by Jorge's cousin Felo, the stepson of his uncle Gustavo, the guerrilla captain. Felo was scheduled to pick up Jorge's sons and daughter and several other relatives before heading to the piers.

In the weeks leading up to the planned departure, Jorge's eldest son, Jorge Félix, had gone through a crisis of conscience. Just a year earlier, he had joined the Methodist church in Guanabacoa, and religion had become an important part of his life. Unable to make up his mind whether to leave with his brother and sister or stay with his mother and father, he left the decision to a higher power. Opening a Bible to a random page, he blindly put his finger on a passage. It was Psalm 74: "O deliver not the soul of thy turtledove unto the multitude of the wicked: forget not the congregation of thy poor forever. Have respect unto the covenant: for the dark places of the earth are full of the habitations of cruelty." He interpreted the words as a clear warning not to go. But Joel and María Victoria were certain that their time had come. Joel, still single, would go alone while María Victoria was leaving with her husband, Ernesto, a butcher, and their ten-year-old son, Juan Mario. She hoped to give the boy a real future, one in which he could not only dream but have a chance to make his dreams come true. In all, seventeen members of Jorge's family trusted their fate to Ramel and the *13 de Marzo*.

While they waited at the San Sebastián house for the signal that it was time to go, Juan Mario fell asleep in his grandfather's bed. María Victoria had filled his backpack with snacks and a drink and told him to get some sleep because they were going on a long ride into the countryside where he would be able to do lots of fun things, including fishing. He'd shown his grandfather a fishing rod he made from a stick with some string and told him he was going to bring back a big fish for dinner. Not knowing when he'd next see the boy he called Juanmi, Jorge held back tears.

"Juanmi, you're always so good to me."

It was an intimate family ritual. "Grandpa," the boy responded, "you're always so good to me."

Jorge kissed him good night.

The tourist bus was late. When Felo finally showed up, he had his wife, Lissett María, and their four-year-old daughter, Giselle, on board, along with Lissett's uncle Guillermo. It was after two in the morning when more than a dozen of Jorge's relatives and friends climbed aboard the bus and drew the curtains. As Joel was leaving, Jorge stopped him in the doorway. He looked into his son's eyes, worried and excited at the same time, and then they hugged. Jorge knew he wasn't likely to ever leave Cuba. And he knew that once Joel got to Florida, he would never come back.

"We'll see each other," he told Joel, "in eternity."

The bus took off and headed toward the traffic circle where Vía Blanca continues toward the seacoast. In a few minutes it stopped in Cojímar to pick up more passengers. They then turned around and headed back toward the port of Havana. María Victoria pulled down the curtains so that Juan Mario could fall asleep. Moments later, the bus stopped and she lifted the curtain, expecting to be surrounded by police. But Felo had pulled into the parking lot of La Benéfica hospital and switched off the engine. He turned on Radio Reloj, an all-news radio station that predated the revolution, and kept it on as they waited a few minutes to be certain they'd arrive at the meeting spot, at the nearby waterfront, at precisely the moment they had planned.

A little before three in the morning, Felo started the bus and exited the parking lot, waving at two guards as he pulled out. Minutes later, he parked near the Salvamento Pier in Havana, where the *13 de Marzo* was docked. Everyone remained on the bus, eyes peeled on the gate. The arrangement they had made was simple. Felo watched for Ramel to walk out. If he wasn't wearing his cap, the trip was off. Cap on, it's a go.

Ramel walked out of the gate wearing his cap.

Felo turned off the engine and left the keys in the ignition. Everyone got off the bus quickly and walked single file through the gate and onto the pier. The tug's crew urged them to board quickly and go below deck. "Be careful not to slip," they told the sleepy travelers, most of whom had never boarded a boat. "Stay away from the motor. Stick close to the hull."

"Mamá, where are we going?" Juan Mario kept asking.

"Camping. We're going for a ride, out to the countryside. We're going to have a good time."

But the boy kept whining. Even he knew they should be on the highway heading to the mountains or the coast. Instead, they were still in the city, boarding an old boat in the dark with people he did not know.

"Shush," she told him. "Shush."

Despite Ramel's mandate to keep everything secret, word apparently had seeped out, and at the last minute more people than he expected showed up. At around three-thirty, when the old tug finally pulled away from the pier, sixty-eight people were crammed on board. Fifteen of them were children, aged five months to twelve years, and fifty-three were teenagers and adults, the youngest sixteen and the oldest a little over fifty.

It was a dark night, with a thin crescent moon. The harbor was quite still. María Victoria felt uneasy down in the engine room and decided to go back on deck. Her husband tried to keep her below, where the crew had told them to stay, but she insisted that it was better on deck. She urged him to come along, but he refused, so she grabbed Juan Mario's hand and climbed back up the steep staircase into the night air. The *13 de Marzo* gently stole away from the pier without turning on its lights. Ramel didn't expect much activity on the water at that hour, and he didn't want to call attention to his boat.

María Victoria found a spot at the stern and tried to make herself comfortable. She sat next to a wooden pole that held up an awning and had a large bell hanging from it. Juan Mario sat on a coil of rope next to her. She tried to persuade him to go back to sleep because they had a long trip ahead, but he was already too wound up. Few moments can be as dark and disorienting as being on the water, at night, without lights. The boy was intent on keeping his eyes open, peering into the night as the city shrank behind them and the vast obscurity of the open sea yawned ahead.

Then he thought he saw something.

PART TWO

RECKONING

CHAPTER 10

Mommy, what's that light?"

María Victoria had already caught sight of it and told him not to worry. "It's just another boat." But the boy could tell that something was not right. His hands were shaking, his eyes wide with fright.

"Mommy. Mommy. It's getting closer."

She heard someone in the pilothouse yell that they were being followed, and then she felt the *13 de Marzo* pick up speed. She peered into the night and could just about make out what was happening: In the black water behind them were two other tugboats, the new Polargos that Ramel had helped bring back from Europe a few years earlier. They were bigger and faster than the *13*, fitted with steel hulls and firefighting water cannons that could shoot a powerful stream of water more than 150 yards. They were no more than thirty feet away when they aimed the cannons at the pilothouse and blew out the windows.

Unsure about what was happening, María Victoria held her son tight and turned away from the approaching tugs to try to shield him. The water from the cannons hit her back so hard it felt like nails were being hammered into her skin. It plastered down her waist-length hair and ripped open the seams of her blouse.

"Mommy, what's happening?"

"Don't worry. They'll stop." She could hear the other mothers below deck screaming. "The worst will be over soon," she told Juan Mario. "And then they'll leave us alone."

But both of the pursuing tugs stuck close and kept the torrents of water trained on the smaller vessel. Some of the women who were still on the deck with María Victoria were knocked off balance and, worrying that they would be pushed overboard, took shelter below. They squeezed into the bunk room or pressed their backs against the hull in the engine room, trying to calm their frightened children.

On the bridge, Ramel ordered Raúl Muñoz, the skipper he'd brought along, to go full speed ahead. After they passed beneath El Morro Castle, protector of Havana since the sixteenth century, Muñoz steered toward the open sea, trying to make a beeline for Key West. But a third Polargo that had been hiding off the coast joined the chase, quickly catching up with the others and, like them, hosing the tugboat with its water cannons. The *13 de Marzo* managed to get as far as seven miles from the shore, but it was no closer to freedom. The pursuing Polargos tried to box it in, but in open waters there's almost no way for a tug to be halted. No way but one.

Muñoz shouted to the other boats to back off and leave them alone. "Can't you see there are women and children aboard?" he yelled across the water. He told some of the women to come up on deck again to show themselves. But knowing they'd be blasted with water, many stayed where they were. María Victoria turned around and held Juan Mario in front of her, hoping that if the approaching crews saw the boy they'd take pity on them and stop the attack. They were Cubans too. They may even have been from Guanabacoa. Surely they'd stop if they saw that children were on board.

"This one's coming right at us," Juan Mario screamed. From where they were standing, the approaching Polargo rearing up to attack them looked like a giant steel shark. They watched in stunned horror as the tug closed in on them. Muñoz demanded that the other boats pull back, but they kept pounding the *13 de Marzo* with water, drawing so close that from the bridge Muñoz could make out the faces of the crew members he now believed were determined to sink his boat. He sent out a distress signal on the international radio channel, pleading for help.

Battered and sore, María Victoria felt her strength ebbing. She kept her grip on the awning pole as the old tug heaved from side to side. The still night was filled with the terrified screams of the women in the hold and the insults coming from the pursuing crews. When water from their cannons flooded the engine room, steam shot out in such thick clouds that some thought the *13 de Marzo* had caught fire.

It was a nightmare none of them had imagined. But as bad as it was, nothing could have prepared them for what came next.

Realizing there was no way he could outrun the three newer and faster tugs, Muñoz cut the engine. The worst that could happen, he thought, was that they'd be towed back to port and arrested for attempting to leave the country without permission. He and the other men would probably be thrown in jail, but the women and children would be allowed to go home. It wasn't what they had hoped for when they left Salvamento Pier, but he could live with it.

As the *13 de Marzo* drifted, one of the pursuing tugs did not cut its engines. It steered directly toward them, then rammed the *13* hard from behind. It did not stop there but rose out of the sea and mounted the stern, crushing the wooden deck.

"We give up," Juan Mario screamed. María Victoria felt him trembling. "We surrender."

The collision tore apart the wooden deck and punctured the hull. Ramel was knocked overboard. The *13 de Marzo* took on water. Knowing that most of the women and children were still below, Muñoz desperately tried to pry open a hatch cover on the forward deck to save them from drowning. He and another man pulled on it with all their strength. They could hear the women banging on the hatch, screaming, "Open it, Raúl! Open it!" The cover was held down with heavy bolts that the men couldn't budge. The old tug listed sharply, sending seawater rushing across the deck and down the stairs to the engine room. Muñoz pushed the other man out of the way to make one last desperate attempt to pry off the lid by himself. Then suddenly the banging from below stopped and he knew that he was too late. Seconds later he felt the deck slip away beneath him. He heard a loud burst of air escape from the hull behind him as the inflowing seawater blasted the remaining air out of it, and he knew all was lost.

It was so dark, and there was so much confusion, María Victoria couldn't tell if the waters were rising or the tug was sinking. She quickly arranged Juan Mario's legs around her waist and told him to wrap his arms around her neck.

"Hold on tight." She summoned whatever strength she had left before the waters swallowed them completely. "And don't let go. Take a deep breath and keep your mouth closed."

"Okay, Mommy."

His voice was so weak she barely heard him.

It took just minutes for the *13 de Marzo* to disappear below the waves.

María Victoria and her son were swallowed by the dark sea, and for a few terrifying seconds they could do nothing but sink deeper. It's a strange reality that although no point in Cuba is more than sixty miles from the sea, most Cubans—including her—never learn to swim. But she was a young mother with the fate of her only son literally on her shoulders, and she knew enough to kick her legs and kick them hard. She bobbed to the surface briefly before going under again. She kicked harder. Juan Mario held on.

"Juanmi!" she cried as she surfaced a second time, gasping for air. Juanmi was what everyone called the boy with the big smile. Who always did his chores without complaining. Who wanted to bring his grandfather a big fish for supper.

"Juanmi!"

She did not hear him answer. He was still holding on, but he was very still. She thought he'd fainted.

She managed to tread water as she flailed her arms trying to find something to grab on to. She caught a glimpse of what, in the dark, appeared to be a board or maybe a raft. She lunged for it but was horrified to find that it was not a board but a body. She recognized the red blouse that Rosa, one of the women she had heard screaming in the engine room, had been wearing. She could tell that Rosa was dead, but she couldn't know that Rosa probably had suffered a heart attack, and that had kept her body afloat. All María Victoria knew then was that she would die too, unless she held on to Rosa with all her remaining strength.

"Help! Somebody help me," María Victoria yelled, fearing that she would drown with her son still on her back, his legs still around her waist, his thin arms still draped over her exhausted shoulders. She watched the three Polargos circling the wreckage and for a second thought they would throw out lines to rescue them. One trained a search light on the survivors, but then, nothing. Nobody threw them a life preserver or set out in a lifeboat. The circling tugs caused the water to swirl, making it even harder for her to stay afloat. All around her, people screamed for help. She searched frantically for her husband and brother but didn't see either of them anywhere. All she could make out were the heads of the other survivors bobbing just above the surface.

She didn't know how much longer she could keep going when she glimpsed something hopeful. People were clinging to a large cooler that had broken loose from the tug. "Ernesto! Joel!" she shouted. There was no answer.

"Hang on tight," she told Juan Mario. She pushed Rosa's body forward. When she was an arm's length away from the cooler, she let go of the cadaver and reached for the box. Someone grabbed her arm and pulled, enabling her to inch herself up the side of the cooler. For a few seconds, she allowed herself to think that they were going to be saved. But then a man grabbed her legs from behind, and as he attempted to pull himself onto the cooler, she panicked. María Victoria lunged for the edge of the cooler, hoping to keep from being yanked off, but her rough movement caused the whole box to tip over. People who'd been holding on lost their grip and tumbled on top of her. Arms and hands clawed and tugged, and in the confusion, in the desperate attempt to survive the unthinkable in the lightless open sea, in that night that had started so innocently before veering off into tragedy, María Victoria felt her only son slip silently off her back.

"Somebody grab him!" she screamed. "Get him before he drowns!"

She lost him right in front of her eyes.

He was gone.

All of them were gone.

CHAPTER 11

GUANABACOA

July 13, 1994

After everyone had left on the bus, Jorge García knew he'd miss them all, but he also rejoiced in the knowledge that they would, in just a few hours, be far away from all that had made their lives so bleak they couldn't bear to see another sunrise in Cuba. In the dark, he and La Flaca dreamed aloud about what their lives would be like without them. Someday, if the insanity ended, perhaps their lives could return to something like what they remembered from the time before Cuba had stopped being the place they knew of as Cuba.

They stayed close to the telephone. They expected to hear from Ramel's brother, who lived in an apartment in Old Havana that had a view of the port. He'd promised to call when he saw the *13 de Marzo* embark, but when they didn't hear from him they didn't panic. Phone service was so unreliable. They turned off the lights and tried to sleep, anticipating that María Victoria or Joel would telephone from Florida soon to tell them that Juanmi and all the others were, at last, free.

But they were far too anxious to sleep for very long, and as soon as day broke they were up. They turned on Radio Reloj and, as they sipped their customary cup of strong espresso, they listened to the loudly ticking clock that backed up the news readers all day long. They hadn't finished that first cup when what they heard shook them awake. A ship—it wasn't named—had capsized a few miles off shore. People had drowned, but no number was given.

They strained to hear details, but there were none. There was no mention of a tugboat. Nothing about women and children being aboard. The winds had been tranquil, with just a few clouds high up in the night sky. Ramel had assured them that the old tug was in tip-top shape and that nothing, nothing, could go wrong.

Jorge's uncle Carlos was the first to show up.

"Hey, are you getting the news?" he asked as he walked in.

"I don't think they're talking about our boat," Jorge told him, unwilling to think the unthinkable, despite what he'd heard on the radio.

At around nine, Jorge was looking outside when two men entered the neighborhood's CDR office down the street. When they drove off with Angelita, the CDR president, he began to worry that something indeed could have gone wrong. Had Ramel's tug had engine trouble? Did they get stuck in a freak storm or strike a reef? He kept his worrying to himself, trying not to upset La Flaca.

At around eleven, María Victoria's brother-in-law rushed in with more bad news.

"Now they're saying it was a stolen tugboat that capsized," he told them.

The news reports were infuriatingly vague, but there was no question that, for them, each one was worse than the one before. By noon, Jorge's patience had run out. Sitting around waiting for news—bad news—was agonizing. Ester, Ramel's wife, lived nearby. "Maybe she's got information," he said. As they were getting ready to leave, a white Lada sedan drove up to the medical clinic next to the school down the street. Everyone in Cuba knew that white Ladas were state cars. Waiting outside for his wife, Jorge watched a man in a green military uniform enter the clinic. Shortly afterward, the officer came out with the local doctor, and both of them got into the Lada. It drove slowly down San Sebastián Street and stopped in front of Jorge's house.

The officer got out stiffly. He opened the rear door and extended a hand to a strange, bedraggled figure. It took Jorge a few seconds to recognize his daughter. He was horrified. María Victoria, then twenty-eight years old, looked nothing like the person who'd left the house just a few hours before. Her long, dark hair was stuck to her back like seaweed, and she smelled of diesel fuel. Her blouse was ripped and her face, arms, back, and legs were covered with black and blue bruises. Her shoes were gone, her eyes were glazed. As they entered the house, the doctor urged La Flaca to sit down. Jorge heard that and braced for the worst. The officer pulled him aside.

"I don't like getting involved in any of this, but I was given orders," the officer said, his voice low so La Flaca couldn't hear. "There's been an accident."

Jorge looked to his daughter. Trembling, she said "Papá, Joel is gone."

Hearing that, La Flaca let out a scream that could be heard several houses away.

"And Ernesto too."

"And Juan Mario."

The officer looked at Jorge. "I should leave now," he said. Neighbors who had seen the Lada and heard the scream came to the door to find out what was wrong. Jorge led his daughter to the rooftop to get her away from the crowd.

"Tell me what happened."

She told him all about the water cannons, the ferocious jets of water that hit them and hit them and would not stop hitting them. She showed him the bruises on her face and arms where the water had pounded her until she could hardly breathe.

"I even picked up Juan Mario to show them there were children on board and—I couldn't believe it—they turned their cannons on him and hit him with the water until I covered him."

"And the others?" he asked. "Who else made it?"

"Iván," she said. "Dariel. And me."

"But the others?"

"They're gone, Papá. All of them."

"What are you two talking about?" La Flaca was slowly climbing the stairs.

There was no way he could tell her the gruesome truth, that all of them— their son, their grandson, their son-in-law, their brother-in-law Ramel—in all, fourteen members of their family were missing, along with Spike and other dear friends and neighbors they'd laughed with just hours before. Of the sixty-eight adults and children who had boarded the 13 de Marzo earlier that day, thirty-seven had died. María Victoria was one of the thirty-one survivors, but Jorge could see that she had been scarred both physically and mentally. It surely would break what was left of La Flaca's heart to know the extent of the tragedy. Instead he told her that the radio had lied. Radio Reloj had called it an accident. But what María Victoria had been through was no accident.

Jorge funneled his grief and anger the only way he knew how. No Cuban reporter would touch the story they had to tell, so he reached out to a foreign correspondent he had met through his work with dogs. Fernando Ravsberg, a longtime freelance foreign correspondent in Havana, had recently interviewed him about his Dobermans for a BBC report from Cuba. He called Ravsberg on the night of the sinking and told him that what Radio Reloj was reporting was not true. Bring your camera tomorrow, Jorge told him, and María Victoria will tell the truth about what actually happened.

Contradicting the government's account would surely bring repercussions, but she didn't care. What more could she possibly lose? Her husband was gone. Her son was gone. Her brother, her uncles, her cousins, all gone. The grief and the chaos inside the San Sebastián house made it impossible to do the interview there, so they arranged for Ravsberg to set up his camera at the house of María Victoria's father-in-law, Santiago, who lived in Guanabacoa. When Ravsberg turned on his camera, María Victoria related in terrifying detail how the other tugboats had deliberately sunk the 13 de Marzo and later ignored survivors' pleas for help. She broke down in tears in front of the camera when she described the hellish last moments when Juan Mario slipped off her back, and she made it clear that there had been a deliberate attempt to leave no survivors. She said she could see a Cuban Coast Guard cutter standing by doing nothing to help until a passing freighter flying a Greek flag drew close. Only then did the Coast Guard throw them life preservers and pull them out. She did not see anyone make an effort to recover the bodies of the dead, not even Rosa's. After she and the other survivors were brought ashore, the women and children were questioned briefly, then released. The men were taken to Villa Marista, Cuba's state security headquarters, and were being held there.

María Victoria's heartrending account contrasted starkly with the government's version of events. *Granma*, the official newspaper of the Communist Party of Cuba and the primary source of information in a country that did not tolerate an independent press, reported that a group of antisocial elements, the description used for anyone acting outside expected standards of discipline, loyalty, and revolutionary fervor, had taken the tugboat by force in "an irresponsible act of piracy." The first article about the sinking—all of three paragraphs published on the bottom of page two on July 14—said that the tug "capsized" about seven miles off the coast and that the Cuban Coast Guard had acted "heroically" in rescuing thirty-one survivors. The article mentioned an "undetermined number" of victims but gave no names.

Ravsberg's interview with María Victoria made it to Miami, where it was broadcast on channel 51, a local Spanish-language channel, on July 15. Nobody in Cuba would have known about it except for Cubans' inventiveness in times of necessity. Miami broadcasts were routinely picked up with makeshift parabolic antennae that were made from coffee cans and metal scraps. So long as the dishes were kept hidden from the government, people could find out what the regime didn't want them to know.

But even with such resourcefulness, relatively few people in Cuba, outside of a small, sad circle of relatives and friends in Guanabacoa, knew the truth of how thirty-seven people had died seven miles off the coast.

In subsequent days, *Granma* published several reports about the incident, without expressing a word of outrage over the loss of so many lives. Under threats of extended imprisonment, some of the survivors contradicted María Victoria's account—a version of events that *Granma* never published or even acknowledged. One of the most damning descriptions of what happened came from her cousin Dariel Prieto Suárez, Ramel's son, while he was in prison and under extreme duress. He was a member of state security who worked as a driver for an officer in the Interior Ministry. In an editorial published in *Granma* about ten days after the sinking, he was quoted as saying from Villa Marista prison that responsibility for the deaths lay squarely with his father, as well as every adult who had decided to bring children on such a risky and illegal excursion.

A BITTER LESSON FOR IRRESPONSIBLE PEOPLE was the headline that *Granma* ran on the rare, full-page signed editorial that was intended to be the last word on the incident. It portrayed Ramel as a calculating schemer who had drugged a night watchman, cut chains, and broken locks in order to steal a leaky wooden vessel that was 115 years old and known to be unseaworthy. When the tug was last inspected, the article reported, several leaks in the wooden hull had been discovered. The inspection report concluded, according to *Granma*, that the *13 de Marzo* should be "limited to work within the port."

The tug sank, *Granma* reported, when one of the Polargos attempted to keep the thieves from stealing property that belonged to the Cuban people. It accidentally rammed the older tug, breaching its hull. Blame for the deaths—no number was given, nor were names ever published, except for Ramel's—clearly rested on the irresponsible adults who risked their children's lives. "Just the act alone of heading out to sea with only four life jackets on board for more than sixty people is an indication of the level of irresponsibility of those who came up with the idea," the newspaper lectured. "If today thirty-one of them are still alive it is because of the actions of those who fought so hard in the middle of the night to save them."

Dariel's brother Iván also was held in Villa Marista. He had survived the sinking by squeezing through the bottom part of a door in the pilothouse that had been busted apart by the Polargos' water cannons. Unlike so many others, he had learned to swim at school, and that may have saved his life. When security agents questioned him, they told him to be thankful he was safely in prison because people were furious with the adults who'd endangered the children. They brought him a copy of *Granma* with his brother's damning comments but did not mention a word about María Victoria's television interview that told an entirely different story.

THAT SUMMER OF 1994 was one of the hottest on record, adding to the misery of Cubans trying to just make it from day to day. The same suspicion and hostility that had led to María del Carmen being accused of illicitly enriching herself with precious seafood effectively branded Jorge and his family enemies of the state. The house on San Sebastián that he had sacrificed so much to build became a prime target of the Rapid Response Brigades, groups of party loyalists who stood outside chanting insults and denouncing Jorge and his family for endangering the children they had brought aboard the tug. "Worms," they shouted. "Antisocial counterrevolutionaries!" They claimed that the family was controlled by the "Miami mafia," Cuban exiles who so hated Castro that they would do anything to bring down his regime.

Jorge was consumed with grief and anger, but he also felt tremendous guilt for his role in enlisting Eddy and Ramel and encouraging Joel and the others to go. At the same time, he was outraged by the obvious lies the government was spreading. Ramel drugging the night watchman? Ridiculous. Thieves? If they were stealing anything, why would Felo have left the keys in the ignition of the tourist bus so his agency could recover it the next morning? What disturbed him most was the way the operators of the Polargos that had rammed the tug were being portrayed as heroes and not as murderers.

One day not long after the sinking, a man dressed in civilian clothes showed up at the house on San Sebastián.

"I'd like to speak with you," the man said, "in private."

By then, Jorge had become suspicious of people just showing up at his door. But there was something compelling about this man, about the quiet but insistent way that he said he had important information to share.

Jorge led him upstairs, away from the rest of the family, and shut the door. "What is this about?"

The man pulled a sheet of paper from his pocket. On it were names and addresses of the Polargos' crews.

Jorge wasn't sure what to do next. He recognized some of the addresses as being in Guanabacoa, but he had no way of knowing whether the men on the list had actually manned the tugs. What if it was some kind of trap, setting him up to be accused of making threats or false denunciations? All he knew was that he had to do something. He mounted Joel's bicycle and set out to find the one person he most needed to challenge—the man on the list identified as captain of the Polargo that had rammed the *13 de Marzo*. The address was familiar, a few houses away from the home of María Victoria's father-in-law.

Jorge found the man he was looking for, and the confrontation out in the street was not pleasant. The captain admitted that he had been involved in the attempt to detain the *13*, but he denied that his boat was the one that sank it. (Radio Martí identified him and broadcast his name: Jesús Martínez.) He refused to accept responsibility for the deaths, but he did say something that convinced Jorge that the *13 de Marzo* had been ambushed. Martínez hadn't been scheduled to work that night, but he blurted out that at the last minute he was told to come in right away because there was going to be "an operation."

As the official press in Cuba ignored or downplayed the sinking, Radio Martí ran with the story, laying out all the tragic details and breathlessly reporting that tensions in Havana were rising along with the soaring summer temperatures. The Cuban government scrambled Radio Martí signals but couldn't block them completely. Rumors began to swirl through the baking hot streets of Guanabacoa and Havana that a fleet of private boats would soon be on its way to Cuba, and another Mariel boatlift was going to take place. The rumors were just that, the result of wishful thinking by exhausted and angry Cubans who had already suffered through several years of the special period, repeated and magnified by overly optimistic Cuban Americans in Miami who desperately wanted to believe that Fidel's days were numbered.

With the capital city primed to explode, some of the most desperate people decided that they could not take it any longer. Just as María Victoria and the others had looked to the harbor as the route to freedom, so did small groups of Cubans who tried to use the pint-size Regla ferries as their ticket out. Two weeks after the *13 de Marzo* sank, on the traditional 26th of July anniversary marking the failed attack on the Moncada barracks that sparked the Castros' revolution in 1953, a ferry named *Baraguá* was hijacked as it made its way slowly across Havana Harbor. A handful of men took control of the crowded ferry and pointed it toward the open sea. They made it to international waters, where they were intercepted by a U.S. Coast Guard cutter.

Fifteen passengers who wanted to go on to the United States were taken aboard. The ferry and remaining passengers were allowed to return to Cuba.

Just over a week later, another ferry was hijacked, this time with an unusual passenger on board. Jorge's nephew Iván had just been released from Villa Marista, but his brother Dariel was still being held. Iván was heading to Havana with his mother to see a lawyer who they hoped could help get Dariel released. Afraid to get back on the water after his ordeal on the *13 de Marzo*, Iván waited over an hour for a bus, but none ever arrived. Reluctantly, he and his mother squeezed onto a harbor ferry called *La Coubre*. It was so overcrowded that people hung from the open sides, their feet dangling inches above the dirty water. The ferry was moseying across the harbor when Iván heard shouting. At first, he figured it was just another argument among people packed too close to one another. But when the crowd pulled apart, he saw a man holding what looked like a hand grenade, and someone else who was waving a pistol and a knife. They ordered the pilot to head to Florida.

The ferry made it to international waters before running out of fuel. An American Coast Guard cutter intercepted them and gave the 190 passengers aboard the choice of being taken to Florida or returning to Cuba. For Iván, it was a bewildering turn of events. His father had died trying to give people the same chance to flee that he, by some miracle, now was being offered. All he had to do was say the word and he would be free. "Go ahead," his mother urged him. "I'll take care of your brother. Don't you worry."

Of the 190 passengers on *La Coubre*, 117 decided to take their chances in Florida. Iván was not one of them. Unwilling to leave his widowed mother alone while his brother was being detained, Iván returned to Cuba with her and seventy-one others aboard the Cuban Coast Guard cutters that had been sent to get them. As the ships steamed toward Cuba, Iván stood on the deck peering toward the coastline. Swimming, martial arts, and other physical activities had given him broad shoulders and a restless spirit. He heard a noise and looked up. The small white-and-blue airplanes of the Brothers to the Rescue group from Miami flew overhead, searching for rafters attempting to escape from Cuba.

When the Coast Guard cutters docked in Cuba, they were welcomed back with cheers. Here were real Cubans who had rejected the disingenuous invitation of the Americans. Here were symbols of the resolve of the revolution.

Including Iván.

Just three weeks earlier *Granma* had denounced him as irresponsible, an antisocial criminal.

Now he was a hero.

ON AUGUST 4, the day after the *La Coubre* incident, the *Baraguá* ferry was commandeered yet again. The hijackers threatened to harm the passengers unless the pilot took them to Florida. The *Baraguá* didn't get very far this time. No one had brought extra fuel, and the little ferry ran out of diesel while still inside Cuba's territorial waters. The engine died, and the tide pushed the ferry back toward shore.

The hijackings were symptoms of a desperate people on the verge of coming completely unhinged. Then, on the morning of Friday, August 5, rumors spread that yet another ferry had been commandeered. People flocked to the waterfront to see, but as the crowd grew larger, police pushed them back. There was some shoving, and shots were fired. New rumors spread that the flotilla that Radio Martí had reported on was about to leave Florida, drawing yet more people to the waterfront. They jammed the seawall, peering toward the horizon, searching for the boats that they hoped would take them to freedom.

CHAPTER 12

HAVANA HARBOR
August 5, 1994

Even in the most wretched days of the special period, when the electricity in her house was off far longer than it was on, when propane gas disappeared and she had to invent a way to cook using kerosene that smoked like hell, when she found herself hoarding plantain skins that with some culinary magic and the power of suggestion she could coax into substituting for meat, Miriam Díaz understood that life continued. Babies were still being born, young girls still celebrated their *quinceañeras,* and her youngest son, Adalberto, planned to marry a nice Guanabacoa girl. The wedding was scheduled for the end of that very hot summer of 1994. Miriam, a proud mother of three from an old-line Guanabacoa family, was intent on looking her best. She could make her own dress and she had some old jewelry hidden away. But the only shoes she had were scuffed and worn down. They served their purpose when she worked as a hostess in a nightly cabaret, but special period or not, wearing them to Adalberto's wedding was out of the question.

With the big day just a few weeks away, she took the number 29 bus from the center of Guanabacoa to nearby Regla, then boarded the ferry to hunt for a decent pair of heels in central Havana. She'd heard about the ferries being hijacked again and again over the previous few days, and she had been saddened by the news that her friend Spike had drowned with so many others on the *13 de Marzo* back in July. But there was one thing about Cubans:

regardless of whatever was going on around them, they could focus on themselves and their needs so intensely they simply didn't expect anything bad to happen to them. These were crazy, unpredictable times, but at this moment, nothing was more important to her than finding shoes for the wedding. And taking the ferry across the harbor was the only way to get them.

Miriam was forty-seven, old enough to remember when the fancy stores along Obispo, Galiano, and San Rafael in Havana were well stocked with the latest fashions from all over the world. But that was under the capitalism that had been expelled from Cuba decades before. In its place was the communism/socialism that she supported and that had brought hospitals, schools, and greater opportunities for women like her. Sure, it was inconvenient that every one of those grand old emporiums was gone, replaced by state-run outlets that carried only cheap, unattractive clothing. And forget about shoes! She'd come to accept that there always would be trade-offs in life, and until the special period ended, she'd simply have to make do with what they had. The consolation was that everyone else had to do the same.

As the little ferry crossed the harbor, Miriam hoped that the consignment store on San Rafael would have a pair of someone else's shoes that were not so outdated that they'd make her look frumpy. Maybe she could get the right color and, if she was truly blessed, the correct size. Her mind was focused on the hunt for shoes as she got off the crowded ferry with the other passengers. But when she expected the crowd to thin out, the waterfront remained jammed with people lined up as far as she could see. Was the carnival already being set up? The heat was stifling, and she thought it would be cooler by the water, but there were so many people she couldn't get close. She crossed to the other side of the street and ran into more crowds.

"What's going on?" she asked someone on the Malecón.

"The boats. We're waiting for the boats to come."

Miriam scanned the horizon but didn't see any boats. When she turned around, she faced a sea of people. On the edge of the crowd, she noticed several police motorcycles, with uniformed officers standing nearby. She tried to get through to one of the side streets jutting off the Malecón and stumbled into a crowd of angry young men, shirtless in the oppressive August heat.

Many of them held rocks or sticks, and they were shouting words that exploded in her ears. She'd never heard such things expressed in public before: "Down with Fidel!" they yelled, their eyes fierce with anger. "Freedom!" Some had started to run when a man climbed up on the hood of a white Lada sedan and pointed a gun. People who stood their ground around him shouted, "Murderer! Murderer!"

Then from somewhere in the crowd—there were so many people—came a truck. Men stood in the open bed. When it drew near, she could see that they wore civilian pants and T-shirts printed with the words CONTINGENTE BLAS ROCA CALDERÍO, a government-controlled construction unit named after an influential Cuban communist. But it was plain that they weren't construction workers because each one held a police baton. Miriam had heard that when there was trouble, the government sent out police in disguise to give the impression that it was ordinary workers, and not police agents, who were trying to quell the disturbance. As the men hopped down from the truck, a woman was being pushed through the crowd toward them. Miriam was sickened when she saw that the woman's head was covered with blood. When she heard people around her again shouting "Murderer!" she became frightened and tried to get away, crossing the potholed street and continuing past broken-down buildings and garbage-filled lots. She turned a corner and kept going, crossing over San Rafael Boulevard without bothering to look for the consignment store. When she reached the National Theater of Cuba she stopped to catch her breath. Several women were standing there with their children and a number of large packages. They said they had come downtown because they heard there would be boats to take them away. And you, they wanted to know, are you waiting for the boats too?

"I just came to buy a pair of shoes for my son's wedding," she told them. "That's all."

She didn't know what she'd gotten herself into and she didn't want to find out. She made her way to a bus stop, hoping to get away from the disturbance. She'd have to come back for her shoes another day. After a long wait, a bus finally came. The driver said it was too dangerous for him to take the regular route around the harbor to Guanabacoa. Instead, he was heading to the neighborhood of La Víbora, away from the port. One of Miriam's aunts lived there, so she boarded the bus, keeping her head down as the driver advised in case rocks were thrown.

That night, Miriam watched the TV news with her aunt. The anchor reported that people had been drawn to the waterfront by false rumors from the "mafia in Miami" and then had turned violent, leaving two policemen dead and thirty-five people injured. As temperatures rose, the crowds had grown larger until they surged forward, breaking windows. At the Hotel Deauville on the Malecón, near where she had been, a nasty confrontation had broken out between the police and what the newscaster described as delinquents, drug addicts, and antisocial troublemakers.

"That's a lie," Miriam told her aunt. "What they're saying is a lie. Believe me. The people that they say were drug addicts? I saw it with my own eyes, and it wasn't like that at all."

She'd been there, felt the anger of the crowd, seen the frustration in the faces of the protesters. She'd seen just a small portion of what went on that day on the Malecón, but there was no doubt in her mind that it hadn't been caused by delinquents. It was a spontaneous public demonstration against Castro's government—the first she'd ever seen. The first anyone in Cuba had seen. The crowds were protesting the hundreds of days without electricity, overheated apartments, bad food, dirty clothes, mind-numbing television—when there was electricity. What had once been inconceivable—that the Cuban people would turn on Fidel, denounce the revolution, and pour into the streets like an angry, desperate mob, breaking windows, stealing from the stores, and agitating for the end of the government—had happened right across the water from her own Guanabacoa. There was only one national news program in Cuba, and what was being reported about that day simply wasn't true. And if this report was a lie, she had to consider, what about all the things that she'd heard on TV or read about in *Granma* but hadn't seen for herself? What about the hijacked ferries? What about Spike and the tugboat?

A week later, Miriam took the ferry again, crossing the dirty harbor and disembarking in Old Havana to continue her quest for wedding shoes. This time, she found them. They weren't cheap, costing several months' salary. But at least she knew she would be presentable for her son's wedding. One problem had been resolved. But the uneasy feeling that the government had lied to her, had lied to everyone, and that somehow she had been living a lie for a long time, lingered.

NINETY MILES, THE DISTANCE BETWEEN Cuba and Key West, was what the protesters on the Malecón believed separated them from freedom. Ninety miles also was the distance between Havana and the beach at Varadero where Cary, Pipo, and the rest of the family were ending another sun-filled holiday on the same day the protest erupted on the Malecón.

When they'd arrived in Varadero earlier that week, they'd been in their glory. Pipo's father had once again booked rooms for them at the Iberostar Barlovento Hotel, jointly owned by the Spanish hotel chain and the Cuban government. For the week that they stayed at the luxurious resort, it seemed they had been transported to another country. While Miriam Díaz and Jorge García were frying grapefruit rind, the hotel's buffet table was laid with real meat and fruit and bread, anything you could want, and as much of it as you cared to eat! This was one of the ways that Fidel had reacted to the loss of Soviet aid—opening up Cuba to international tourism for the first time since taking power. There was a beautiful pool for Oscar and his cousins to play in. Cary and Pipo had their own room. So did Esperanza and Miguel. Zenaida had a third room, where she was in charge of watching the boys. It wasn't in-expensive, but they could handle it easily. Cary was director at a major manu-facturing company, and Pipo, on the advice of a friend, had taken a job as head of services at a recreation center and state store in Cojímar. There, along with his salary, he was able to purchase groceries at discount prices, sav-ing them more money and allowing them to avoid ever having to eat fried grapefruit skin.

On the Friday that Miriam shopped for wedding shoes, Cary and her fam-ily were hoping to pack as much fun as possible into their last full day of vaca-tion. It was hot, the crystal-clear waters of Varadero were cool, and they spent most of the morning on the powdery white sand beach. In the early afternoon they headed back to the Barlovento for lunch. Passing through the lobby,

Cary happened to glance at a television, and what she saw stopped her short. The hotel captured foreign TV broadcasts, including CNN. Cary stood in the lobby watching video of the angry mob running wild on the Malecón, breaking windows, throwing rocks and sticks, and shouting, though she could hardly believe it, "Down with Fidel!"

"Look," Zenaida said, teasing Cary. "There's your Havana. Look at it, coming apart right before your eyes." Cary and Esperanza adored their mother, but her view of Cuba's revolutionary government had grown increasingly distant from theirs. Zenaida had once believed wholeheartedly in Fidel and the revolution, and she personally had benefited from the changes he brought to Cuba. But as a young girl, Zenaida had heard her own mother cursing the socialism she thought had infected Jamaica, and the frustrations and disappointments of her own life had revived those fears and resentments in her. Her long search for housing had left her embittered, and the special period had drained the last of her loyalty to the revolution. She was too old to leave and start over somewhere else. But she was concerned about what was happening to her family, especially Cary, who seemed to have placed party above family.

Cary responded to Zenaida's taunt like the *partidista* her mother believed she was. "That's not Cuba," she said, pointing to the television. "It's just the enemy putting together images to make people think that's what's happening here."

"Oh, you think so? Look! Look at what's going on!"

Zenaida's mocking words resonated as Cary stared at the TV. Still, she refused to believe that what she was seeing was real. "You know what the enemy can do. It's just a montage of images that they found to make it look like a protest. But it's not real." She stormed out of the lobby, dragging Oscar up to their room. She turned on the television and watched with mounting worry as the screen filled with more scenes of the mob at the Malecón.

Cary refused to believe that her own people could behave like that, attacking government property and shouting hateful words in such an ungrateful way. She knew that the special period was much more difficult for others than it was for her; she saw that at the aluminum plant every day. But Cuba had been through many challenging times since 1959, and people had never responded like this. *Maybe it's the special period and what they've been eating that are making them go crazy,* she thought, *awful things that have blinded them so they can't see that this is just a pothole in the road, not a dead end.* It was inconceivable that any members of her generation, people who had invested so much in the new nation they were building, would revolt against the party or do something as risky as commandeering a ferry and fleeing to Florida.

She tried to put the images of the Malecón out of her mind and stay focused on the precious time remaining in their vacation. The following day they'd have to head back to Regla. Why waste time worrying about something that wasn't even real?

MIRIAM DÍAZ HAD STUMBLED INTO the worst part of the protests; most Cubans never saw what she saw. Nor could they see what Cary saw on the foreign newscast. For most Cubans, what happened on August 5, 1994, was not the first and only mass protest by Cubans against Castro's Cuba, but a firm demonstration of the people's affection for their leader. State media played down the protest, attributing it to a few delinquents who were stared down by loyal construction workers, and focused on the moment when Fidel's green army jeep pulled up to the Malecón and the comandante himself waded into what quickly transformed from an angry mob into an adoring audience.

"I had heard that there had been acts of violence. It was an essential duty to come here," Castro told the Cuban reporters who had been dispatched to record his arrival. "I had to see what was happening and, above all, to promote composure, calm."

Cary watched that scene play out on TV that same night. This was the Fidel she admired, the leader who did not fear his own people, even when they were angry as hell. "Of course, this does not surprise me," Fidel said as he stood outside the open door of his jeep, surrounded by people. "These provocations have been organized in advance." He then linked all of the events of that summer, from the ferry hijackings to the disturbances that day on the Malecón to the single incident that had set everything in motion. "One of the most infamous acts ever is what the United States did regarding the tugboat accident." He said everyone knew what really happened to the *13 de Marzo* a few weeks before. "It was actually the tugboat workers who did not want to let them take their boat away. They did everything possible to prevent the hijacking. Unfortunately, an accident tragically took place as part of the workers' efforts."

Castro then laid out his latest gambit, turning the worsening crisis on its head. Cuba was not preventing its people from leaving; it was keeping the United States safe. "We take special measures. We are truly guarding the U.S. coasts, and in exchange, when there is an incident, any accident, they accuse us of cruelty, murder, and all that."

Cary embraced this idea. She now believed that what she'd seen on the hotel TV was not a forgery but an actual protest, but one that, as Fidel said, the United States somehow had triggered through manipulation and deceit. "This was a deliberate provocation," Fidel said. "This is what the United States is seeking."

A Cuban reporter, apparently picking up on the rumors from Miami, asked Fidel if he was considering allowing another Mariel boatlift. "We are not opposed to anything, to letting those who want to leave, leave." Then he directly threatened the American government, accusing Washington of inciting the riot and encouraging the hijackings, as well as politicizing the sinking of the *13 de Marzo*.

"Either they set things in order or we will stop guarding the U.S. coasts."

Castro relished the tight spot into which he had painted the United States. He accused President Bill Clinton of using the tugboat incident to whip up anti-Cuban sentiment. Clinton had called the sinking of the *13 de Marzo* "a human tragedy" and "another example of the brutality of the Cuban regime."

"There we go again with the sinking of the tugboat," Castro said during the televised news program *This Very Day* (*Este Día*) a few weeks after the unrest on the Malecón. He accused Clinton of slandering Cuba by suggesting that the tugboat had been sunk deliberately, and he made clear what he thought of the sinking and the deaths of thirty-seven people who were aboard when he labeled it "the incident that began this entire process."

——◆——

As Cary and Pipo were returning from their vacation at the beach, Castro made good on his threat, ordering Cuban security forces not to stop anyone attempting to flee the island by water. It was a warm summer night when they heard a commotion in the street and came out of their apartment at SP79 to see what was going on. Cary held Oscar as she watched a group of young men and women in a horse-drawn cart hauling an inflated truck inner tube with wooden boards strapped to it. People ran down the street alongside it, cheering, "They're going! They're going!"

Cary had never seen anything like it, and she had trouble making sense of it. When the Mariel boatlift had taken place, she was studying in Kiev. Now, as she watched the rafters parading down the street as though they were heading to the carnival, she felt like crying. It hurt her to see people of her own generation so determined to risk everything and throw themselves to the sharks. She'd never forgotten what it was like being on the *Kazakhstan* when the sea turned ugly and waves rose as high as the deck of the ship. No matter how little food there was in Cuba, or how dark the streets of Havana got at night, she couldn't understand why anyone would risk everything to cross the Straits of Florida in a fragile homemade raft.

She didn't realize then that she was playing a part in helping them go.

The rafters used whatever material they could find to fashion makeshift vessels that could float them to freedom. The only source of building material was state enterprises, including Cary's own aluminum plant. At first it was wooden shipping pallets. The slats were ideal for making a rigid platform on top of inner tubes, like the raft Cary had seen from her building. But Novalum had something far more valuable. One of Cary's allies in the plant came to her in confidence to tell her that workers were stealing aluminum sheets and selling them on the street for around one hundred dollars apiece. The malleable metal was easily transformed into sturdy prows for the homemade rafts. The party loyalist in her felt aggrieved that her own workers were helping people abandon the country, to maybe end up as food for sharks. She had to do something.

Cary called a meeting before the first shift started one morning that August. More than 160 men gathered near the open gate of the large central workshop, early morning sunlight deepening the shadows inside. Cary knew that the men had resented her since she had held a meeting in the same spot when she took over as director a few months earlier. She knew she had to be careful about the way she addressed the issue of stealing when conditions in Cuba were so desperate that blankets were being cut up, cooked with tomato sauce and onions, and stuffed in bread for sandwiches.

"We are living in historic moments when people, large numbers of people, are making the decision to leave the country." She wore a skirt and T-shirt and cheap sneakers with rubber soles, the only new footwear available during the special period. The men watched intently as she laid out her defense of the revolution and what she felt was the patriotic duty of state workers.

"The objective of this meeting is not to persuade any of you not to go. That's your own decision. But our role as a state enterprise, and my role as a director of this enterprise responsible for all the goods and resources that are here, is to remind you that all of this is property of the state. As I am the representative of the state here, all I ask is prudence. Don't take a piece of metal that is supposed to become one of our products and sell it to people who are going to throw themselves into the sea. Don't do it. Please don't do it."

There was silence. "Do you agree or disagree?" she asked, looking from stone face to stone face. Nothing. "Does anybody have anything to say?"

Finally, an older worker, a solid supporter of the regime, spoke up. "You're right. We'll make sure nobody steals anything."

A few men cheered. Most murmured agreement, then turned and walked away. Not for a second did Cary believe that simply asking her employees not to steal would prevent more thefts. But she felt that she had done her part to defend the revolution, and she had done it in a public way that left no doubt about her allegiance. Still, it bothered her to see so many people abandoning Cuba when she thought of her country's future as brilliant. Things were changing. The brutal economic conditions were forcing the old men in the government to modify their concept of socialism and open some Cuban businesses to the outside. Hadn't Fidel already legalized the use of the despised

U.S. dollar? As director of Novalum, she now had the power to write checks, with a government cosigner, on the Novalum account, as if it were her own company. Surely Cuba was moving toward more openness and opportunity but doing so without turning its back on the promises of equality that were at the heart of the revolution.

By some measures, Cuba made unmatched strides toward leveling out Cuban society in the first decades after the revolution, raising the standard of living for the poor, but at the cost of limiting the ability of anyone to earn more than others. Racial discrimination had been outlawed in the 1976 constitution, and women now were being given a chance to lead. It was all so clear to her, and yet those people on the Malecón didn't see it that way. And the ones throwing themselves to the sharks, how could they be so blind?

ONE MONTH AFTER MARÍA VICTORIA had watched Juan Mario slip away from her, she and her father, along with other survivors of the doomed voyage, as well as family and friends from Guanabacoa, planned a tribute to those who were lost. Miriam Díaz wanted to go so she could toss a flower into the surf at one of the beaches in East Havana, to prove that her friend Spike and the others who died would not be forgotten. She had done the same to commemorate the disappearance of Camilo Cienfuegos, one of Fidel's most charismatic guerrilla commanders, whose plane went down mysteriously before the end of 1959, and she believed that the victims of the 13 de Marzo were just as important. But a few days before the planned ceremony for the tugboat, a local police officer showed up at Jorge García's house on San Sebastián Street. Word had gotten out about the ceremony. The officer was there to tell them they couldn't do it that day because August 13 was Fidel's birthday.

"We are not going to permit you to have any kind of meeting on that day," he warned Jorge.

"His birthday doesn't mean anything to us," Jorge said.

"You can't do it."

"We're going to throw flowers into the sea on August 13. You do what you have to do, and so will we."

Jorge changed plans but told only his immediate family. Miriam Díaz and the others were left in the dark and never made it. Early on August 13, Jorge took a circuitous route from Guanabacoa to the colossal public housing complex known as Alamar, determined to shake off any police who might try to follow them. They made it to the water's edge without being stopped, but then two strange things happened. They watched a group of men push off in a homemade raft, bound for Florida. They wished the men luck, understanding full well the danger they faced. Then they threw in their flowers. As the flowers floated out to sea, several ducks swam by. Jorge thought they probably had escaped from some Santería ceremony.

One of the ducks waddled out of the water and headed directly toward María Victoria. It stuck close to her and followed her back to the car. She took it with her. With all the shortages, it wasn't easy for them to find things to feed the duck, but they managed. And no matter how bad things got, they all knew they could never kill and eat it.

BY THE END OF THAT CHAOTIC MONTH of August, the wave of Cubans seeking to escape the island threatened to engulf southern Florida. President Clinton ordered the Coast Guard to intercept rafters at sea and transfer them to the Guantanamo Naval Base. In just one week, the U.S. Coast Guard picked up 10,190 rafters. More than 30,000 Cubans eventually were held at Guantanamo before being processed and admitted to the United States. Clinton then tightened the screws on Cuba, prohibiting Cuban Americans from sending money to family on the island, limiting the number of charter flights to Cuba, and threatening to take to the United Nations accusations of Cuba's violations of human rights, including the sinking of the 13 de Marzo.

The disturbances along the Malecón became a pivotal moment in Cuban history, undermining Fidel's boasts that the lack of public protests proved that people supported him and his policies. For the Cuban people, the day came to be known as the Maleconazo, and most every Cuban on the island remembered it in one way or another depending on their politics. Cary and Pipo were dismayed by it while Zenaida saw it as proof of the revolution's decay. María del Carmen was working on the waterfront that summer, and when she heard about the riot, she was glad that she was locked inside the comfort and security of the house on Corralfalso. She had taken off that day to care for her mother, who was confined to bed, her kidneys failing.

In their new home on the outskirts of Guanabacoa, Arturo Montoto and María Eugenia watched knots of excited, scared, and desperate people cheering as they made their way to the sea. But what happened out in the street had not affected them. They possessed the same self-centeredness as Miriam Díaz, which enabled them to ignore the big picture and focus on their own survival. They planted fruit trees at their home in the Santa Fe section of Guanabacoa and scraped by on their meager salaries. It had become difficult for Arturo to paint; when he planned a still life, he had to borrow a tomato from a neighbor. His neighbor made him promise to return the tomato. She needed it for her daughter's lunch.

CHAPTER 13

GUANABACOA

August 1994

After Jorge García tossed flowers into the surf at Alamar on Fidel's birthday, he could no longer hold on to any delusions about the horrors of the night the tug was sunk. Even though no bodies had ever been recovered, and the government made no attempt to bring the wreckage of the *13 de Marzo* to the surface, fourteen members of his family were gone. For good. The finality of it came home to him when he was summoned to the office that oversaw the government's supplemental food program. Spike's wife, who ran the office in Guanabacoa, demanded that he sign papers officially removing Joel, Juan Mario, and María Victoria's husband, Ernesto, from the *libreta* even though death certificates had never been issued for them, or for any of the victims.

His final words to his youngest son, "We'll see each other in eternity," haunted him as conditions on San Sebastián became more oppressive. Rapid Response Brigades continued to harass him and his family. María Victoria was fired from her job at the store in Guanabacoa where she had worked with Ernesto. Jorge was not allowed to teach, drive, or take any job with the state. He was even expelled from the local rescue squad. Guanabacoa, where he had lived his entire life, had become a prison cell.

But he was determined not to give in. He still had his golden voice and the tape recorder he'd brought home from Africa, and he used both to eke out a living selling recordings of popular songs and hosting girls' *quinceañeras*. La

Flaca was still by his side, her grief so great that it strained her weak heart almost to breaking. He still had María Victoria, though it was difficult to imagine how she could go on with her life in anything like a normal way after the nightmare she'd been through. And he still had his dogs, even after he was stripped of his position as vice president of the canine sports club.

Jorge felt that he owed the dead justice. It was painfully clear that the government wanted only its version of the incident to be known. Getting the truth out would take an extraordinary effort. María Victoria continued to tell her story. In an interview with the *Washington Post* a few months later, she said that she thought Fidel really believed that what had happened was an accident because all of the people around him were lying to him. "He needs to know the truth, that this was murder." Jorge understood that his daughter couldn't shoulder all responsibility for spreading the truth by herself. He'd have to get involved. He wasn't looking for revenge, but it was important that the voices that had been silenced be heard. The damning testimony that *Granma* had attributed to some of the survivors couldn't be left as the only record of the crime. He knew of only one way that the true horror of that night could be known and that someday—no matter how long it might take— justice would be achieved.

He took out Joel's Chinese bicycle and began his quest for truth. He knew many of the people who had boarded the *13 de Marzo*, and he was familiar with every street and alley in Guanabacoa. Slowly, over the course of weeks, then months, then years, he tracked down the stories of all sixty-eight people who had boarded the tug. Sometimes La Flaca went with him, riding side-saddle on the bicycle frame. He gathered photographs of all those who had drowned and managed to get some details from their families so they would be remembered as more than just names. He found out that the youngest victim, Hellen Martínez Enríquez, who was six days shy of six months old when she drowned, had dark eyes like her father and a white birthmark on her thigh. The oldest, Manuel Cayol, was a retired steel worker whose adult children were already living in the United States when he boarded the *13 de Marzo*.

Jorge pursued every one of the thirty-one survivors. Some didn't want to talk to him. Susana Rojas Martínez was only ten when Jorge sat with her in her home. Her hands were shaking as she recalled how the tug sank so quickly that her mother, Daisy, and three-year-old little sister, Dadney, fell off one side, and she fell off the other. "When I grow up," she told Jorge, "I'm going to be a lawyer so I can defend people who have problems."

It took Jorge three attempts to find the tugboat's skipper, Raúl Muñoz, and when he finally tracked him down, Muñoz made it clear from the outset that what happened was no accident. "In no country of the world, in no ocean, in no sea, anywhere, from the point of view of navigation should one vessel try to approach another. In no circumstances and for no reason. And less so if the vessel being approached is transporting people or worse, children, some only months old."

The twenty-five-year-old skipper did not mince words. "It was a massacre. They decided in advance to sink the *13 de Marzo*, not to stop it."

Sometimes Jorge had to use guile to get past the Rapid Response Brigades that kept watch on the homes of survivors to prevent them from talking. When he pedaled over to the apartment of Gustavo Martínez Gutiérrez, a thirty-eight-year-old electrician who had tried to help Muñoz open the hatch on the *13*, Jorge had to tell a small lie to find him.

"Excuse me." He approached two older women in the neighborhood where he believed Martínez Gutiérrez lived. "Look, I just returned from Moscow and I want to see the family of a friend from work. But I've been away two years and I don't remember the address. I was here once, but now all the buildings look the same."

"What is this person's name?"

"Gustavo." Then he added, "And his wife's name is Yuliana."

The women looked at each other skeptically, then one told him to follow her.

Jorge had to wait several hours until Martínez showed up and reluctantly agreed to talk. He described listening to the screams of the people trapped below as he desperately tried to help Muñoz open the deck hatch, knowing that his own wife and infant daughter, Hellen, were down there. Only his son,

Yandy, ten, had survived. Martínez was an electrician, not a sailor, and he had never had his head below water. He said the Polargos circled the wreckage of the tug, taunting them: "This is what you wanted!" He finally reached the floating cooler where his son was hanging on. When the boy saw him, he began to cry, asking where his mother and sister were. Martínez told him they were okay and had been picked up already. But he knew differently.

In interview after interview, Jorge heard the same story. That no one had cut any chains or drugged anyone to get onto the pier. That the other tugs had acted aggressively toward them right from the start, using their water cannons as weapons. That after their tug sank, the other crews did nothing to help. One survivor brought Jorge to tears again. Jorge Luis Cuba Suárez, known in the neighborhood as Pimpi, was with Jorge's son Joel in the hold of the tug when it was rammed. Joel took off the silver chain with a medal of the Virgin of Guadalupe that he wore around his neck and asked Pimpi to hold it for him, maybe in a premonition that he wouldn't make it out. Pimpi safeguarded the medal in his pocket just as seawater flooded in. He managed to get to the metal staircase and climb out in time.

Joel did not.

Pimpi was hauled off to prison with the other survivors. The day after he was released, he visited the house on San Sebastián and handed Jorge the medal.

Along with his interviews, Jorge gathered information to refute the government's argument that the condition of the *13 de Marzo* had doomed it from the start. He talked to a graduate of the naval academy who argued that the tug could not have been 115 years old as the government claimed. Regardless of its actual age, its wooden hull had to have been well protected for it to still be in the water and working in the busy harbor. The articles in *Granma* claimed that with more than sixty-five people aboard, the *13 de Marzo* was grossly overloaded, an argument that Jorge found ironic. He, along with every Cuban his age, knew that in 1956 Fidel and Raúl had crossed the Gulf of Mexico in a grossly overloaded fishing yacht named *Granma* with eighty-two men and arms, ammunition, fuel, and food aboard.

The *Granma* had a wooden hull.

———◆———

MARÍA VICTORIA GARCÍA SUAREZ'S POWERFUL interviews with foreign correspondents had no noticeable impact on Cuban officials, but they helped trigger investigations outside of Cuba. In January 1995, the U.S. Senate Foreign Relations Committee heard the testimony of survivors who had managed to escape in the months following the sinking. Despite knowing that there might be reprisals against their families in Cuba, several gave damning accounts of the government's actions. Sergio Perodín, who had celebrated a birthday, along with Ramel's Doberman, the night the *13 de Marzo* pulled away from the dock, pushed off in a homemade raft a few weeks later. He was intercepted by the U.S. Coast Guard and taken to Guantanamo before being allowed to enter the United States.

Perodín told the committee that while he was at the base, he met a man who said he was the carpenter who had worked on the *13 de Marzo* in the months leading up to the departure. Perodín said the carpenter told him that the government had prepared the Polargos to go after any vessel that was commandeered. "And if any tugboat were to try to go to freedom," the man had said, "the orders were to sink it."

The Organization of American States (OAS) heard testimony from several survivors, including Arquímedes Lebrigio, who had lost his twenty-eight-year-old son Jorge in the incident. In *Granma*, Lebrigio was reported to have said the tug sank because there were too many people on board. "It was overloaded," the paper quoted him as saying. "It was very old and made of wood. When I got on it, I realized that it wasn't going to hold out. Whatever happened there would have happened a few miles farther out to sea."

Shortly after the sinking, Lebrigio made another attempt to escape Cuba, this time on a raft. Like Perodín, he was intercepted and brought by the U.S. Coast Guard to Guantanamo, and eventually to Florida. Seated before the OAS commission in 1995, he told quite a different story from what *Granma* had published. He said government interrogators had pressured him to say that the tug had sprung a leak. He had been below deck when the *13 de Marzo* weighed anchor and did not see water leaking in anywhere. In his view, the old tug could easily have made it to Key West if the other boats hadn't attacked it.

The OAS faulted Cuba for not attempting to recover the bodies of the victims, even when the Brothers to the Rescue group offered to fly over the area to spot debris. When it asked the Cuban government for its version of the sinking, a response came from the Cuban Interests Section in Washington, which took the place of a Cuban embassy while diplomatic relations with the United States were suspended. The seven-paragraph statement concluded that blame for the "unfortunate accident" lay solely with the leaders of the expedition.

Amnesty International called on the Cuban government to launch a thorough investigation and make its findings public. When that didn't happen, Amnesty conducted its own investigation and, in 1997, several years after the sinking, issued its conclusions:

"Given the grave accusations of the survivors, the contradictory official accounts of the incident, and the failure of the Cuban authorities to carry out a full and impartial investigation and to make the findings public, as well as the fact that those seeking such an investigation or even simply to commemorate the incident have faced intimidation and harassment, Amnesty International believes that there are serious reasons to doubt the official version of events." The group discounted the government's explanations that the workers on the pursuing tugs had acted on their own. It was likely an official operation, Amnesty concluded, and "those who died as a result of the incident were victims of extrajudicial execution."

Despite the broad range of condemnations, the Cuban government never veered from the position outlined initially by Fidel and then, in a speech two weeks later, by Raúl Castro, who was then head of Cuba's armed forces.

"We reject with all our energy the hypocritical and venomous anti-Cuban campaign orchestrated around this incident," Raúl defiantly declared. "And we reject any interference in the internal affairs of our sovereign country by the United States or any other country. The State Department, the Congress, or President Clinton have no right whatsoever to meddle in an event that is the exclusive jurisdiction of the sovereign government of the Republic of Cuba."

CHAPTER 14

GUANABACOA
September 1994

Life in Cuba was going from difficult to impossible. People were being packed like cattle into long trailers called "camels" to get to and from work. Elevators in high rise buildings stopped working, converting sweltering apartments into prisons. Women were breaking open old batteries and using the black paste inside for hair dye. Cary found out that one of the workers at Novalum was stealing a harsh chemical that was used to clean and etch aluminum before it was painted. He boiled the chemical in a pot on his kitchen stove and put the melted goo into ice trays to cool. When they had hardened, he used the cubes of industrial-strength detergent as household soap.

Those Cubans who were not desperate enough to join the thirty thousand rafters who'd been taken to Guantanamo, along with the unknown number lost at sea, were forced to come to some reckoning with the wreckage of the revolution while continuing to live in what Cuba had become, regardless of how much that reality differed from their dreams. María del Carmen had been offered another chance to get away when friends left space in their homemade raft for her. But there was too much of her great-grandmother Eustoquia in her system, and the enameled ring of faith, hope, and charity on her left hand reminded her of her great-grandmother's vow never to venture onto the open seas again. More important, Mari's mother, Amelia, was quite ill, and she often stayed at home to nurse her through her final days. With

Román usually at sea, and her father and Tata having died years before, there was no one else but Mari to help.

The little house on Corralfalso that had been a refuge for Eustoquia became that for Mari as well. She had been holed up there on the day the Malecón exploded in protests. She also was home a few weeks after the disturbance when she was ordered to do an unscheduled inspection of the sanitary conditions on a fishing boat before it left Havana Harbor. She told her boss that she couldn't leave her mother right then. She thought she could catch up with the ship when it reached the port of Matanzas, about sixty-five miles away, but she couldn't get there before dark, and the idea of boarding a ship at night frightened her. She asked for the inspection to be held off until the following morning, and her boss agreed. Arrangements were made for her to be driven to Matanzas. Then a tug would take her out to where the ship would be anchored about a mile off shore and bring her back after she completed her work.

At around six the next morning, she put a few snacks and the thermometer she needed for her work into her backpack, checked on her mother, locked the front door, and waited outside until a car with three of her coworkers pulled up. They drove to Vía Blanca and continued heading east, arriving in Matanzas by eight in the morning. A tugboat was waiting for them at the pier. After her three male companions were on the deck, she handed up her backpack and was ready to climb aboard when a state security agent yelled at them to stop.

"Where do you think you're going?" the guard demanded.

"They're taking me out to the ship so I can do my inspection," Mari said.

The guard was skeptical. Memories of the tugboat hijacking were still fresh, and there had been rumors that one of the tugs in Matanzas, maybe even the one that Mari and her companions were about to board, had already been hijacked and taken to Florida once and then allowed to return.

The guard wanted to know what kind of inspection she was supposed to be doing on a ship. Mari told him she normally checked temperature and sanitation while the ships were docked in Havana, but this vessel was on a tight schedule and had pulled out of Havana before she'd had time to monitor conditions on it. He didn't believe her. He hadn't heard about any inspections being scheduled, and besides, a woman boarding a fishing boat was unheard of. Mari was one of only a handful of women working with the fishing fleet or anywhere on the Cuban waterfront in those years.

"Show me your papers," the guard demanded. Mari had to admit that she hadn't been given any.

"No, we can't let you go," the guard said. "You'd better come with us until we can clear this up." She and her coworkers were taken to the customs office at the sugar-exporting terminal in Matanzas and questioned.

While they were detained, Mari tried to explain that the captain of the port of Havana had sanctioned her boarding the tug, and the others had simply accompanied her. There was no email at the time, and it took hours to contact the right person in Havana, locate the authorization papers, and get them delivered to Matanzas. By the time the papers arrived and the officials' suspicions were erased, it was nighttime. Mari then had to board the tug in the dark and be taken out to the larger boat a mile from shore, exactly what she had hoped to avoid.

Mari would be reminded of those difficult days for many years to come. Her neighbors knew she worked at the port, and many asked her what really had happened down there that miserable summer of 1994. And when she attended mass across the street at Los Escolapios, she'd see one of her classmates from La Milagrosa, Caridad Guerra, folded into one of the old pews, her hands clasped in prayer. Mari knew that Caridad's daughter, her granddaughter, her brother, and her son-in-law Felo, the stepson of Jorge García's uncle Gustavo, all had drowned on the 13 de Marzo. But Mari never felt it was right to reopen her friend's wounds by asking her about the tragedy. If she ever wanted to talk about what happened, Mari would be there to listen. Until then, she just prayed for her.

Mari stopped taking the Regla ferry after that summer, frightened away by the possibility of another hijacking, as well as the new security measures the government had instituted. Guards had started to paw through the pocketbooks, backpacks, and packages passengers carried aboard, searching for anything that could be used as a weapon. It would have seemed trivial in any other country, or even in Cuba at any other time, but Mari also steered away from riding the ferries because she knew that if she overlooked a nail clipper or eyebrow tweezer in her handbag, an overzealous guard would confiscate it. Replacing such things would have been close to impossible. It was a small thing, certainly, but for Mari, maintaining her appearance was one of the ways she fought against the declining civility of Cuba. She decided to simply forget the ferry and take the bus instead. It might take hours, but she was almost certain that no one would ever try to commandeer a bus.

Only Román continued to take to the water. He worked with the tuna fleet through the difficult years when the government did not have enough cash to buy replacement parts or pay for repairs. By 1998, the Cuban tuna fleet had all but ceased to exist. The boats were either sold or left to rust at their landings until they were s' rapped. The docks where they unloaded their catch were left to rot. Mari was forced to switch jobs, but she stayed close to the port, supervising quality control for a refrigerated trucking company in Regla.

Román found work on a Jamaican fishing boat. When his new boss came to Cuba on a business trip, Román asked Mari to meet him at the airport. She dressed up in her best skirt and blouse and, as always, nylon stockings even in the searing heat of Cuban summers. And she strapped on a pair of tall red platform sandals that Román had brought back from one of his voyages, shoes that were a luxury few women in Cuba could dream of owning. As she climbed the stairs in the terminal, the sole of one of her sandals broke off. Luckily, she happened to have a roll of tape in her handbag, and she used it to hold the pieces in place. Román shook hands with the owner and presented Mari to him. Despite the mishap, she felt she at least had made a good impression, and such impressions were still important in Cuba.

At least they were to her.

CHAPTER 15

REGLA
October 1995

Cary, we've got a problem, and it's urgent." It was Pedro Hernández Rifas, director of the textile union, a position in Cuba equivalent to the head of an industrial sector. Hernández had shown up unexpectedly at the door of apartment 24 in SP79. He knew Cary from the meetings where she had defended the changes she'd made at the aluminum plant, and he thought of her as someone who knew what she was doing and who could get the job done.

Through her hard work and boundless ambition, Cary had impressed many people. In 1993, she had joined the municipal committee of the Communist Party in Regla, and a few years later she became president of the economic commission of the party for the entire province of Havana, the most economically important region in the country. That put her in a position to see up close the ways Cuba was managing the impact of the Soviet collapse and the loss of more than half of Cuba's economy. It was clear that to avoid a repeat of what happened on the Malecón in 1994, the extreme idealism of the revolution would have to be tempered. Castro had already swallowed some of his socialist pride and lifted legal prohibitions on the hated American dollars. He then opened specialty stores where diplomats, tourists, and Cubans with dollars could buy appliances, clothing, and food not available at state stores that accepted only Cuban pesos.

By the end of 1994, even more radical reform was needed to keep the economy from collapsing. Cuba changed its foreign investment law, making it easier for outsiders to get involved in tourism and other industries. Even though their closest market, the United States, was still out of reach, Cuba believed that it could attract significantly more visitors from Canada, Mexico, Spain, and Italy, along with Russia and other countries from the dissolved Soviet bloc. After years of neglecting Havana, the government gave the city's historian, Eusebio Leal, vast new powers to restore hotels and open restau-rants and specialty stores that catered to tourists. He transformed entire blocks of Old Havana that Fidel had left to rot, bringing back parts of the fabled city to their former glory. Leal then did something that hadn't been heard of in Cuba since the revolution. He invested the proceeds in other projects in Ha-vana's urban core, rebuilding more hotels and starting trade schools that taught specialized restoration skills.

Recovering from the loss of Soviet aid was a slow and painful process, and there were many setbacks. In October 1995, Cuba was hit by another damag-ing hurricane that left a trail of destruction across the island. Hernández told Cary that the hurricane had devastated many manufacturing plants, includ-ing several operated by Puntex, a large state company. Puntex was an impor-tant part of the textile industry, but it had lots of troubles even before the storm. The same man had led it for more than two decades, and it was an ad-ministrative and operational mess. Delayed maintenance had idled much of its machinery, and, by any standard, its accounting was chaotic and its supply chain unreliable. Puntex could not handle any more complications.

"We want you to take over," Hernández said, surprising her. Cary had known for a while that she was being groomed for higher administrative po-sitions. The Communist Party kept track of individuals with the right apti-tude and proper attitude to handle more responsibility and brought them along from position to position. But this was not just another step up for her. It was a leap.

Puntex was a sprawling state-run company with twenty-six textile plants and a workforce of 2,500—most of them women. As director of Puntex, Cary also would run Texpun, a textile importer and exporter. In workshops all over Central Havana, in Guanabacoa and throughout the province of Havana,

Puntex produced T-shirts and men's and women's underwear, often using material imported by Texpun. A large new mill in Santiago also came under her control.

Cary was back in her element, handling the textile operations that she knew best. She didn't have to imagine how rolls of aluminum resembled bolts of cloth. Now stitches, textures, and materials once again were her world. She regularly traveled from Havana to Santiago, learning more about her industry and seeing firsthand the way the revolution had seeped into the lives of Cubans in other parts of the country. Workers at the new mill in Santiago begged her to send more red yarn because red—the Communist Party color—sold well in Cuba's second city.

Cary thought she saw at Puntex a clear solution to the despair that had led so many Cubans to risk their lives on the open seas. Here was a new way for Cuba to operate, one that more resembled the kind of go-getting attitude that Zenaida had instilled in her, an approach that could rebuild pride in her homeland and in the revolution. But she also found that despite decades of promises about equality, some things hadn't changed. Just as at the aluminum plant, she was thrust into a den of jealousy, resentment, and subtle but undeniable racism. On the central office team of ten supervisors that she inherited, nearly all were men and not one was black. In the twenty-six textile factories, only one manager had skin that looked like hers. To her great disappointment, she found her formal introduction to the Puntex staff distressingly familiar. Her team assembled at Puntex headquarters on Concordia Street in central Havana. She walked into the small conference room with theater seating to find the first three rows empty. Right then she felt that the vacant seats were a sign of their unwillingness to accept her.

"Don't be afraid. Come closer," said the minister who was to introduce her. He had to call some of them by name to get them to move to the empty rows. Cary already knew from a friend who worked there that she was seen as an unprepared interloper—a young black woman with braids who was rising too fast. She recognized the code words, and she expected the same cold reception she'd received at Novalum. This time, though, instead of factory workers, she was confronting managers and directors who, like her, had college degrees and a level of experience in the professional world. Some were jealous because they had spent years in the business, hoping for promotions, only to be passed over. And here came Cary, with her degree in economic engineering, whatever that was, but without enough hands-on experience to put together a single pair of socks. She might understand the complexities of labor flow, and she could plot the production process for making an aluminum jug. But she had never set foot in a textile mill or run one, let alone twenty-six.

When the minister finished his introductory remarks, he turned the floor over to Cary. She took a few seconds to look over her new colleagues. She had become an expert at reading faces, and the expressions of those in front of her showed anything but admiration. The message she was receiving was clear: *I've worked twenty years with the director who's being forced out, but now I've got to work with this know-nothing?* The room was tense with their resistance, but Cary thought that if she engaged them as equals, she could win them over.

"You are my colleagues," she said in her most professional tone, "my school friends." She was reaching out to let them know that although she was in charge, she didn't think she could do her job without them. "Since we graduated fifteen years ago, I've gone through several different jobs at different places, but you, you've been right here, and you really know how this place works. I know you're better at this than I am, and that's why I want to make it clear: I need you."

In truth, she didn't need all of them. She revamped the staff, promoting some who had fresh ideas and who she felt supported her, while gently telling veterans who had been there too long that they'd be better off working somewhere else. She handled the negotiations respectfully, and most of the changes went off without a hitch. But one economist resented the moves. "I worked with the owners under capitalism," he argued, indignant that he was being asked by someone without experience to give up his post. In the end she won, and he left.

As she replaced Puntex's old guard with younger people, Cary's leadership grew stronger. Given the ability to import and export, she pushed Puntex into areas where it had never operated. She negotiated directly with foreign buyers and paid European suppliers with checks she wrote in dollars. The new freedom was intoxicating but risky, as she found out when she negotiated a large contract for T-shirts in a unique shade of green.

Italy was one of the countries that Cuban officials courted after the new foreign-investment laws had been passed. Italians already had taken over part of the decrepit Cuban phone company, which had been confiscated from ITT after Castro took over. No eyebrows were raised when a different Italian company solicited bids for a large purchase of olive-green T-shirts. Wages in Cuba were so low that Puntex beat out competitors in India and other developing countries.

The initial order for a sample of one thousand shirts specified a very particular tone of green, one that required mixing several dyes. The Italians sent over a specialist to prepare the Cuban machinery for the thread that needed to be dyed. When the Italians were satisfied with the color and quality of the sample, they signaled that they were ready to place the complete order for 250,000 T-shirts, with options for future orders at least as big.

As the shirts were being made, Cary's phone rang.

"Cary, do you know where those T-shirts are heading?" she was asked.

"We sold them to the Italians."

"Yes, we know that. But do you know who's behind the Italians?" She didn't. "The enemy."

The reason the tone of the olive-green dye had been so specific was that the Italian company planned to sell the shirts to the North Atlantic Treaty Organization (NATO) at a substantial markup.

"How does it look if a state-run, socialist Cuban business is selling shirts to NATO?" she was asked. But since the shirts had already been produced, they were quietly sold to the Italian company, which resold them to another company that then delivered the Cuban-made T-shirts to NATO.

And Cary received strict instructions never to try something like that again.

The NATO misstep wasn't the only time she found out that as director she did not have complete control of the business she ran. It was the middle of December in 1999, when she and a coworker celebrated their birthdays on two consecutive days. They had partied together in previous years, and the idea of combining the celebrations had made them more fun. On the night of the joint party, she returned home at around two in the morning and went right to sleep. It was almost three-thirty when the phone rang.

"I'll put on the minister."

Cary worried that there had been a fire at one of her factories, or some other disaster.

"Relax, Cary," the minister said. "Everything's fine. But we need to speak with you immediately. Would you be able to handle a big order for T-shirts very quickly? I don't know exactly how many, but I think we're talking about two hundred thousand or so."

"Of course I can," she replied, recalling that the NATO order had been larger.

There was a catch. "We need them by the end of the month."

She did a quick mental calculation. With just twelve days left in the month, she'd have to produce around twenty thousand shirts a day to fulfill the order. She figured that twenty of Puntex's twenty-six plants could be switched to T-shirt production, making it a cinch to turn out the two hundred thousand on time.

"Yes, I'm sure of it," she said. It was a matter of personal pride to be called by the minister at that hour. "We can go over the details in the morning," she said.

"No, Cary," the minister said. "I'm heading over to your house right now." A short while later he showed up at the door of her new home in Guanabacoa. She and Pipo had recently given up their apartment in SP79 in exchange for a different home. Although there was no legal market for selling houses in Cuba at the time, the government had turned a blind eye to an informal system of house swapping called *permuta*, where people exchanged one dwelling for another to accommodate their needs. Through a complicated set of deals, Cary and Pipo traded the paid-for three-bedroom apartment in Regla for an apartment in Bahía, close enough to Zenaida to see her balcony from theirs. It made sense then because Zenaida was caring for Oscar after school, Pipo worked nearby in Cojímar, and Cary had her state car. Two years later, they exchanged dwellings again, this time moving into the first floor of a private house in a section of Guanabacoa called Habana Nueva, a midcentury modern real estate development of single-family houses with driveways and yards that was started before 1959 but never completed. An accountant at Novalum whom Cary knew from her time there had inherited the bottom floor of the house, which was located just a few blocks from the aluminum plant.

"Look, Cary, this is a really important assignment" were the minister's first words when she opened the door of the house in Guanabacoa for him. That's when she realized that the order probably was coming from Fidel himself. There was to be a huge rally at the end of the month to demand the release of Elián González, the five-year-old Cuban boy who had been found by American fishermen three miles off the coast of Fort Lauderdale after the raft carrying his mother and others had sunk. His photograph was going to be printed on T-shirts that would be given out at a rally in front of the former U.S. embassy. It was a photograph Cary knew well, as did most Cubans, and it frightened her. It showed Elián in a multicolor-striped pullover, his cheeks pink, his hair black, and his eyes dark marbles. She had been at Puntex long enough to understand that printing the boy's image in all those colors would require several passes through the presses. Getting them right would take time. And only two or three presses in the country were capable of printing that many colors.

Cary checked with one of Puntex's most experienced production managers to ask whether they could do what she had assured the ministers they could easily accomplish. She was disappointed to hear that if they printed all four colors, they couldn't produce more than fifty thousand shirts by the end-of-the-month deadline. He told her the only way to meet the original goal was to print the shirts in black and white. The final decision was not up to her, but she thought she could try to influence it.

Cary had her designers work up five different versions of the Elián T-shirt—some in four colors, some in the red, white, and blue of the Cuban flag, and some in black and white. She called in a favor with a Spanish textile company that rushed in ready-made T-shirts. Then she waited for a decision about what to print on them.

Cary hoped that having T-shirts ready for Fidel's rally was more important than the colors on the shirts. She was relieved when the black-and-white design was selected. She believed that Fidel himself had probably made the final decision, leading her to think that despite his reputation for bombast, Fidel genuinely did listen to others, at least some of the time.

Once before, she had encountered a reasonable side of Fidel, and she'd been charmed. It was during the Fifth Congress of the Communist Party in 1997, the very day that Oscar received his kerchief as a *pionero por el comunismo*. Cary hated missing her son's ceremony, but as head of the party's economic committee for the province of Havana, skipping the Congress was not an option. Pipo took her place at school.

The congress was held in the same huge auditorium in Havana where the National Assembly customarily met. Sitting in the cushioned seats for the first time, she felt the hypnotic aura of hundreds of individuals ready to accept a single shared vision, one that at that moment aligned with her own expectations. Whenever a vote was called, every hand was raised in affirmation. In the economic panorama painted by Fidel in a six-hour speech that day, she detected a new way of thinking for Cuba that promised a brighter future, despite the wretched state of Cuban society in the aftermath of the worst moment of the worst year of the darkest stage of the revolution.

She was seated alongside Eusebio Leal, the Havana historian, when he told her to be prepared because Fidel might ask her a question. She already anticipated something like that. "*Oye, negra,*" the Communist Party official at Novalum had said when he called her a few days earlier, "the comandante might call on you when he talks about substitution of imports." Her decision to use some of the money she raised selling aluminum scrap to repair the machinery for making cigar tubes apparently had caught Fidel's attention.

The congress got under way, and when the discussion turned to the economy, Cary was called on to present the figures she had prepared. With all the revolutionary spirit she felt at the time, she added that the machines had been repaired and the cigar-tube line returned to production in *tiempo récord,* a standard that seemed to apply to everything important the government did.

That's when Fidel, the party's first secretary as well as president, interrupted her to ask a question.

"But how can a woman run a factory with all those men?"

"Yes, Comandante, I'm a woman and I ran the factory, not loudly but firmly."

She was seated in the vast hall with hundreds of other party members, but she could feel Fidel's eyes trained on her. She'd put her faith in Fidel, saw him as the indispensable leader, a man of history.

She apologized, saying she wished she had spoken louder.

"I can hear you," he said. He asked her how much each of the imported tubes cost. Eleven centavos a piece, she answered. And the ones you made? Six centavos.

She spoke as confidently as she could, projecting into the microphone and rattling off her production figures.

"That's good, Ingeniera," Fidel told her. "Keep up the good work."

The discussion moved on. She'd spoken to Fidel for only a few seconds, but for her it was enough. She knew that if you went on too long and said too much, you could blurt out something that contradicted the party line, and that could get you into a lot of trouble. Better to keep it short, respond to the question, then sit back down and revel in the moment when the comandante spoke directly to you.

As CARY ADVANCED IN HER CAREER and in her standing within Cuba's hierarchy, Pipo was content to play second fiddle at home. His own skill set was taking a careful, step-by-step approach to solving problems—an orientation that, along with a considerable dollop of patience, had enabled him to oversee the construction of a five-story multifamily apartment building, as well as to wait in line to buy chicken and cooking oil and other groceries for his family. He left it to Cary to draw the blueprints for their life together. He bicycled to his job at the Cojímar recreation complex because Cary did not think it was right to use her state car and driver to get him there.

The Cojímar complex included a social club called La Costa, where he sometimes helped out. He was inside the club one day when he noticed a new employee, a huskily built young man with close-cropped hair who deejayed at dances. He lived in the area, but Pipo didn't know him. His name was Iván Prieto Suárez, and later on, Pipo heard that he was the son of the man who led the doomed *13 de Marzo* tugboat expedition. The same Iván who, rumors had it, after surviving the sinking of the tug, was aboard one of the Regla ferries when it was hijacked in the summer of 1994.

After he was brought back from the sea that second time, Iván had developed a deep and abiding suspicion of the state security apparatus. He couldn't forget how harshly they had treated him during his three weeks at Villa Marista, and he knew that his brother, Dariel, had suffered even more. Now he was once again doing what he loved, playing music and keeping the party lively. But when he found out about all of Pipo's affiliations with the Communist Party, he kept his distance, assuming—without any proof—that the skinny guy who was always running around taking measurements was probably an informer.

Everybody in Cuba, at one time or another, suspected nearly everyone else of being an informer, or of somehow working with or for the government, and getting something in return.

CHAPTER 16

After borrowing a neighbor's treasured tomato for one of his still lifes, and watching family and friends abandon Cuba for better lives elsewhere, Arturo Montoto reconsidered his own strapped existence in Guanabacoa. His dream had been to make art, not teach others how to do it. Weary of the bureaucracy at the art institute, he was certain that all his training in Cuba and the Soviet Union destined him for something greater than a classroom. Compared with the majority of Cubans, who were barely scraping by or who never had a chance to pursue the careers they had studied for, he already enjoyed a great deal of freedom. But it wasn't enough for him. Improbable though it must have seemed while Cuba was still struggling with blackouts, food shortages, and strict rationing of essentials, he asked his wife to support him so he could immerse himself in his art. When María Eugenia said she would, he left the good job he had as chairman of the Department of Painting at the Superior Institute of Art and took up his brushes and canvases on the back roads of Guanabacoa.

At last, he was on his own, free to paint what he wanted. But he understood the limits of what the regime would tolerate. It was 1994, the low point of the special period, and escaping on a raft was the only form of dissent that didn't end in jail. Fidel's mandate, "Inside the revolution, everything; against it, nothing," remained the first commandment for every Cuban artist, and

Arturo was no exception. His still lifes ruffled no feathers, and foreign tourists liked the way he handled the ordinary objects of life in Cuba, the ironic combinations he painted of hard and soft, dark and light, new and old, and the way he used shadows in the baroque style he had learned in Moscow.

For a time, selling his paintings required almost as much creativity as painting them. After striking a deal with a tourist from Colombia or Mexico, he'd have to wait outside the tourist's hotel to get paid. Then, like a scene from a Cold War spy novel, he and the buyer walked toward each other. As they got close, Arturo grabbed an envelope from the buyer's hand and kept on going. The tourists paid in American dollars, which gave Arturo access to all that the black market offered, even though any Cuban caught with even a few greenbacks at that time could be sent to prison. Selling his art eventually got easier after the government legalized the dollar. Following that big change, Havana immensely complicated the lives of ordinary Cubans by introducing the convertible peso, which was pegged to the dollar, while retaining the old peso for workers' salaries and sales in *libreta* stores.

He sold a few paintings, mostly for dollars or convertible pesos, and organized small exhibitions in Havana. But he continued to struggle until he once again realized the benefits of working within the system. Early in 1995, his friend and former art institute classmate José Villa Soberón encouraged him to join the National Union of Writers and Artists of Cuba. Arturo's experience with the Young Communist League had soured him on participating in state-sponsored organizations, but Villa Soberón, one of Cuba's foremost sculptors, convinced him that the benefits far outweighed any downside.

Soon after joining, Arturo realized that Villa Soberón was right. Just as when he had belonged to the Young Communist League, Arturo reaped advantages from being part of the system's artistic hierarchy. He was invited to participate in an exhibit of Cuban culture in Cayenne, the capital of French Guiana. It was his first trip outside of Cuba since returning from the Soviet Union, and the freedom he experienced being away from the island left him yearning for more.

Geography had long been a pivot point for Cubans. Some reveled in Cuba's position as the largest island in the Caribbean, a land blessed with ideal climate, superb biodiversity, and warm, crystalline waters that wash onto some of the most spectacular beaches in the world. For others, those same geographic details made Cuba not a paradise but a prison. Arturo was one of them. The thought of living on an island terrorized him, and he often quoted Cuban poet Virgilio Piñera, who wrote that the sea encircled him "like a cancer." Even from his privileged position as an artist supported by the government, he felt that the surrounding waters condemned him to the excesses of revolutionary Cuba. He would have much preferred to live in the middle of a huge continent, anywhere that he knew he could get in a car and drive and drive without ever reaching the end of the land.

After returning from French Guiana, Arturo became restless, but not enough to try escaping on a makeshift raft. In 1996, he found his ticket out of Cuba. Again, his good standing within the system helped him. Cubans were not allowed to leave without first securing an exit visa from the Cuban government, and the government tightly restricted them. Only a few artists were authorized to travel out of the country, but they were not allowed to take their spouses or their children—the communist government's way of making sure they were careful about what they said while they were away, as well as ensuring that they did not defect. Minister of Culture Abel Prieto thought there was a better way. Believing that giving loyal artists more freedom to travel would lessen the likelihood that they'd criticize the government while outside Cuba's borders, Prieto loosened the regulations and allowed Arturo to leave with María Eugenia. He already had a visa to work in Chile. A Chilean businessman had offered him a position as a designer with a firm that produced women's pantyhose, giving him a way to establish legal residency in Chile.

Arturo and María Eugenia moved to Valparaíso, where he set up his easel and started painting. Soon he was invited to exhibit his work in a local gallery. They quickly became popular, and the gallery owner invited him to give professional art classes. In time he immersed himself in the Chilean art scene. As his prestige grew, he took advantage of his newfound freedom and branched out. Some of his paintings were exhibited in galleries in the United States, and those sales produced a reliable flow of American dollars. His life had turned around almost completely from the dark days of the special

period in Guanabacoa, but he still wasn't able to reach his full artistic potential. He felt hemmed in not by the kind of political restrictions he had railed
against in Cuba, but by the sky above him in Chile.

It was the light, or the absence of it, that troubled him. Valparaíso, on the
Pacific coast of central Chile, was far colder and rainier than Havana, and for
much of the year it was wrapped in thick fog that swept in from the ocean,
diffusing the light. At times, the sun would disappear for disheartening days
on end. He'd suffered through the Soviet winters and was certain that the
absence of the sun had affected the quality of his work there.

With an average of about 330 sunny days a year, Cubans become addicted
to the sun. For many, daylight on the island can be as enlightening as a personal reckoning, as intense as a memory of a mother's kiss. Although he felt
welcome in Chile and enjoyed the freedom he had there, after living with the
cold and fog for three years, he was desperate for someplace warmer and sun-
nier. But not Cuba. María Eugenia's cousin in Mexico City had a good position
with a company there and lived in the comfortable suburban neighborhood of
Lomas de Chapultepec. In 1998, he invited Arturo and María Eugenia to stay
with him. He even cleaned up a garage so that Arturo could use it as a studio.

In less than a month in Mexico City, Arturo completed three paintings.
He showed them to dealers, and they sold quickly. With the money he earned,
they were able to find their own place to live and work. Just as he had in Chile,
he integrated himself into the local art scene, making connections in the
worlds of culture and business. The money from his paintings allowed him to
live comfortably, and under the fabled light of Mexico he worked steadily.

He earned enough to purchase a house in South Florida and to pay for
frequent trips back to Cuba to care for his ailing father-in-law, who still lived
in Guanabacoa and believed in Fidel.

These were boom years for Arturo, and as his renown grew, he found that
Cuba was eager to claim him as a successful homegrown artist even though
he had turned his back on his homeland and the socialist system of government. In 2004, he mounted four different solo expositions, three in Cuba and
one in Miami. He caught a lucky break when he installed fifteen of his paintings in a small exhibit in Havana that caught the eye of Mexican developer

Kemil Rizk, an avid art collector who had gone to Cuba looking for paintings for his office. Rizk had become familiar with Arturo's work in Mexico and was quite taken with what he saw in the exhibit.

"Arturo's work reminded me of the Russian impressionists that I really liked," Rizk recalled. He offered the artist a deal. He was willing to take all fifteen paintings to a gallery in Mexico where he was sure they'd sell. When they didn't, he reached out to an acquaintance who owned a gallery in the resort town of Vail, Colorado. The owner, James Tylich, was a keen collector of Russian art. He was intrigued by the combination of Arturo's training in classic Russian style and his Cuban background. Cuba was still off limits to most Americans, which gave any Cuban art a certain cachet. But Tylich wasn't sure how well Arturo's paintings would sell in the American resort town. He agreed to show them on the condition that at least two of them were sold in the first month. Within three weeks, five had been purchased, and the rest were bought soon after. When Tylich asked for more, Arturo sent larger canvases, along with some drawings on paper. All sold well, and the proceeds poured into his U.S. accounts.

Arturo's relationship with Rizk continued to deepen. When Rizk built a new resort in Playa del Carmen, Mexico, years later, he used six of Arturo's paintings as templates for glass murals that he installed in the resort's high-end restaurant.

Arturo was working successfully in Mexico, but he knew something was missing. He still wasn't inserting politics into his work. He neither painted for the system—as artists in the Soviet Union had been forced to do—nor against it, which he could have done while in his self-imposed exile. Instead, he infused his paintings with the essential Cuban trait of irony, and in the static arrangements of objects in his still lifes he planted subtle social commentaries. The objects often had a contradictory relationship to each other, which was the way he saw Cubans relating to the system they lived under but never had freely voted to accept. Ordinary objects like a pickax or a hatchet stood next to a delicate piece of fruit, one representing aggression, the other softness or compliance. Or he leaned a long steel bar against a jagged concrete step—one whole, the other broken.

He rarely found that kind of contradiction in his exclusive Mexico City neighborhood, and without that source of inspiration, he focused on the interplay of opposites, and the relationship between dark and light. It was as if he were haunted by light, and terrified by its absence. Cubans have a profound relationship to light, a strength (or sometimes weakness) that has become an aspect of *cubanidad*, the essence of Cubanness. Cubans can become obsessed with the light in their homeland, a quality so spectacular that it resides within them even when they are separated from it. "With all that light, Cubans have a hard time letting go," Cuban writer Carlos Eire once put it. "Even if they only lived in the place for one day before being whisked away, the sunlight is forever trapped in their blood."

While they lived in Mexico, Arturo and his wife became Mexican citizens. But under Cuba's "once Cuban, always Cuban" laws, they were still considered Cuban citizens, and they were subject to all the restrictions placed on Cuban citizens whenever they were in the country. With both his Cuban and Mexican passports in hand, and his reputation solidly established throughout the hemisphere, Arturo Montoto—so well known by this time that he could go by just his last name—moved back to Guanabacoa, ready to reconcile himself to the revolution he never accepted, the system he never respected, and the life he never wanted.

In exchange he reclaimed his splendid sun.

CHAPTER 17

GUANABACOA

1998

Jorge García never attended another political rally or May Day parade after 1994, and he didn't worry about the repercussions of skipping them. There was no need for him to keep up any kind of pretense. He thought he had nothing left to lose and nothing but hatred for the Castro regime. In 1998, he wrote a critical essay for a competition organized by the Cuban Commission on Human Rights and National Reconciliation and won. The modest prize, five hundred pesos and a radio, was awarded to him at a small private ceremony in the home of Elizardo Sánchez, a leading Cuban dissident who, with Ricardo Bofill of Guanabacoa, had founded the commission, Cuba's first dedicated to human rights on the island.

In his winning essay, Jorge sketched out the history of the defense of human rights and pointedly criticized the Cuban government for systematically violating the rights of its people. "Although the Cuban government has had achievements in the areas of education, culture, sports, and health," he wrote, "it has been a systematic violator of the remaining human rights."

Not long after the ceremony, two men dressed in civilian clothes showed up at his door. They told him they were interested in buying a puppy, but he was suspicious. Eventually they admitted they were from state security.

"We need to search the house," one said.

Jorge knew he could not refuse to let them in, but he asked what was going on.

"We understand that you have a computer here."

"Everybody in Cuba knows I have a computer here. That's how I do my work."

"A computer was stolen from the hospital."

"Wait a minute. The computer I have is not the one you're looking for." It was the Olivetti he'd purchased with the earnings from his book on Dobermans that had been published in Spain.

"We have to search the house."

The computer was sitting in plain sight. The agents dragged it out to a van, along with Jorge's printer, a bunch of his CDs, and other electronic equipment. Then they escorted him to a patrol car and told him he was under arrest. It was an old trick. They would not charge him with stealing the computer, but since he couldn't produce a receipt for it, they'd accuse him of receiving stolen property. Jorge was certain he was being punished for writing the critical essay, but it was more likely a reprisal for his continued crusade for the 13 de Marzo victims. He was brought to the police station in Guanabacoa and formally charged with "illicit economic activity," a catchall denunciation for which there was practically no defense. The charges were typed up, and he was told that as soon as he signed a form admitting his guilt, he would be released.

He refused, insisting that he had done nothing wrong. As he was arguing with the police at the booking desk, the chief of police entered the station.

"Jorge, what are you doing here?"

He explained. "Come into my office," the chief said.

The two men were not strangers, both having lived in Guanabacoa for many years. The chief looked at Jorge sternly and asked him to level with him about the computer. When Jorge assured him that he had purchased it with the proceeds of his book on Dobermans, the chief said he'd see what he could do about having the charges dropped. But first he had one favor to ask.

"I've been looking for a hunting dog. A pointer." A male, one with black-and-white markings.

Jorge stood in front of the man who had the power to make his life hell.

This was the kind of corruption that he believed had bankrupted Cuba, and he despised it. But he decided that this time he'd go along with the powers that be in exchange for a brokered peace.

"You've got it," Jorge said.

ALTHOUGH JORGE HAD MANAGED to avoid a major confrontation with the police, life in Cuba was becoming increasingly unbearable for him, with no end in sight, until an unexpected sequence of events turned everything around. Earlier in the same year Jorge was arrested, Pope John Paul II made his historic pilgrimage to Cuba, the first ever visit by a pope to the island. Foreign correspondents swarmed all over Havana, and while they waited for the Pope, they researched other stories. The crew of Ted Koppel's *Nightline* program had read in the American press about the tugboat incident and reached out to Jorge. He and María Victoria were brought to an apartment in Havana that ABC had rented for the pope's visit and recorded a long interview. After it aired, the U.S. Interests Section contacted Jorge and offered to help him seek asylum in the United States. By the following May, the papers had been arranged for Jorge and his family to be brought to Florida as refugees. La Flaca and María Victoria were eager to leave, but at the last minute, Jorge's son Jorge Félix balked. He had read too much in *Granma* about violence and drugs in the United States to want to raise his two sons there. Besides, his family was getting more heavily involved in the Methodist church in Guanabacoa. They would stay behind and take over the house on San Sebastián.

One problem remained, and it was a big one. Despite the police chief's assurance that he'd clear things up in exchange for a puppy, Jorge still had a court date pending on the charge of illicit economic activity. If immigration officials at the airport saw that on his record, he wouldn't be allowed to leave, and the others might be detained as well. They also had become well known as critics of the government because of the *13 de Marzo*, forcing them to try to slip out without calling any attention to themselves. On the day they were to depart, they left packed suitcases with Jorge Félix and came out of the house on San Sebastián carrying little more than what María Victoria and the others had had with them when they boarded the *13 de Marzo* five years earlier. They didn't say goodbye to neighbors or friends.

When they got to the airport they split up, so that if Jorge were detained, the women still could get out. From where he stood in front of the immigration officer, he glanced at his wife and daughter waiting in other lines. He remembered the moment when he'd said goodbye to his son Joel and wondered if he'd ever see them again. The officer checked his passport, took his photo, made a few keystrokes on his computer keyboard, and waved him through.

La Flaca and María Victoria also passed through without any problem. They were on their way. Jorge put his bag through the X-ray scanner at security and was startled when the security officer yanked it off the conveyor and emptied it. Among the few items that tumbled out was a plastic CD case with a photo of Princess Diana on the cover. Inside the case were two CDs that contained the transcripts of all the interviews Jorge had done about the sinking of the tugboat.

"That's what set off the machine," the official said.

Jorge had to think fast. "Look, I'm a Princess Diana fan, and I've always had that with me. It's got her whole history up to when she died in the accident. Wouldn't it be okay if I take it with me?"

The security guard looked right at him, then at the CD. Jorge held his breath. "Go ahead."

He put the case and everything else back in his bag and entered the waiting room. When he saw La Flaca and María Victoria, he winked at them to let them know that everything was okay. They boarded a Mexicana Airlines jet for the short trip to Cancún, then transferred to an American Airlines flight to Miami, flying over the same water the *13 de Marzo* had tried to cross five years before.

They arrived safely in Miami on May 25, 1999. Two days later, they held a news conference at the Cuban American National Foundation. Even in a new country, a world away from Guanabacoa, the tragedy of that night did not leave them.

Jorge vowed that it never would.

———◆———

PLENTY OF EXTRA SPACE OPENED up for Jorge Félix and his family after his parents and sister left. The San Sebastián house was big enough for him to build a photography studio. He quit his job as an ambulance driver and set up his own business recording birthday parties, weddings, and other events. As Cuba began the long process of dragging itself out of the special period and into the mixed economy that Cary was attempting to master at Puntex, Jorge Félix carved out his own existence between his new business world and his newfound religion. The house that had witnessed such tragedy became a comforting, stable place that made him feel satisfied with his life, banishing the events of 1994 that had wrecked his family.

He got so involved in the church and in his business that he hardly noticed when, in 2003, nearly a decade after the *13 de Marzo* had been sunk, a group of men desperate to leave Cuba hijacked one of the old Regla ferries and demanded to be taken to Key West. It was a cruel reminder of the summer of 1994 for those Cubans who had lived through that time, and it raised concerns in Castro's government about a rerun of the violence on the Malecón.

When the ferry ran out of fuel about thirty miles from Havana Harbor, the Cuban Coast Guard cutters that had been in hot pursuit convinced the hijackers to let them tow the ferry back to the port of Mariel to be refueled. It was a ploy. Once at the port, the hijackers were arrested.

This time, the Cuban government was in no mood to tolerate anything like the unrest of 1994. Within a week of the failed attempt, all eleven hijackers were put on trial, and all eleven were found guilty. Fidel personally intervened, ordering the judge to issue the maximum punishment in order to send the sternest warning possible.

The three alleged ringleaders were sentenced to death and shot that same day.

CHAPTER 18

GUANABACOA

November 2000

No matter how many times it happened to Cary, whenever a white Lada sedan with white license plates pulled up in front of her house, she assumed that something had gone wrong. White Ladas with white license plates were reserved for the highest-level ministers in the Cuban government. If one of them parked outside, it must mean trouble was brewing. As director of Puntex and Texpun, she tried to keep on top of everything that was going on, including foul weather and labor unrest, but sometimes that simply wasn't possible.

"What happened?" she asked, opening the door.

"Relax, Cary." Standing at her doorstep was the minister of light industry, a man she had worked under since returning from Kiev nearly two decades earlier, along with two of his vice ministers.

"Is somebody sick?"

"No. Nothing like that."

Then what? she wondered. Had she messed up? Were they still upset about NATO, or the Elián shirts?

"You're doing a great job at Puntex," the minister said. That was a relief. But then what did they want?

"Hell, *Negra*, I was really impressed with all the reports that came to me about you." At the same time, he said, he'd been getting signals from his superiors that Light Industry was top heavy with white men, and that, at times, they had lost sight of what was most important to women.

"So now I'm going to take care of the problem," he said. Cary's experience at Novalum and Puntex, her training in Kiev, and her membership in the party made her the kind of person they were looking for to take over a position of responsibility.

"And besides," he added, "you're a black woman."

She did not consider the minister's tone offensive, but Cary got the message. Being identified by her color was a fact of life for her, and people being surprised that an Afro-Cuban woman was intelligent and skilled was an unintended insult she'd heard many times before. Friends whom she worked with and whom she liked had told her often, "Cary, it's like you aren't even black," believing they were paying her a compliment.

The minister offered her a promotion to the post of vice minister of light industry for all of Cuba.

Pipo and Esperanza encouraged her to jump at the new post, but Zenaida told her point-blank to be careful. The government is using you, she said. They only want you because they need a black woman in a position of authority. You will get hurt.

Once again, Cary ignored her mother and accepted the job. Despite what the minister had told her about needing someone like her, she soon realized that being accepted there wasn't going to be easy because of who she was. At meetings she'd sit uncomfortably at the same table with the other vice ministers, all men. They'd use vulgar language unapologetically, as if she wasn't there. When they acknowledged her presence, they'd say, "*Oye, Negra.*" She was used to that; it was no more insulting or less blatantly obvious than when a thin Cuban woman was called "La Flaca." Cubans had no filter when it came to identifying individuals by their physical appearance. They routinely rubbed two fingers on a forearm to silently indicate a person's color; the more vigorously the fingers were rubbed, the darker the skin. The insensitivity knew no boundaries. Raúl Castro had long been disrespectfully called "El Chino" behind his back because he couldn't grow a bushy beard when he was in the mountains with Fidel. A robust man was routinely known as "El Gordo." "La

Rubia" (the Blonde) could be any white woman, no matter the color of her hair, or any black woman who was thought to act like a white woman. And a black woman like Cary was invariably "La Negra" (the Black Woman).

Cary knew that just holding a position of authority in Cuba wouldn't protect her from the kind of racial and gender discrimination that remained despite prolonged efforts to reverse them. She'd experienced it at Puntex from the moment she was introduced to her staff. One time she was stopped as she tried to enter the fancy Meliá Cohiba Hotel to head a Puntex staff meeting. Seeing a young black woman at the entrance to the expensive hotel, the security guard blocked her way. "You can't come inside," the guard told her. She had to show her personal identity card and her ID as director of Puntex before the guard believed that a young black woman trying to enter an upscale hotel in Havana could be something other than a prostitute.

When she sat at the table with the vice ministers, she felt that she was being slighted again. It was the way her colleagues pigeonholed her that got under her skin most of all, giving her unpopular tasks or assignments that were based solely on her race and gender, not on her skills. They'd send her to a factory at the other end of the country where there were labor problems, expecting her to be able to deal with the workers because she, like them, was a black woman. She was ordered to investigate thefts from state-owned factories—not the petty theft of one-hundred-dollar scraps of aluminum but the wholesale robbery of state resources that meant factory directors themselves were taking bribes. It was the kind of assignment that wouldn't win her any friends and had a good chance of making her many enemies.

Still, Cary realized that she had reached a peak in her career that she could never have imagined when she boarded the cruise ship to Kiev. But she barely had settled into her new position when her world turned upside down. Her mother had retired when she was fifty-five, the standard retirement age for women at that time. Now seventy-two, she was diagnosed with advanced colon cancer. As she got sicker and needed more care, she moved into the spare room in Cary's house in Guanabacoa.

Under Cuba's universal health care system, hospitalizations were free, but individuals usually had no choice about where to be treated. Each neighborhood had a local doctor and a first-stop medical office for consultations and routine health issues. More serious cases were sent on to a polyclinic in the vicinity, and the most critical patients were transferred to the hospital closest to their neighborhood. But when Zenaida needed to be hospitalized she was not taken to La Benéfica, the mediocre general hospital near Guanabacoa. Because she was a vice minister's mother, Zenaida Ewen was rushed to Cuba's best hospital, the Hermanos Ameijeiras Hospital in Havana. One of the most imposing buildings in the city, the twenty-five-story brick tower had been designed as the National Bank of Cuba when construction began under Batista. After a long delay, Fidel ordered the work to be completed, and in 1982 the building opened as a showcase of Cuba's medical muscle.

At Ameijeiras, Zenaida was treated not like a retired auxiliary nurse but like a VIP. Doctors doted on her, making sure she had everything she needed. Cary regularly received phone calls from the central government offices inquiring about her mother's condition, asking whether there was anything more they could do for her. When she was discharged, Zenaida returned to Cary's house in Guanabacoa, but the extraordinary care continued. Oxygen tanks were delivered and refilled regularly. Hard-to-find adult diapers appeared at the front door. Zenaida wasn't forced to use cheap colostomy bags from China that fit poorly—only the best ones for her. A wheelchair to help her get around? Others might have to wait months or years. For Zenaida, one showed up immediately.

When doctors told Cary her mother had only months to live, they offered to provide palliative care. Cary had Fran, her former neighbor at SP79 who had become her driver, use her state car to transport her mother to the hospital for the sessions. After each treatment, Fran drove Zenaida back home to Guanabacoa.

In her final days, Zenaida watched with growing concern as Cary scurried from home to work and back again. She was proud of what her plucky daughter had accomplished, but she still worried that the government was exploiting her. One day, she called Cary into her bedroom and handed her a sheet of paper. On it she had written a list. On top of the list she had put "Business Improvement," followed by "System of Payments and Bonuses," "Corruption,"

"Illegality," "The Party," "The Eastern Provinces," and finally, "The Matienzo Family."

"What's this?" Cary asked.

"Those are your priorities, Caridad."

As she lay dying, Zenaida felt that Cary would someday regret having given up so much in return for so little. Cary tucked the list away in one of her books. She did not want to argue with her mother while she was so sick, but she was certain that her work was not a waste of time.

On November 2, 2002, Zenaida Ewen died in the house in Guanabacoa with Cary at her side. By Cuban custom, it was Cary's responsibility to prepare her mother's body for burial. As a former nurse, Zenaida had long before stopped being squeamish about death, but she once told Cary, "You don't know anything about how to bury the dead." When an old person dies, she said, nobody knows what clothes to dress her in to get her ready to be buried. To make it easier for her, Zenaida had set aside a clean white sheet and put everything else they'd need in one drawer, including underwear, a change of clothes and two pairs of socks.

Cary washed her mother's body, then sprinkled it with talcum powder and a spritz of Violetas Rusas, the flowery perfume that Cubans splash on from infancy to old age. Then she dressed her mother in the clothes she had left in the drawer. Before covering her with the sheet, she pulled one pair of socks onto her mother's feet. She unrolled the other pair over her mother's hands, knowing that in two or three years it would be time to exhume the remains from the tomb and inter the bones in a small vault. When they opened the tomb, they'd have to pick through the fraying pieces of cloth and old shoes to find all her bones. The tiny ones in Zenaida's hands and feet would be held neatly together like sacks of marbles inside the two pairs of socks.

The reality of death in Cuba meant that it could be as difficult to find a place for the dead to rest as it was for the living to find a place to dwell. Families that controlled a burial plot reused it continually, placing the newly deceased into the tomb and then retrieving the remains a few years later so the space could be reoccupied. But Zenaida had come to Havana from Tacajó, and there was no family burial plot in either place. Before she died, she told

Cary she did not want any ceremony or memorial stone. "I'll still be with you wherever you go," she told her. "If you feel a breeze on your cheek on a warm day, that will be me reaching out to touch you."

After a traditional viewing and overnight vigil at the funeral home in Regla, Zenaida's body was placed in a common grave in the cemetery at the center of town.

Years later, when it was time to exhume Zenaida's remains, Juanita, Cary's former secretary at the aluminum factory, showed up with an oversize aluminum box to hold them. In the cemetery office, Pipo negotiated with the manager for a bone vault. The manager was accustomed to the reality of death in Cuba.

"If you don't have your own place, we'll keep them here," she told Pipo. She pointed to boxes in her office, long thigh bones in one, smaller arm bones in another, and skulls apart. But if something else was desired, for a certain fee she said she probably could find an appropriate place. It cost them forty dollars, two months' salary, for Zenaida's remains to be placed in a vault reserved for members of the union of hairdressers and barbers of Regla. She had never worked as a hairdresser, but she had been a regular customer of Delia, a Regla beautician, and that was sufficient, along with the forty dollars, to have her included in their ranks for eternity.

STILL GRIEVING HER MOTHER'S DEATH, Cary threw herself into her work at the ministry, hoping to mask her distress beneath her additional job responsibilities. Whenever she was called to handle a problem at a distant workplace, she didn't hesitate to hop on a plane or get into her car. She and Fran often spent long hours in her state-issued Lada heading to a faraway factory or warehouse. Sitting in the back seat reading reports and memos, she had plenty of time to think. There was one image she couldn't shake, and that was of her mother being waited on so solicitously at the Hermanos Ameijeiras Hospital. Cary was taking to the road every week, going hundreds of miles from home, devoting so much time and energy to her work, and doing it with a deep and abiding faith in the Cuban system. The same system that had built and funded that imposing hospital and trained the skillful doctors and nurses who had looked after her mother with such care. But as much as she did not want to accept it, she knew that if she hadn't been a vice minister, if she hadn't been a ranking member of the Communist Party, her mother would have suffered in a local hospital without receiving the care she needed.

She still believed in the revolution, but she could no longer gloss over this glaring inconsistency. Other people who needed the same care as her mother were forced to endure unspeakable pain and discomfort simply because of who they were, or who they were not. Coming to grips with the ugly reality of inequality on top of the lingering sadness over her mother's death stressed her so much that she started to grind her teeth, eventually wearing them down to the point where she needed dentures. She was torn because she knew she should have been grateful her mother hadn't suffered. She was, but at the same time she was acutely aware of the injustice of others who did not have the same privileges as her being forced to do without. And it wasn't just in the hospital where that was the case. She found herself edging into open conflict with her colleagues over the equality debate raging inside her. She'd be at a meeting of vice ministers to discuss plans for putting workers on a double shift to increase production at a factory, and she'd ask, "Are you going to increase their meal allowances?" No, Caridad, she was told. There's no money for that. "Fine, but neither can we work them to death." She argued for raising salaries and providing bonuses for midlevel managers when their enterprises did well, but that too was shot down.

In the fall of 2004, Cary was sent to handle a labor dispute in the city of Guantánamo, where she had been born forty-eight years earlier. The local printer that put out *Granma* newspaper was wracked by thefts, not because people clamored for the newspaper's coverage, but because newsprint often substituted for difficult-to-find toilet paper. The scale of the losses could not have been possible without the cooperation of the Coraza division security guards, who were her responsibility. Her mission was to bring the guards back in line. She was at a meeting with plant managers when she first felt a pain in her chest. It stopped after a while, and when the meeting ended, she had Fran drive her back to Guanabacoa, a trip of more than sixteen hours.

When she got home, her legs were swollen to several times their normal size. That concerned her, but not overly so. She was young and strong. She didn't bother mentioning it to Pipo, figuring the swelling would go down. All she needed was a shower and a good night's rest.

She recovered enough to go to the office the next day, but she didn't feel right either physically or emotionally. A thought had started to form inside her while she was in Guantánamo. The people she talked to there seemed much more fragile than people in Havana. Many of them were dressed in rags. Their houses were humbler, their demands more desperate, the incentive to steal so much greater than she had imagined. She was becoming aware of a difference she hadn't noticed before, and it left her unsettled. Two weeks after the trip to Guantánamo, she woke up feeling so miserable that she missed the weekly directors' meeting. Instead, she walked down the street to the neighborhood medical office and asked the doctor to check her pulse. It was just thirty-five. She told the doctor she'd always had a very slow heart rate, that's just the way her body worked. He sent her to the polyclinic to which she was assigned, and a doctor there, a friend, ordered an electrocardiogram. When the results came in, he didn't like what he saw.

"I think you may need a pacemaker, but don't worry," the doctor told her. "Go back home, and I'll make some calls."

Pipo came from work to be with her while she rested. When the doctor called to say that an ambulance was on its way, Cary objected. She didn't want her neighbors to see, but the doctor insisted. When she heard the ambulance pull up in front of the house, she was determined to walk out on her own. Pipo helped her up, but they made it only as far as the front door before she had to sit down and wait for the crew to get her.

They were rushed to the Centro de Investigaciones Médicas Quirúrgicas (CIMEQ), the elite hospital where Zenaida had undergone her palliative treatment. The admitting doctor asked them where they lived. When Pipo told him Guanabacoa, the doctor muttered, "You don't belong here," and told them to go to Miguel Enríquez, the formal name of La Benéfica, their not-so-great local hospital. Pipo wanted to avoid a conflict that could upset Cary. But

before they left for La Benéfica, the hospital director came striding down the
hallway toward them.

"Caridad Limonta, where are you going?" the director asked.

"We were told to go to Miguel Enríquez, so we're going," Pipo told him.

The director gave the admitting doctor a dismissive look and ordered that
Cary be taken to a private room, one with its own television set. It was very
nice, clean, and perfect in every way.

And that was what bothered her.

Cary had lived her whole life with the deeply entrenched revolutionary
concept that every Cuban was equal, that all of them had the same rights, that
the system of free health care that Cuba so often boasted about was available
in equal measure to all. She'd taken such pride in arriving in the Soviet Union
carrying a suitcase that was identical to the suitcases the other Cubans carried, wearing shoes and pants that were the same as everyone else's, pulling
on underwear labeled "Made in Cuba" that every other Cuban wore, believing
all the promises that Fidel and Raúl and Che had repeated about socialism
delivering equality for all Cubans, black or white, man or woman, government official or common laborer.

She could no longer hide from the truth that she'd been avoiding almost
since the day she had returned from Kiev, full of idealistic, even naïve, visions
of the new egalitarian society that Cuba boasted it could create. In her work
at the textile industry offices, she'd seen how some workers received more
than others, and how some were promoted not because of how hard they
worked but because of who they were related to. Then, when she was in and
out of the gynecological hospitals with her many miscarriages, she picked up
subtle signs of how some women received better treatment than others because of who their friends were. She had willfully ignored all those clues that
the classless society Fidel promised was a mirage until her mother became ill.
It was clear that had she not been a vice minister, her mom would not have
been admitted to the best hospital in Cuba. There might not have been oxygen
tanks at home. Or a wheelchair.

When she confronted her own health emergency, her doubts about the revolution became undeniable. She now saw how she had been shielded by the advantages of her own fortunate background. Unlike the majority of Cubans, she'd had few if any unmet needs in her own life until her mother's illness. Facing the imminent death of someone so dear to her, she needed access to the best care Cuba could provide, and she got it. But her own ironclad sense of social justice now forced her to open her eyes to the truth. Socialist Cuba promised social justice and a fair distribution of resources. Socialist dogma was supposed to ensure that all goods and services were allocated evenly to everyone who needed them. But Cary and her mother had been pampered in their time of need not because they were Cubans. Not because they were socialists. Not because they believed.

But because they were more important than others.

CHAPTER 19

After doctors installed a pacemaker in Cary's chest, she recuperated quickly and eagerly returned to work. But the new contraption near her heart didn't seem to be functioning the way it was supposed to. When she complained, doctors told her the pacemaker was doing its job; she just had to give it time. It was a medical student at the hospital who finally came up with the correct diagnosis: when the pacemaker had been implanted, she had picked up an infection that had gone straight to her heart.

The deadly diagnosis deepened the apprehension she had been experiencing since Zenaida confronted her with that damning list of upside-down priorities. Cary knew she was being poisoned from inside, and yet she had gone back to work and was giving her all to support a system that had deceived her. She had spent the better part of her entire life rising through that system, taking on more and more duties, neglecting Pipo and Oscar, even after all she'd suffered to become a mother. Now, all that she had worked so hard to achieve was put at risk by the very surgery that was supposed to help her. Doctors warned her that the kind of open-heart surgery she needed to treat the endocarditis had only a minuscule chance of success. What if she didn't make it? Oscar was only thirteen. He needed both his parents. She already regretted the time she could have spent with him but hadn't because she was focused on giving her all to Fidel's Cuba instead of her own.

As she was being taken into the operating room, she sang "Pregúntale a las estrellas" to herself to keep from panicking. The surgeons cut her chest open and put her on an artificial heart machine while they removed the infected pacemaker and scrubbed the infection out of her heart. They then installed a new pacemaker near her waist, as far from the contamination as was feasible.

Cary took several months to recover, and by the time she felt well enough to return to work, she asked to be relieved of her position as vice minister, feeling she no longer had the strength, or the desire, to continue in the high-pressure job. She was given a special position as assistant to the woman who replaced her. But then she found that although her title had changed, her work was as strenuous as ever. To keep from being overwhelmed, she paid a woman who had recently moved into the neighborhood to help her around the house. Cary and her new neighbor found that they shared a similar background. María Luisa Durand Hernández—everyone called her Lili—also had followed her mother from sugar country in Cuba's far east to remake herself in Havana. Cary took a liking to Lili, though they were ten years apart in age and leagues apart in their training and achievements. Still, as they got to know each other, Lili came to think of Cary as a model communist. And Cary saw Lili the same way.

LILI CAME FROM A FAMILY of campesinos in Banes, a small city not far from Tacajó. When she was just a girl, her mother took off for Havana and left her with her grandparents on their small subsistence farm. Her revolutionary indoctrination began early. She attended Heroes of Girón School, and when she was fourteen, she joined her local CDR. Her grandparents were caring but rigid in an old-fashioned way that seemed out of touch with what she thought was the spirit of revolutionary Cuba. They didn't allow her to go to parties or have a *quinceañera*. When she was old enough to attend high school, she told them she wanted to live in Santiago, where her father, José, worked as a stevedore and where she had aunts and cousins who'd keep an eye on her.

Lili grew up adoring Fidel and hating Batista, the dictator who had been born in Banes. When she attended her first May Day parade in Santiago, surrounded by thousands pledging themselves to the revolution, passion stirred inside her, and she vowed to always show her dedication to communism openly and proudly. The aunts and uncles who were supposed to watch over her didn't do such a good job, and when she was seventeen, Lili became pregnant. She named the child Juan José after his absent father and strong-willed grandfather. She was not at all ready to raise a son. She left the baby, who everyone called Joseíto, with her aunts in Santiago and took off for Havana. She'd heard tales about the great city, where the streets pulsed with excitement, and she wanted to be there.

The old capital deceived many young women from the east who made the journey with great expectations only to find that life there was just as difficult as it had been where they came from. Lili joined her mother in Casablanca, a squatters' village across the bay from Old Havana. Thousands fleeing the crushing poverty of the eastern provinces built shacks there or set up housing in whatever locations they could find, eventually including an old Soviet power plant. As the capital grew more overcrowded, the government imposed new restrictions, and without authorization to move from their home province, many people became illegal immigrants in their own country. Without the right permits, they couldn't work, and they did not qualify for either housing or the *libreta*.

But it was easier in 1979, when Lili moved in with her mother in Casablanca. She was able to find work in the nearby naval hospital, cleaning emergency rooms and operating salons after surgery. She pursued a course at the technological institute attached to a psychiatric hospital in Havana, then returned to the naval hospital, where she did her mandatory social service.

She was at the hospital late one night when an ambulance brought in a military officer who had been injured in a serious crash. The officer needed surgery, but before he was taken to the operating room, Fidel showed up. The hospital staff lined the corridor, buzzing with excitement. Fidel came through acting like just another visitor. He greeted Lili and the rest of the staff, asked how they were, and then inquired about the condition of the injured officer. He was given a surgical mask and gown to put over his uniform so he could enter the prep area where the officer awaited the surgeons. The officer was still conscious, and as Lili watched, Fidel bent over the gurney to tell the badly injured man that everything was going to be all right, the doctors would give him the best of care.

Seeing Fidel up close cemented Lili's already worshipful admiration for *el comandante*. She had grown up with heroic stories of the revolution, and she burned with revolutionary fervor. True to her teenage vow, she took part in nearly every rally, every march, every May Day parade. For her, the revolution was a living thing, a force that she could see and feel. It had given her the opportunity to study and provided her with meaningful work. After ten years at the naval hospital, she went to work as a security guard for state enterprises, including Novalum, pulling twelve-hour shifts as night watchman or minding the front desk during the day.

Cuba would never be perfect; Lili knew that. But following the example of Fidel, she believed that Cubans could achieve greatness. "I am a revolutionary communist," she proudly told anyone who listened. "I like my communism. I like my country." She was certain that Cuba could have advanced much further if it hadn't been isolated by the U.S. embargo since before she was born. Despite the hardships that came with being on America's enemy list, she knew that Cuba had many allies around the world, and it had achieved so much with so little. "Here in our country health care is free. Education is free. Here, if a child gets sick or has a life-threatening illness, it's something sacred. What am I saying? Not just a child. Older people, anyone who gets sick, they all are taken care of."

Her faith in the righteousness of the revolution was absolute. She lived with her mother and mentally handicapped sister in Casablanca during the summer of 1994, but she knew little about the sinking of the *13 de Marzo*. Unlike Jorge García and María del Carmen, she did not know any of the victims, survivors, or grieving relatives. The government's explanation that a group of lawbreakers had threatened guards, stolen a decrepit boat, and recklessly tried to make off with the people's property was all the explanation she needed.

ONE DAY IN THE SPRING OF 2006, Cary was eating lunch with her colleagues, listening to them complain about work. She sat there silently, brooding over her inadequate new position and the discontent welling up inside her. She didn't get along with the new vice minister she was supposed to assist. It might have been an impossible pairing to begin with—two strong-willed, independent women who were both used to giving orders, not taking them. The stress of dealing with all the same problems but without the authority to make decisions, compounded by the lingering sadness of losing her mother and the growing disillusionment with the imbalances in the socialist system, overcame her.

She got up to leave. "Don't talk about me when I'm not here," she told those at the table. "If you have something to say to me, tell me now."

"Cary, no," they told her, sensing her distress. "Just sit down. You've been awfully tense."

It might have been the fish she ate, or it might have been the contortions of her spirit, but when she returned to her office, her lunch came up. Cary realized that her body was telling her something. She grabbed a few personal items from her desk, including a photograph of her mother relaxing in the patio of the house in Guanabacoa. Then she called Fran and told him to get the car ready. "I'm going home," she said.

He drove her around the harbor in the new Kia automobile with white license plates that had been assigned to her as vice minister. When she got to the house, she told Pipo that she had decided to quit her job at the ministry. "Are you crazy?" he said. Without her position and her privileges, the comfortable tableau of their lives would collapse, leaving them all at a loss.

It was a moment of reckoning for Cary. Suddenly the intense sunlight of Cuba seemed to illuminate things she'd never seen before. It was like the time she had asked Fran to drive her to a clinic in Guanabacoa. As they drove up Corralfalso she looked out the car window and noticed a large mound of garbage near Los Escolapios church, almost directly in front of María del Carmen's house.

"*Oye,* Fran, what happened here? Where did all this garbage come from?"

"It's always been there, Cary," he responded.

"I've never seen it."

"That's because you never look out the windows. You've always got your nose in a report."

He was right, and Cary knew it. Just as she now knew that Zenaida's list of her skewed priorities had been accurate all along. She had been living in a bubble of her own creation for so long that she couldn't recognize the reality of the world around her. There never had been true equality. She'd always had more than others—more vacations, more education, more food, a bigger apartment, a state car and computer. And just as she'd been oblivious to that mound of garbage on Corralfalso, her rigid concept of party loyalty had blinded her to the reality of the Cuba that existed from the dirt roads of Tacajó to the crumbling asphalt of Guanabacoa. She had traveled across the Cuban mainland for her work, and she had seen—though it didn't register till now—that even at its worst, Havana was an abundance compared to the rest of the island.

Neither discontent nor a lack of loyalty to the revolution fed the transformation taking place inside her. It was the real world that her newly opened eyes were seeing. She was fifty years old, with a chest full of scars, a memory filled with broken promises, and a heart that, though weakened by disease, still brimmed with love for her bedeviled island home. And then, as if to prove that the revolution itself was sick, in July 2006 an ashen-faced broadcaster on the national television news announced that Fidel had been felled by an unnamed illness and would be replaced provisionally as president by his brother Raúl.

The revolution was as old as many of the bulky American cars that lumbered along Cuba's roads, and like those aging behemoths, Fidel and his revolution barely resembled their original selves. But one thing had always remained constant. For as long as Cary could remember, as long as she'd been alive, every Cuban life, every Cuban moment, every grain of corn or liter of rum produced on the island owed its very existence to the oversize figure of Fidel. There was not a single statue of him in all of Cuba, nor any school or hospital with his name. There didn't need to be.

Fidel was Cuba.

Cuba was Fidel.

And if Fidel was sick . . .

PART THREE

RECONSIDERATION

CHAPTER 20

GUANABACOA

2006

Cary stood in front of the mirror and cried. Her eyes went right to the ugly scar above her right breast where the first pacemaker had been implanted and then had to be torn out. Down on her left side, inches above the cesarean scar from Oscar's birth, was another gash where the new pacemaker had been sewn in. She raised her hand and touched the beef roll that ran from her sternum practically to her navel, a thick braid of keloid scar tissue that made her look like some clumsy seamstress had sewn her together, which was how she felt about her life. She had walked away from her job as vice minister, a position that confirmed her accomplishments and hard work, and left behind the entitlements that had made life bearable for her family, all in exchange for what?

It was not the first time the mirror had made her cry. Her first surgery, the relatively minor procedure to implant the initial pacemaker, had left a single scar that so disgusted her that she'd asked her friend Dunya to sew new blouses with high collars so it wouldn't show. Dunya tried to convince her not to be ashamed of the scar, telling her it was a sign of the obstacles she'd overcome. But Cary was headstrong and, she admitted it, more than a little vain. What she saw in the mirror repulsed her, and she was certain that anyone who looked at her would feel the same. She even kept herself covered up when she was intimate with Pipo because she didn't want him to see what had become of her.

Then the additional scars made everything so much worse. She felt as though she had been stripped of her dignity and her future.

Many people she once had considered friends suddenly disappeared. When she quit as vice minister, she gave up her car, her driver, her cell phone, her computer—all of it along with, she assumed, any advantage that being a high official in Cuba bestowed. She and Pipo would be on their own. They had some money saved, but not much, and they knew it wouldn't last long. She had officially retired, and her pension came to about twelve dollars a month. That wouldn't go far when a pound of laundry detergent could cost a dollar, and a cotton dress fifty. Oscar was still a teenager, and he needed her. Pipo needed her. And she needed to feel that she was still alive, still able to fight back, still in control of her own destiny the way she had been since she was a young girl skipping down the dirt streets of Tacajó.

For days, she closed herself in the house trying to figure out what to do next. Nothing seemed right. Then one day she wandered into her mother's old room, which doubled as a big closet. She couldn't remember what she was looking for. Maybe nothing at all, just the spiritless meandering of someone searching for an answer. On the shelves were pieces of cloth, and boxes with the discarded buttons and zippers that her mother had trained her to safeguard. And there in the corner was the old Union Special treadle sewing machine that Zenaida had given her as a gift for completing her studies in Kiev.

She missed her mother terribly and thought about her constantly, especially as she drifted through those gray days without work. Zenaida's damning list of Cary's priorities often came to her mind, and now she was tortured by the conviction that her mother had been right all along. She had allowed her world to be flipped upside down, giving her energy—and practically her life—to a political ideology that turned out to be hollow, just as her mother had warned. What would Zenaida think about what had become of her, with her scars and her disappointments? Her Santería devotee aunt made her feel even worse when she told Cary that Zenaida had come to her in a dream. She was crying, her aunt said, and her tears were a strong message meant for Cary. Your mother was saddened by what you have done with your life, she told her.

Then she offered to use her prayers, incantations, and secret rituals to try to appease Zenaida's spirit on her behalf.

It was more than Cary could handle while she was feeling so low. Along with everything else she was ejecting from her life, she'd had enough of Santería. She knew her mom better than anyone, and despite their differences, she was sure that Zenaida had not lost faith in her. "That woman you saw crying was not my mother," she told her aunt. "If Mami is in heaven, I know that she is very happy for me just because I am alive." She asked her aunt not to be angry with her, but after all she'd been through, her soul was wounded and she needed to look for something more spiritually meaningful for her than Santería.

Cary knew one thing for sure: Zenaida had never simply sat back and waited for what she wanted to come to her. She was incessantly ambitious, always hunting for opportunity, always ready to exploit whatever possibility she encountered. To survive, Cary would have to do the same. And the old sewing machine from Zenaida was the answer she was searching for.

But first she'd have to address one small problem. She didn't know how to sew.

Cary had been involved in the textile industry for a quarter century and knew all about fabrics. Working with the designers at Puntex, she had acquired a sophisticated flair for fashion that she had honed on her trips abroad. She had overseen the production of hundreds of thousands of shirts, millions of pairs of socks and underwear, but she had never sewn together a single blouse on her own. She stared at Zenaida's Union Special sewing machine. To operate it, she had to pump the pedal; that much she knew. And she understood the theory behind assembling individual elements of fabric and thread, zippers and buttons, into a finished piece someone might be willing to buy. If she could oversee the production of aluminum jugs and fancy cigar tubes, if she could deliver two hundred thousand printed T-shirts in a few weeks, if she could make factories all over Cuba run smoothly and safely, surely she could operate an old sewing machine, couldn't she?

Once she had decided what path to follow, she put her mind to accomplishing it the way she had tackled every other goal, taking it step by well-thought-out step. She headed for Regla, where she knew of a store that sold old hotel sheets. Like the aluminum discs that Novalum turned into pots and pitchers, she considered the soiled and torn sheets her raw material. Back home, she laid them out on a table and cut out the stains and worn spots. Her idea was simple. Cuban women traditionally buy elaborate crib sets, called *la canastilla*, for their newborns. The sets consist of necessities such as tiny sheets, blankets, and pillows, along with playful extras like shiny piping or cartoon characters sewn into mosquito netting. Times might be tough, but new mothers always seemed to find enough money to outfit their newborns in finery. She sat down at the sewing machine with a clear picture in her mind of what she wanted to make, but no matter how hard she tried, her hands refused to do what she wanted. She had watched the seamstresses in the Puntex workshops zip through yards of material in machine-gun bursts, but her Union Special just wouldn't move the way she intended. Material bunched up, stitches wavered crazily, seams didn't match.

It took her the entire day and more than a few tears to complete one crib set that she felt might be good enough to sell to a neighbor. Day after day, she sat at the machine, determined to do better. Soon she could finish as many as three complete crib sets a day, including the netting material that she bought in Old Havana. If she sold each set for about four dollars, she'd match her monthly pension in just a day. But that usually didn't happen. She was learning as much about selling as she was about sewing, and she realized that she wasn't very good at either. If the woman buying her crib set didn't have much money, she lowered her price. She knew that made her a bad saleswoman, but it felt like the right thing to do.

It was a start at a new life, but not a very good start. Cary knew that she needed help, and she had an idea. She went back to Quitrín, the women's empowerment project in Old Havana that she had helped Vilma Espín establish when she was a rising star in the textile industry. She enrolled in one of the classes offered at Quitrín and learned the correct way to use her old sewing machine while picking up useful hints for how to measure, cut, and sew more efficiently. By the time the class ended, she was ready to take on more work. A few times a month, she'd board the old number 5 bus from Guanabacoa to

Havana or walk down to Regla and catch the ferry across the harbor. Sometimes she'd meet Esperanza, who worked in Old Havana then, and together
they'd scour the city for old sheets and cheap manufactured trim. She expanded beyond infant linens. Wearing jeans was no longer considered antisocial, so she bought used men's jeans, cut them down, and sewed the pieces
together to make women's skirts. She'd take a secondhand blouse, add a colorful flourish, and sell it at a profit. When she showed her clothing to friends
and neighbors, she was surprised that they were willing to spend their hard-
earned money to buy them.

With the proceeds from those initial sales, Cary purchased more material.
As she became more adept at using the sewing machine, she turned out bedspreads, fitted sheets, and other household items and sold them, substantially
adding to the meager income she received from her state pension. Feeling better about herself, she let Zenaida's spirit guide her. On her deathbed, Zenaida
had asked Cary to read to her from the Bible. She asked so often that Cary had
memorized Psalm 23 and found in its consoling words strength for herself as
well. From the operating room of the cardiology hospital she had walked
through the valley of the shadow of death, and now that she was getting her
priorities straight, she believed that her soul was being restored. Almost without thinking, she accepted her friend Dunya's invitation to attend a Sunday
morning evangelical service in a small house in Regla that doubled as a church.
She went back the following week, and the weeks after that. Eventually, she
acquired her own Bible and dutifully underlined the important passages with
a green pen as the pastor, José Luis Pino, invoked them during his sermons.

Slowly, she was putting her life back together, reformulating what, for her, it
meant to be Cuban. And belonging to the Communist Party was no longer part
of that formula. When she tried to hand in her red card, the party didn't accept
her resignation. Slow down, they told her. Get involved in the local party in
Guanabacoa. But she would have none of it. She no longer had faith in the system that had failed to live up to the promises of the revolution. Eventually, she
was allowed to separate herself from the party. When she was completely free
from it, and from all the blind allegiance it demanded, she realized that she had
stopped being a revolutionary, but she had not stopped being a patriot.

She still loved Cuba.

As she felt better about herself, she stopped applying salves and ointments to her scars and accepted them as part of who she was. She was an independent businesswoman, a rarity in a country that did not yet officially recognize private enterprise, although it had started to accept a few small-scale ventures. Since the terrible summer of 1994, Cuba had permitted individuals to open family-run restaurants called *paladares* in their homes under strict guidelines that limited the number of tables and did not allow anyone but family to work in them. In theory, Cubans would not be allowed to enrich themselves on the backs of others. The waiters and housekeepers at the fancy resort hotels in Varadero would argue with that premise, but officially, socialist orthodoxy remained the rule.

After Raúl Castro filled in as president in 2006, he started to put his own mark on Cuba, and he was far more open to traces of capitalism than Fidel ever was. After running Cuba's armed forces for nearly half a century, Raúl was used to placing practical needs ahead of ideological ones. It didn't take much vision to see that Cuba was getting poorer every year, and that the centralized economy was so stagnant that the popular street saying "They pretend to pay us, and we pretend to work" seemed like doctrine. Raúl's government decided that the best way to stimulate growth was to give a limited number of Cubans a chance to work on their own, creating a mixed economy with fewer nonproductive state workers coexisting with a carefully managed, and rigorously restrained, non-state sector.

Cary understood that language well. As soon as they were available, she applied for and received a license to work as a self-employed seamstress, a role she had unofficially occupied for years. It didn't take long before the reality of a semi-open market hit. Suddenly, other women in and around the capital had the same idea about starting their own business producing crib sets, household linens, and repurposed clothing. In addition, mass-manufactured clothing brought from Mexico, Panama, and other Latin American countries by enterprising Cubans who had special permission to travel was flooding the market, often at prices lower than what Cary could charge. Once more her thoughts turned to Zenaida, and that led her back to a part of Cuba that occupied a special place in her heart.

A few times a year, she boarded an intercity bus at the Havana terminal in the late afternoon and rode through the night with bags of blouses, bedspreads, and crib sets that she had made at home. If the bus wasn't overly crowded, she could sleep most of the way there and be ready to start selling as soon as they pulled into the city of Holguín the next morning. She'd drop off a bag of clothing and bedding at the home of a friend who had agreed to sell them for her. Then she'd catch another bus to Tacajó, her sugar-town home, where Cuka—the daughter of the woman who twice had taken in Zenaida when she desperately needed support—would help sell the rest of her inventory, taking a cut of the proceeds for herself.

In Tacajó, Cary found that although several decades had passed since she lived there, life still revolved around the sugar mill and the dull whistle marking the beginning and end of every shift. After Flora had destroyed much of the town, a whole new section had been built. They called it Canta Rana for all the frogs that croaked constantly and sometimes slipped inside the houses. The people who lived in Tacajó were so isolated, and so poor, they only rarely got to shop. They wore clothes until they fell apart. Cary charged less for her clothing there than she did in Havana, but that didn't bother her, because she knew that people had less money to spend.

As Cary rebuilt her life, and felt good about it, she was constantly reminded of how little control she actually had over her destiny. During a physical checkup, doctors told her that the battery in her pacemaker needed to be replaced, and they wanted to use that opportunity to move the mechanism from where it was, down near her abdomen, to where it should be, high on the left side of her chest. It meant yet another surgery, and another scar, but this time she didn't care. She had already started wearing blouses that left no doubt about how disfigured she was. Harder to accept was the reality that the surgery would force her to rule out trips to Tacajó until she recovered. Then two events changed her life yet again.

In 2011, Raúl Castro ordered a sweeping overhaul of Cuba's centrally controlled socialist economy, declaring that Cuba could no longer afford to be the only country where people did not have to work. He tried to push through measures that would have eliminated about one million nonproductive state jobs. That number later was cut in half, but dumping five hundred thousand workers onto the street still threatened chaos. Under the guise of opening the economy, Cuba greatly increased the number of self-employed work licenses to more than two hundred. Some of the restrictions on *paladares* were loosened, allowing the private restaurant industry in Havana and other cities to grow significantly. But many of the categories of self-employment were so laughably specific that they'd never put a dent in Cuba's severe economic troubles. License holders were limited to one-man ventures like peeling fruit, or cleaning automobile spark plugs, or operating a kiddie cart pulled by a goat. In reality, the government was offering its people not freedom to better themselves, but permission to eke out a level of survival the government could no longer provide. On top of the limitations it slapped onto their entrepreneurial vision and capacity to amass wealth, the government required would-be capitalists to buy their licenses for relatively hefty fees and pay heavy taxes, a shock to people who had never paid taxes before. The goal, as outlined by the government, was to make Cuba a rich country without rich people.

Cary took out one of the new licenses for making clothing, broadening her economic possibilities. She now could legally hire up to five employees, which was important to her because it allowed her to provide economic opportunity for other women. But just as she was assembling the pieces of her new project, Pipo had a health crisis of his own. He worked as a manager at a shipping company in the port of Havana, overseeing the maintenance of the heavy equipment that was used to move containerized cargo. One February morning, a hose ruptured on a key piece of Chinese-made equipment. He checked his records for a replacement and sent a laborer to the warehouse to get it. Every minute the equipment was down, the enterprise's productivity dropped, and that reflected badly on him. Minutes went by. The laborer finally came back empty-handed. He'd looked for the hose in the place where it was supposed to be, but it wasn't there. Pipo had heard that excuse countless times before. The inventory control and scheduled maintenance that he had learned in Kiev still seemed foreign to the military officers that Raúl had put in charge of many Cuban enterprises, including port operations. It was frustrating, and as his frustration grew that morning, he felt a pain in his chest. Suddenly, he had trouble breathing.

He didn't think he could wait for an ambulance, not the way he felt. The nearest hospital was La Benéfica, and this time he wasn't worried about its reputation. Besides, Cary no longer was vice minister, and he couldn't expect special treatment. He wanted only to see a doctor as quickly as possible. Pipo's company didn't have a single car available to take him to the hospital, but a coworker who owned a motorcycle with a sidecar said he could get him there right away. Clutching his chest, Pipo slumped into the sidecar as they sped off into traffic.

He was in such bad shape when he stumbled into the emergency room that doctors had to revive him with electroshocks. He had suffered a massive heart attack, and the doctors literally brought him back from near death. He underwent days of intensive therapy before being sent to CIMEQ, the same cardiology institute where Cary had received her pacemaker. The doctor who had taken care of Cary then examined Pipo. They were old friends who'd known each other growing up in Cárdenas. After reviewing test results, he doubted that Pipo needed a pacemaker. A stent and medication would do the trick. His bill: $0.00.

He was released from the hospital and put on medical leave. During Pipo's recuperation, Cary again stopped taking trips to Tacajó. Instead, she focused on growing her home business, facing up to the challenges of being a self-employed entrepreneur in a country that did not quite trust private business. There was almost no credit available, the tax system didn't make sense, and, worst of all, there was no legal wholesale market where private businesses could buy the basic materials they needed.

Without a wholesale market, self-employed Cubans struggled. *Inventando* was how they described the process of finding raw materials, but in essence what it often came down to was stealing. For many businesses, the state was the only wholesale market. Government employees diverted material from factories and warehouses and sold it on the black market. By prohibiting a legal wholesale market and restricting imports, the Cuban government un-intentionally encouraged corruption. The petty theft that Cary had tried to stop at Novalum in the 1990s had spread to every corner of the Cuban economy, and almost every Cuban—whether an entrepreneur with a small business or a parent searching for dinner—became a criminal in one way or another. *Inventando* largely replaced the word "stealing" in Cuban vernacular, and the rules of civil society changed so that stealing was condoned, so long as what was being stolen came from the state and not from a neighbor or a friend. In the new Cuba, *inventando* was a way of leveling the playing field and making up for the miserable dollar-a-day salaries that state workers received.

After half a century of socialist central planning, overemployment, and low productivity, most Cubans who took out licenses and went into private business did so without the practical skills they needed to succeed. The government itself seemed unsure about the fledgling private sector, tolerating it but not supporting it or allowing it to grow beyond a very limited and easily managed size. It was capitalism running on cruise control, with the speed set at two miles per hour.

While Pipo recovered, he decided that, like Cary, he too had outgrown the Communist Party. After spending more than forty years in the Young Communist League and the Communist Party, he handed in his resignation. But just as had happened to Cary, the party did not at first accept his decision. When he insisted that it was time for him to leave, the party took the step of sanctioning him and sending his case to the local party office in Guanabacoa. There, his revolutionary activities and his long history with the party were scrutinized. After considering the way he had handled his administrative duties, the local leaders lifted the sanctions against him and allowed him to surrender his red card. He retained his good standing in civil society, suffering no consequences for turning his back on the Communist Party after belonging to it for most of his life.

He was only fifty-six, too young to retire but too weak to return to work on the piers. To give him something to do, and hopefully bring some extra money into the house, Cary arranged some of her clothing on hangers and attached them to the fence outside their house. Sitting next to the blouses and

T-shirts, Pipo chatted with passersby and sold whatever he could. To their surprise, the fastidious engineer had a knack for retail. And he liked it.

With all the restrictions imposed by the government, and all the interruptions caused by their health emergencies, Cary's business was stagnating. When a friend invited her to enter an instructional program that would take her business to the next level, she figured she ought to give it a try. The brand-new, privately run program met in an antique building not far from Havana Harbor that had been a Catholic seminary before the revolution. The Centro Cultural Padre Félix Varela served as a demilitarized zone between the Catholic Church and the Cuban government. The center was permitted to hold public discussions on such general themes as "Are Cubans Happy?" so long as it did not openly encourage resistance to the regime. With financial backing from Cuban exiles in Florida, the center had started a business incubator program called Cuba Emprende (Cuba Initiates), that offered eighty hours of training in business practices and ethics.

In June 2012, Cary attended her first class. She was at least twice the age of everyone else and hadn't sat in a classroom since Kiev. She had already been running her own business for six years and was familiar with many business terms and economic concepts, but not free-market ideas. She expected the classes to be a kind of financial refresher course, but what she experienced in the classroom took her by surprise. This was nothing like her classes in Kiev, nor any she had taken in Cuba. Her professor began by asking the students to introduce themselves, but without using their own names. Instead he directed them to pick the name of an animal that was spelled with the first letter of their first name and describe how they were like that animal. When it was her turn, she blurted out the first thing that came to her: *caballo*, horse. A horse is strong, and swift, full of life, she said. But she didn't say what she really felt at that moment: after all she'd been through, the horse contained inside her was a tired beast, worn out and overworked.

The classes addressed details of running a business, including financing, accounting, merchandising, and sales. Much of what she learned there contradicted her two decades working in a controlled economy, but it reinforced what she instinctively felt about running her own business. All of it was helpful, but the most important concept she learned was that she, with her experience and skills, her deeply rooted desire to control her destiny, was her business's most important resource. Not the state. Cary. She left the course convinced that she could run a flourishing business within the framework of a changing Cuba.

Buoyed by her new confidence, and taking to heart the advice that she was more valuable to her company than any other resource, Cary came up with a name for her business that was a reflection of herself. She called it Procle, a mash-up acronym of the words *produciones comercializadora* and part of her name, Luisa Ewen. She envisioned Procle producing and selling a range of products, from bedroom linens to uniforms for the burgeoning number of private restaurants in Havana. Turning to old contacts for favors, she imported five industrial sewing machines from Europe. Before 2012 ended, Pipo ran a 220-volt electric line around the perimeter of their Guanabacoa living room, converting it into a small workshop. She hired women who had lost their state jobs. Most important, her business plan left room for Oscar, who was now twenty-one, to eventually take over—if that was what he wanted. The struggle to retain its young people was widely considered to be one of the principal dramas of Cuba, an aching sore point for officials, intellectuals, administrators, and, most of all, parents. Cary hoped to build in enough opportunity so that her son might believe he had a future in a new Cuba, one that she saw changing and, in some ways, finally delivering on the promises that she and so many other Cubans had waited for throughout their lives.

CHAPTER 21

MIAMI
May 1999

The day after they had landed in Miami, Jorge García, La Flaca, and María Victoria were picked up at the house where they were staying with Jorge's brother-in-law Elio and driven in a black limousine to the headquarters of the Cuban American National Foundation, an anti-Castro political powerhouse in Miami. They walked into a room full of TV cameras and reporters and held a news conference. "We are very hurt that the Cuban government has denied responsibility here. That incident was murder, and the government keeps claiming it was an accident," María Victoria told the reporters. Five years had passed since she had lost her family on the *13 de Marzo*, and the hurt had not lessened. "Our life is not, and never will be, a real life without them." She described her uneasy existence ever since the tugboat sank. "Even today, I look back and can't help but think someone may be following me," she said. "We're speaking out here now so that the truth of life in Cuba can be known."

For the first time outside Cuba, her father declared that the sinking of the *13 de Marzo* five years earlier had not been an accident, as the Castro government claimed, but "an assassination." He described how, when the man he presumed was a state security agent had come to his house with the list of names, his first impulse had been to grab a knife and seek revenge. "But then I reconsidered it and learned to live with the heartache in my chest."

Like many of the 1.5 million Cubans who have gone into exile since the triumph of the revolution, Jorge remained deeply Cuban. He still loved Cuba, but it was the Cuba of his youth that endured in his heart, the Cuba of sun-drenched afternoons around the park in Guanabacoa, of big dogs and houses filled with family and friends, that he clung to, and not the Cuba he had fled. After he rented a ranch-style house near a boatyard in Miami, he tried to put that other Cuba behind him. He had taken very little with him from there— some clothing, the CDs with his interviews and transcripts hiding under Princess Diana's profile, and a few photographs. He hung one of those photos in a back room he used as an office and workshop. It was a picture of his son, Joel, looking directly at the camera with a big smile and no hint of the tragedy that would swallow him and his family.

It wasn't easy for Jorge to start over in a new country, especially one just entering a fierce presidential election campaign that would turn in part on events in Miami involving Elián González, the Cuban boy who, a few months after Jorge landed in Florida, would be rescued at sea by American fishermen. The boy's relatives in Miami took him in, but when his father—who had stayed in Cuba—demanded he be returned, it set off a fierce international struggle that enraged Fidel and exposed an ugly, fanatical side of the Cuban American community. After Cary had managed to print the Elián T-shirts for the big rally outside the embassy in Havana, Attorney General Janet Reno's authorization of a raid to snatch the boy and return him to Cuba gave Fidel the victory he sought, and it may have deprived Al Gore of the Florida votes that could have changed the outcome of the election.

Jorge was fifty-four years old when he got his first job in Miami as a five-dollar-an-hour security guard. After a few months, he caught a break with the Cuban American National Foundation. With his background making recordings and hosting *quinceañeras* in Guanabacoa, he started experimenting with the foundation's newer audio technology. He began to produce radio spots for La Voz, the foundation's radio station. When La Voz was shut down in 2001, Jorge poured his energy into completing his Spanish-language book *El hundimiento del remolcador* 13 de Marzo (*The Sinking of the* 13 de Marzo *Tugboat*). His passion guided his writing as he threw into the book everything he had, sometimes without obvious order or strict chronology, and without the help of an editor. He included the emotional accounts of the survivors along with the sad testimonies of the families of the victims. He printed grainy black-and-white photographs of the sixty-eight people who had boarded the tug. He even included a photo of La Flaca to go along with the pages about Joel. In that photo, she stares into the camera with deep sadness and pain showing in her eyes. In the middle of the book, tucked between stories of the survivors and the victims, Jorge reprinted the expert's report on the condition of the tugboat and its seaworthiness.

The Fund for Cuban Studies, an arm of the Cuban American National Foundation, had a small number of books printed. Jorge received two hundred as the only compensation for his years of work. Few copies have ever made it to Cuba. Arturo Montoto received one from an American diplomat and kept it in the library he was creating for himself in Guanabacoa.

Jorge went back to working security, and when his supervisors found out about his experience with Dobermans in Cuba, they offered to let him train their dogs. He also found work with La Poderosa, a high-wattage Spanish-language radio station in Miami. He and La Flaca scraped by, their attempts to put down roots in Florida always clashing with the malignant memories of the catastrophe that had altered their lives. She consoled herself when María Victoria remarried, and took comfort knowing that Jorge Félix was happy living in the house on San Sebastián as he got more deeply involved in his church. But her damaged heart ached with the loss of her grandson and of Joel, the son who was not supposed to be, yet was, and then had been brutally taken from her.

She was too weak and too old to renew her teaching certificate in Miami. Instead, she tried to earn some money by doing the washing and ironing at a small nursing home, without ever telling the doctors who ran the place about her condition. She lost more weight and grew ever weaker. Then, on July 13, 2007, thirteen years to the day after she lost Joel and the others at sea, she was rushed to Westchester Hospital in Miami.

Jorge then was pulling night shifts at the cruise ship terminal in Miami. A few nights after his wife had been hospitalized, María Victoria called him while he was on duty and told him to come to the hospital right away. He understood exactly what that meant. He stayed at La Flaca's side through the night. At four in the morning, he watched her straighten up sharply as a monitor let out a single beep. Her heart, though damaged, though it had suffered so much sadness over the years and had been broken so many times, kept on beating for another twenty-five minutes after she was declared brain-dead.

They had been married for forty-four years.

Jorge was still trying to accept that she was gone when a nurse came into the room to tell him he needed to stop by the hospital's main office.

"Do you have a funeral parlor for her?" the hospital administrator asked him.

"No, not yet. What's the problem?"

"There's no space left in the morgue. Are you sure you haven't signed any contract with a funeral parlor that could come and pick her up?"

He had been making payments on a cemetery plot but had not arranged anything with a funeral home. He didn't realize he had to. Death in America was far different than in Cuba. It was just five in the morning, and the hospital administrator was pressuring him. He called a funeral home in Miami's Little Havana and encountered another reality about death in the United States. He was offered various levels of service. The least expensive cost seven thousand dollars.

"Is there any way to lower the price?" he asked. It felt awful to even bring up the idea of cutting costs. They went through the uncomfortable process of bargaining down the price of death. Eliminating the police escort—$600. Leaving the crucifix off the top of the coffin—$180. The donation for the Catholic priest who comes in to lead prayers—$500. When they had scratched everything that decently could be left out, Jorge took out his credit card. He was told he'd also have to coordinate with the cemetery, where an employee explained that although he had purchased a gravesite, there was an additional charge of $2,500 for opening the grave. If he wanted a tombstone with Elisa's name and the dates of her birth and death, the engraving would cost $200. Additional words would cost $5 a letter.

He took out his credit card again.

Jorge already had been deep in debt before La Flaca died. Coming from Cuba, he had been awed by the ease with which he was able to get a credit card, and the purchasing power the little piece of plastic represented. But he didn't fully understand how dangerous it could be. When Jorge Félix had come to the United States on a mission for the Methodist Church, Jorge helped him buy ten thousand dollars' worth of professional video equipment for his business in Cuba, charging it to his credit card. For a while after La Flaca's funeral, Jorge tried to pay off his debt, but interest kept piling up, and when he eventually realized he owed more than he did the day she died, he threw up his hands and declared bankruptcy.

Broke, his spirit crushed, Jorge retired to live on Social Security and whatever he could pick up doing voice-overs. He continued working on his book, publishing a limited second edition in 2017. He was determined to pursue justice for the members of his family whose bodies remained at the bottom of the sea.

Jorge's life had been hollowed out, and so had his soul. He had been brought up in the Catholic faith and in 1994 was initially comforted in his grief by nuns who had come to the house on San Sebastián to console his family. He was grateful that Monsignor Carlos Baladrón had used the pulpit at La Milagrosa's chapel to condemn the repression he and his family suffered before they fled. But in time, even as Jorge Félix drew closer to his church, Jorge turned his back on his own religion. He had suffered so much while the Castros—whom he held responsible for sinking the tug—had never been brought to justice, and probably never would. The faith that had been drilled into him at Los Escolapios was not strong enough to support the weight of his grief and anger.

MANY CUBANS WHO HAD SUFFERED far less personal tragedy than Jorge also turned away from the Catholic Church. During the long years when attending mass was suspect, many Cubans who had been baptized Catholics drifted off into Santería, or abandoned religion altogether, focusing on the next day's meals rather than the next life. The churches themselves, some of them ancient, were beaten down by Cuba's humidity and rain, and with no funds for maintenance and repair, and rapidly shrinking congregations, they fell into ruin. The big churches fared worse than newer chapels like La Milagrosa. The masonry walls of Los Escolapios church grew splotchy with black mold, and its entrance was often draped with dead chickens and putrid fruit left as sacrifices to the Santería gods. After the roof over the rear vestibule collapsed, covering the statue of Christ with plaster and dust, believers like María del Carmen's sad friend, Caridad Guerra, who'd lost her family on the *13 de Marzo*, were terrified when they went in to pray, fearing that the whole ceiling could come down on them.

María del Carmen continued to attend mass either at Los Escolapios or at La Milagrosa with Román when he was home. He continued working at sea until 2009, when his boat was sent to Africa. On the voyage there, he began to suffer headaches so severe that he had to be put ashore in Spain. He recovered enough to rejoin his crew in Las Palmas in the Canary Islands. From there he sailed to Angola, but his health took another turn, and he was sent to a clinic where doctors diagnosed lung cancer. By November 1, 2009, he was back in Cuba.

Román died shortly after coming home. Mari was stunned. She developed a rash on her right hand, an angry red mass that erupted overnight. She considered it a physical representation of her grief. The rash had appeared on her hand in other moments of extreme emotion, and then disappeared just as suddenly as it had come.

A month after Román died, Mari had a mass said for him in the Chapel of Santo Cristo de Limpias, where they had met and where they had been married. After a life at sea, he didn't leave many assets, but there was his old blue Daewoo sedan. It was no Ford, but it ran, and his son, Virgilio, was thrilled to have it.

Mari had never suffered the political reprisals that Jorge felt, and her personal tragedy did not sink to the depths of what had befallen his family. And yet she too reached the point where she wondered what had become of her life. She had worked for forty years, and what could she show for it? She lived in a house that she had inherited. The busts of Caesar and Raphael, along with the sofa and even the rocking chair she sat in, had been left to her by her parents. Román had brought back their stereo and small television from overseas. Her contribution? Nothing that she could see. And now she was too old to leave Cuba, and too young to just give up. How would she get through the years ahead?

There was just one answer, the same answer that she'd sustained herself with since she was a child: Spanish dance. After Castro shut down all the private schools, she had continued taking dance lessons, following her favorite teachers as they held classes clandestinely in their own homes. Her father drove her to classes in his Ford two or three nights a week. In her mid-twenties she took classes with Cuban flamenco master Orlando Vargas. She sometimes wondered what it would have been like had dancing been her career, instead of testing dead fish. For Mari, classical Spanish dance was an entire world, one composed of passion and sensuality, a world where a dancer's every movement had meaning, as opposed to the life she had, almost without meaning at all.

As she got older, the rhythms of classical dance remained her lifeblood. She had her job, but when she clocked out, she went to dances run by the Catalan Beneficial Society in central Havana or at the Spanish embassy. On weekends, she helped teach young students the secrets of the dance, hoping to instill in them the same love that had been so important to her throughout her life.

Mari's son did not share her passion for Spanish dance, but he was as devoted to karate as she was to flamenco. He reached the level of black belt, competing in matches in Guanabacoa that were held inside a building on the other side of Los Escolapios that once housed the Progreso social club. He continued with karate until he entered university and studied to become a dental surgeon.

Mari kept a photograph of Virgilio in his white karate uniform and black belt on the curio cabinet in her living room, beneath a statuette of Jesus and above a tiny porcelain tea set she'd received when she was a girl. Sometimes, when she sat in her rocking chair on quiet afternoons, taking stock of her life, she looked at that photograph and realized that it was the one thing in the entire house that she could truly consider to be an accomplishment of her own.

One that could never be taken away.

CHAPTER 22

GUANABACOA

2008

Once Arturo Montoto and María Eugenia moved back to Guanabacoa, he was eager to paint again under the splendid Cuban sun. The preceding decade had been productive, and his work was well regarded. But he was dissatisfied with some of his output, convinced that the light he had worked under in Chile and Mexico had held him back. He soon discovered, as had Román Calvo after a long sea voyage, that the country he came home to was far different from the one he had left thirteen years earlier. The Castros were still running things, but this Cuba was filled with material shortages, bureaucratic obstacles, and a disheartening decline in civility that would challenge Arturo day in and day out. Raúl Castro had introduced economic changes that would have been unthinkable in the Cuba ruled by his brother, but only by comparison to the worst days of the special period did living in Cuba seem bearable.

Food was still a daily challenge. The days of fried grapefruit rind were over, but farms had become less productive in the years since he'd left, and blights had wiped out citrus crops so that grapefruits had disappeared altogether. Forget about beef, and it was hard to find fish of any kind in the market. Arturo ached for leafy green salads and enough ripe tomatoes to make pasta sauce. Remembering his mother's cod fritters, he obsessively searched for *bacalao*, but rarely found any.

Not tasting cod fritters was a disappointment, but constantly coming up empty-handed when he searched for the paints, canvases, and other material he needed for his work made him question his decision to come back. The most reliable way for him to get what he needed was to buy it abroad and carry it back on the plane. But he had to deal with weight and size restrictions, and as security got tighter, he had trouble bringing in oils and thinners, even acrylic paints. He was forced to use inferior materials, or to abandon a project when he couldn't find enough of what he needed to finish it.

As one of Cuba's most celebrated artists, a master of light and shadow whose works sold for prices most Cubans couldn't imagine, his relationship with the government also changed. State media sought him out, eager to report his standing in the international art world. He was invited to sell his paintings in galleries across Cuba. Most important, his reputation, combined with his dual citizenship, allowed him to travel to Mexico and the United States, as well as to Europe and other parts of the world, without worrying about the government standing in his way. He remained as distant as ever from the regime and its philosophies, and with the fear of retaliation removed because of his fame, his scorn for the system grew, though he still refused to use his art for political purposes. He watched young Cuban artists rake in lots of money selling polemical works in Miami, where anything critical of Fidel or Raúl sold well, and he resented their success. In his mind, such works were crude provocations without technical merit, though the earnings they generated seemed to mock his long years of training. He was satisfied to conform to the quid pro quo that he had negotiated with the regime, surviving in the system by using irony as his principal weapon. He enjoyed an array of privileges because his art did not openly criticize the system. But his personal views surely held it in contempt. Out for a night with friends, he'd ask for a "Ha-Ha-Ha" at the bar. It was actually a Cuba Libre, rum and cola, but thinking of Cuba as being anywhere close to free was for him a cruel joke.

It was the light of Cuba's blue-sky days that made coming back worthwhile. He believed he was strong enough, and independent enough, to confront the challenges Cuba threw in his path, as long as he could paint beneath the dazzling daylight of his native land. But as Cubans endlessly repeated, life is complicated. The years were taking a toll on Arturo, and soon after he returned to Guanabacoa, he had to undergo surgery for two inguinal hernias that had become so painful they often kept him from working. Complications after the surgeries left him unable to paint for months. Even when he was back on his feet, he didn't have the strength to stand before his easel for very long. He put his artwork on hold while he focused his energy on a project that brought together elements of his past and combined them with his vision for a Cuban future.

Arturo had never forgotten how much his own art education had changed his life and helped transform him from that country kid who knew only the "Florentine Giant" into an internationally recognized artist. With the ample proceeds he had earned abroad, he envisioned opening a studio workshop that could double as gallery, exposition space, and classroom for a new generation of Cubans whose lives could be altered by exposure to fine art the way his was. He felt that Guanabacoa's connection to Lecuona, Montaner, and other giants of Cuban culture made it a good place to undertake such a project. His knowledge of the city's architectural heritage convinced him that he'd find a physical space that would accommodate his dream. And he believed that living near but not in the center of Havana would give him the freedom to do things his own way.

He searched for a space that was big enough to contain all the elements of his ambitious plan, and he found it in one of Guanabacoa's neglected historic structures, a large ruin directly across the street from Los Escolapios church, near the historic center of town. The building had once belonged to the Progreso Society of Recreation and Instruction of Men of Color, an Afro-Cuban cultural institution founded in 1899. For many years, the Progreso hall was a celebrated site for cultural performances within the city's black community. After the Castro government seized it, the building became a venue for parties, including private birthdays. Arturo's wife, María Eugenia, celebrated a birthday there when she was a child. Later, when the building was used as a martial arts dojo, María del Carmen's son competed under its roof.

During the special period, money for maintenance disappeared, and despite its significance, the building was allowed to fall into disrepair. Parts of the roof collapsed, and weeds grew in the cracks, splitting concrete from beams. As conditions worsened, the building's role in Guanabacoa changed. Forgotten was its important history for Afro-Cubans. Local people came to see it as a building supply depot, stripping off whatever they needed for their own projects. When the grillwork around every window had been stolen, every bit of ornamentation stripped from the facade, and every reusable bit of stone and concrete hauled away, what remained of the building doubled as a dumping ground.

When Arturo told anyone that he wanted to make the old Progreso hall his art studio, he was met with strange looks. The building, or what was left of it, was on the verge of collapse. In fact, an adjacent building did fall down, knocking over a utility pole that killed a passerby. The remains of that building were torn down and a bank ATM installed in the empty lot. A ficus tree sprouted from the roof of the Progreso hall, and its roots crawled down the walls like gigantic pythons. Trash was piled waist high in spots, and the stink from the dead chickens and other Santería offerings left there pushed people off the sidewalks and into busy Máximo Gómez Street.

Arturo saw beyond the dirt and debris, envisioning a unique space that would become an asset for the community, as well as a touchstone for his own work. If he could get the necessary permits, he had the money to take on the project. His paintings were commanding prices of over ten thousand dollars at international art houses. As he recuperated from surgery and adapted to the new conditions of life in Cuba, he and María Eugenia came up with an overall design for the building. More than ever, he felt committed to the idea of creating an arts center where, through education and expositions, he could restore some of the culture he felt that Cuba had lost since 1959. Almost daily, he was confronted with the petty corruption that had worked its way into most aspects of Cuban life. Theft and insubordination were rampant, and the most basic level of any service could be gotten only with a threat or a bribe.

He confronted this new reality in minor ways every day whenever he dealt with surly store attendants or unruly crowds rushing to get on an over-crowded bus. Then there were incidents that really set him off, like the time he believed he was being overcharged on his electric bill. He got nowhere on the telephone, so he headed to Guanabacoa's municipal building, to an office called "Attention to the Public," located just to the side of the main reception desk in the front lobby. Just about every town in Cuba had something like it where individuals were expected to file complaints about government short-comings, hoping for some kind of resolution. He knocked on the office door, but there was no answer, and when he tried the door, it was locked.

He wasn't surprised. He'd tried to file complaints about other issues, but the office always seemed to be empty or closed, although it was supposed to be receiving citizen complaints every weekday. He took his inflated bill directly to the government utility, which had its own office of "Attention to the Public."

This time, the office was open, and there were people inside. An attendant sat at the front desk, puffing on a cigarette, fogging up the small office with smoke.

"Excuse me, I have this bill . . ." Arturo started to say, but the smoke made it difficult to breathe.

"Please, could you put that out?" he asked politely. "I can't breathe in here."

On the other side of the room, two young women were listening to reggaeton music. The attendant had put out her cigarette, but Arturo felt he was still under assault.

"Could you please turn that off so I can talk?" he said, trying hard to control his temper.

The young women exchanged glances, sucked in their cheeks, and turned down the music.

"So, what do you want?" the attendant asked him, her eyes revealing how she had taken him for another demanding, know-it-all Cuban man.

He felt his back stiffen. Then he blurted out: "From you? Nothing."

Eventually he pulled rank to get the problem resolved. The Ministry of Culture had an office like the one in Guanabacoa that, under the title "Attention to Personalities in the Field of Culture," gave artists special treatment.

"Don't worry, Arturo," he was told. "This will be taken care of." He was instructed to return to the utility's local office the following Monday. When he showed up this time, he was taken right into the director's office. His electric bills were adjusted and the issue resolved immediately, but Arturo left there wondering how Cubans who did not have access to the office of Attention to Personalities in the Field of Culture were supposed to take care of their problems.

It took the better part of three years of haggling with the government to get permission to start work on the Progreso renovation. Local officials had no experience with anything like what he envisioned. He was a private individual, and the ruins of Progreso were owned by the state. Would he have to swap a building for the property, or could he buy it outright? And at what price? Cuba didn't have a multiple listing service, and no one compiled a record of comparable sales because there hadn't been any for half a century, not legal ones anyway. Initially, officials wanted him to buy the building, pay for the restoration, and then leave it to them to run. Arturo rejected that idea. After prolonged legal wrangling, he secured title to the parcel by agreeing to give up the house he owned in Guanabacoa in exchange for the Progreso ruins, as well as paying the local bank an additional amount for the property.

He was delayed further as he pressed for possession of the adjacent lot, for which he had special plans. He argued that the bank ATM had been placed there illegally. He won that issue, and the ATM was removed.

Work progressed slowly because of the scarcity of concrete and lumber. When Raúl Castro's government liberalized the sale of construction material, Arturo was able to buy what he needed. He hired teams of local workers and was on-site personally supervising them so often that neighbors got used to calling him "Bob the Builder," after a popular cartoon character. He added living space for himself and an outdoor workshop for large projects, and in the adjacent lot he had tons of topsoil trucked in to create a replica of the backyard orchard he remembered in Pinar del Río. The only thing missing was a *mamoncillo* tree.

In all, he spent around $160,000 on the studio, living space, and garden, a sum that dwarfed any other privately financed project in Guanabacoa except the lush compound built by Gilberto Martínez Suárez, the Cuban reggaeton artist from Guanabacoa who called himself "Gilbert Man." After Interpol arrested Martínez in 2015 on credit-card fraud and money-laundering charges, his estate was seized and turned into a nursery school.

Arturo moved into his new quarters in 2013. In the main workshop area, he devoted one side to his treasured library. Many of the books he put on the floor-to-ceiling shelves were about art, but he also kept James Joyce's *Ulysses* alongside books by Octavio Paz. On another shelf, Hugh Thomas's *The Conquest of Mexico* sat next to a history of Bulgaria. While most of his books were in Spanish, including Jorge García's testimonial about the *13 de Marzo*, some were in English or Russian, and a few were in Greek, which he had learned in order to study classical philosophy. Once he settled in, he offered free classes in art theory and art appreciation to students from Guanabacoa and surrounding areas. He also lectured on the power of critical thinking. For years he kept a whiteboard in the studio diagrammed with Aristotle's Five Modes of Reaching the Truth.

Arturo restored the Progreso building with his own money. He did receive encouragement from the office of the historian of Havana and the municipal government of Guanabacoa, but no financial assistance. The Escolapios priests across the street had watched with envy as his building rose from ruins while their church sank further into decay. "Maestro, can't you help us a little?" they'd asked. "The pope has money," Arturo responded. "Why don't you ask him?"

Teaching at his own studio, using his own methods, was a joy, but he developed nodules on his larynx that swelled when he spoke too long, and his doctors told him to shut down those classes or risk losing his voice altogether. He continued to provide hands-on studio training for a select group of young artists, his way of paying back the support he had received as he developed his own skills.

The construction project had kept him focused for years after his return to Cuba, and he devoted so much time to it that he painted little. He and María Eugenia grew apart, and after her father died, she moved to South Florida to be with her mother. Arturo began a relationship with a much younger woman, Daily de la Peña, who had an artistic streak. She loved creating fashionable clothing, and as their relationship developed, Arturo offered to buy her a serious sewing machine. One of her friends had told her about a woman in Guanabacoa who had her own clothing company. Perhaps she had a sewing machine for sale.

One afternoon, Arturo and Daily pulled up in front of a pinkish concrete house in the Habana Nueva section of Guanabacoa and rang the bell.

Caridad Limonta came out to greet them, and to sell them one of her sewing machines at what both sides agreed was a fair price.

CHAPTER 23

VEDADO, HAVANA

2014

Cary no longer needed the sewing machine at home because she had taken the business leap that Cuba Emprende had inspired and rented commercial space for her own workshop. It was a big step, one she wouldn't have had the confidence to take without the program's encouragement. Since the revolution, Cubans had developed powerful survival skills that helped them make the best of any hardship. Unable to find a replacement fan belt for a 1958 Plymouth, they knew that a man's dress belt would do. If bakeries ran out of boxes, they learned how to carry home a fancy birthday cake on a crowded bus without smudging a single whipped-cream swirl. But that resourcefulness is also their most paralyzing weakness. Instead of marching to the Plaza de la Revolución demanding change, or locking arms with dissidents to fix Cuba's grim reality, most simply accept and then adapt to the latest privation. Without the Cuba Emprende course, Cary might have been content to continue sewing at home. But once the *caballo* that had been her classroom namesake was awakened, it was champing at the bit to race ahead.

The space she rented for her workshop was at the other end of Havana from Guanabacoa, in the once-posh Vedado neighborhood. It was a first-floor walkup in a six-story 1930s art deco apartment building on the corner of Fifteenth and Sixth, across the street from a small park dedicated to the memory of John Lennon, the Beatle whose image once had been prohibited by the revolutionary government. A statue of Lennon by Arturo's friend José Villa Soberón sat on a park bench, where it was photographed by tourists. The life-size bronze wore a pair of Lennon's classic round wire-rim eyeglasses that were stolen several times. The government then stationed a security guard to watch the statue all day, holding on to the glasses. When a tourist was ready to snap a photograph, he'd put them back on Lennon's nose.

Cary rented the space from the Federation of Cuban Women, which controlled the building. She'd sent a proposal for a combination atelier and boutique where she could create and sell her own fashions. She also promised that she would provide a much-needed community service—altering and sometimes making everyday clothing for neighbors. Because of Cuba's tight restrictions on imports, custom-made was sometimes cheaper than buying off the rack. The federation approved.

Cary's shop quickly became popular with neighbors. They dropped off clothing that needed to be pulled in or let out, and while there, they chatted with *la jefa*. If someone was fortunate enough to get hold of fabric for a blouse or a pair of pants, Cary's seamstresses could turn around the order in a day or two. As the business grew, she started a women's circle for neighbors to discuss their concerns. She was all for opening Cuba to capitalism, but if making money was the only goal, she felt that the previous sixty years had been wasted.

She hoped the workshop would also accommodate another essential element of her plan for the future. Oscar was twenty-four and had lots of ideas. She just wasn't sure what he would end up doing. Or where. She wanted him to stay with her in Cuba, but in her heart, she was painfully aware that he had savored the idea of leaving Cuba since he was a boy.

THE SON OF TWO ENGINEERS, Oscar knew early on that it would be logical for him to pick engineering as a career, but he never embraced that idea, always thinking he was built differently from his parents. But if not engineering, then what? As a youth he liked drawing, and he was crazy about playing the drums, but when he was barely a teenager and tried to enroll in the music school in Guanabacoa, he was told he was already too old to begin formal musical training. He attended the local high school instead, and as he got closer to graduation, his cousin Leonardo, Esperanza's eldest son, introduced him to a friend who was enrolled in the Superior Institute of Design in Havana. With his interest in drawing, Oscar figured he could study any number of fields, from industrial design to fashion. But getting in wouldn't be easy. There was an admissions test, a difficult one. Cary hired a private tutor who charged three dollars a class, a huge amount for them at that time. Oscar learned about perspective, shadows, and depth. When results of the admissions test were announced at a high school assembly, he was delighted to be among the few who got in.

Before he could enter the design institute, Oscar had to complete his compulsory military service, which was shortened from two years to eighteen months because he was headed to university. Cary tried to get him a health deferment. He was short and slight, like many other Cubans born during the special period, and prone to stomach problems and muscle spasms. Nonetheless, he was classified as fit enough to serve. He reported for basic training at a military post in East Havana, where his head was shaved, he was handed a white T-shirt and a pair of green shorts, and he began rigorous physical training. It was the start, he often complained, of the worst year and a half of his life.

He was assigned to a tank battalion, with keep-busy orders to clean equipment and maintain the post. He spent many days at the parade grounds, doubled over as he cut grass with a machete. One time his crew was ordered to whitewash the curbs along a parade route. It was already late in the day, and the skies were threatening. He asked the supervising officer if it made sense to continue painting if it was going to rain, and the answer he got was "Get back to work."

They finished painting just as it started to pour, washing their work into the streets.

Oscar survived his military service and started his studies at the design institute. He found that the tutor had prepared him well. By the time he started his fourth and final year he was so far ahead that he was able to consider a radical change. On Cary's advice, he applied for a license as a self-employed designer working for Procle while he completed his studies. Cary taught him about accounting, cost analysis, and workflow. At first, he had mixed feelings about working for his mother. Although he fully embraced the concept of the private sector, the garment industry held no appeal for him. But as he became more accustomed to the challenge of figuring out schedules, purchases, prices, and deliveries, he realized that it didn't matter what they were making and selling. Aluminum pots or pairs of socks, understanding the manufacturing process, regardless of what was being produced, would make it easier for him to do what he wanted later on.

He graduated in July 2015 with a degree in industrial design and a burning desire, shared by many young Cubans, to get out of Cuba as soon as possible, especially now that something incredible was happening that brought the United States and Cuba closer together than they'd been since Dwight D. Eisenhower was president.

The pages of *Granma* still were flecked with stories about the threats of American aggression, and the drumbeat of protest against the Miami Mafia was as steady as ever. But things were changing under the young black president in the United States who kept saying it was time to put the past to rest and look to the future. In December 2014, Barack Obama and Raúl Castro had surprised people in both the United States and Cuba by announcing that they were going to restore diplomatic relations and jointly take a new path forward. With Fidel sidelined with his worsening illness, Obama and Raúl made it easier for Cubans to visit the United States, and for Americans to visit Cuba. And visit they did, showing up in record numbers and filling legions of Cubans with hope that their long period of isolation was finally ending. Even in Guanabacoa, far off the tourist trail, would-be local entrepreneurs opened the town's first two bed and breakfast operations. One ambitious entrepreneur even built a wine bar, hoping to entice tourists to cross the harbor for a night of entertainment. Secretary of State John Kerry came to Havana in 2015 to watch the American flag being raised over the reopened U.S. embassy on the Malecón, half a century after the two nations turned their backs on each other.

Oscar didn't have a chance to study abroad the way his parents did, but when a friend told him about a program at Florida International University

(FIU) for young Cuban entrepreneurs that was being coordinated through the newly reopened U.S. embassy, he jumped at it. In the summer of 2016, the Roots of Hope course offered forty-five days in South Florida, where students would learn about running a business and have a chance to network with American businessmen. He applied, met all the requirements, and was accepted. At last, he believed, he'd found his ticket out.

His plan was simple. He'd fly to Miami with the group, and once in the United States, he'd ask for asylum. He spent weeks planning his escape without telling his parents what he was thinking. A friend gave him the name of a design institute graduate who had started his own business in South Florida. Oscar shot off an email, introduced himself as a fellow graduate, and was thrilled to receive a return email offering him a tryout whenever he got to Florida.

Deciding to get out of Cuba seemed to be a no-brainer. In his mind, the stress of working in Cuba had nearly killed both his parents. They were in their early sixties, still working hard instead of retiring and taking care of their health. He was just twenty-five, full of self-confidence, with ambitions to fill his wallet with spending money. His Florida contacts assured him that although he'd cause his parents grief when he didn't return, they'd be happy for him once they heard how quickly he was able to get on his feet and start making real money.

He also knew that his mother's own feelings about America were rapidly changing. When she was invited to represent Cuba Emprende at a conference in Florida in 2015, she applied for a B-2 visa that allowed her to travel back and forth between Cuba and the United States for five years. On her first trip to America, she marveled at the aisles of produce in U.S. supermarkets and the internet access that was everywhere, all the time. And although she kept a lookout for mounds of stinking garbage like the one that plagued her corner in Guanabacoa, she never encountered any. In March 2016, when President Obama became the first American president since Calvin Coolidge to visit Havana, she would be invited to join other self-employed Cubans to meet with him. Seated at a newly opened craft brewery on the Havana waterfront, she heard Obama say that it was time to recognize the differences between their two countries and to move ahead, and she agreed wholeheartedly. She had been raised on slogans like "*Cuba sí, yanqui no,*" but seeing a black American president walking the streets of Havana with his pretty wife filled her with hope.

Oscar packed a suitcase with just enough clothes for a forty-five-day stay in Florida. He did his best not to raise suspicions, but Cary knew there was a good chance he might not come back. Despite her own desire to keep her only child nearby, she was determined to let him find his own way. She and Pipo scraped together five hundred dollars for him to spend while he was in Florida studying or starting a new life.

A few weeks after Obama's visit, Cary accompanied Oscar to the airport. They both understood the possibilities that existed at that moment, but neither mentioned them out loud. They hugged briefly, and Oscar kissed her goodbye. While he waited to board the charter flight to Miami, he chatted with other students in the program about their own businesses. He was surprised to hear them boasting about how they had gone from idea to thriving business in a relatively short time. He took note of the clothes they wore, and when they mentioned their cell phones, fancy watches, and other luxuries, his ears perked up. Despite the austerity he'd grown up with during the special period, or perhaps because of it, he appreciated the power of money. He wanted a life where finding enough to eat wasn't a daily preoccupation. Where he could get from place to place easily, perhaps even own a car someday. Where the streets were clean, the sidewalks without cracks. A place without limits.

But something else started to seep into his imagination. If his companions could run thriving businesses in Cuba and live the kind of lives they wanted, maybe it wasn't necessary for him to separate from family and friends. Maybe it was possible to make money in the new Cuba. He started to think that instead of asking for asylum as soon as he landed in Miami, he'd attend the classes at FIU, learn what he could about business, and then, just before the program ended, present himself as a refugee if that was still what he wanted. Waiting would give him time to figure out what was the right move. And no matter what he decided, what he'd learn there would make him better prepared to run his own company, wherever it was located.

When he arrived at the Miami airport, Oscar walked right past the immigration officers without uttering a word about asylum. Outside the terminal, he was surprised to find not a single beat-up American car like the ones in Havana. For a few days he explored the city, astonished at what he saw. A friend took him to his high-rise apartment near the waterfront in downtown Miami. The rooms dazzled him, but nothing compared to what he saw from the balcony. It was twilight, the lights of the city had come on, and the streets sparkled with a brightness that matched the shining points of light on the water and in the sky. Oscar realized then how far behind Cuba had fallen. Free to explore without any kind of government minder, he gawked at the shelves of the Publix supermarket he was taken to. The sidewalks were so clean he thought they were closed, and nowhere did he come across mounds of trash like the one near his house. He had seen American movies where a man walks into the street, raises his arm, and a taxicab appears, and it was true!

Cary's course at Cuba Emprende had focused on starting a business. The FIU program concentrated on running an existing business. The students met with company officials from PayPal and American Airlines, and they had a chance to talk to the Cuban-born founder of Perry Ellis International, George Feldenkreis. They had a session with business leaders from Miami's chamber of commerce who seemed eager to invest in Cuba. His month-and-a-half stay in Florida was a whirlwind of new ideas. Before the course wrapped up, the students had a chance to pitch an idea for expanding their own business. When it was Oscar's turn to stand in front of the microphone, he outlined a venture to custom-design logos for companies and special events, then have the design printed on canvas bags he'd manufacture and sell at a profit. Nothing new for Florida, but a bold new concept for Cuba. After he pitched, the other students told him that when he was ready to move forward, they'd be willing to help. The future suddenly seemed as bright as a Cuban afternoon.

After all he'd seen and heard, and after all the conflicting ideas that had taken root in his head, Oscar decided it was not the right moment for him to abandon Cuba. He returned home confident about making it in the private sector. He had developed contacts whose commercial and personal successes he wanted to imitate, and he thought that a multiple-entry B-2 visa could be what he needed to make his life in Cuba manageable.

Cary and Pipo were relieved to have him back and delighted to hear about his plans for the new venture. They called a lawyer friend to help draw up papers and went with Oscar to the bank to apply for a loan. It would have been impossible without Cary's substantial help because the bank had almost no experience making loans to individuals, another of Raúl's recent concessions to the open market. She walked the bankers through the process of approving a twelve-thousand-dollar, ten-year loan to cover equipment, material, and start-up costs. Then she signed a ten-year lease with a ten-year option to extend on a second-floor industrial space on Neptuno Street in central Havana. At the lawyer's suggestion, Oscar filled out the legal documents that he'd need to do business with state enterprises as well as private entrepreneurs.

The lawyer brought him his first customers, organizations looking not for tote bags but T-shirts and promotional material that Oscar would design. In a few months a neighbor told him about a state-run store in Old Havana that packaged custom-mixed perfumes in small canvas bags imprinted with the store's name, 1791. The store had been purchasing the bags from a company in Spain, but they had grown increasingly expensive. Oscar put in a bid to make them for substantially less, and guaranteed delivery of five thousand a month, even before he had produced a single one. Cary helped him secure a limited supply of canvas from a dance troupe in Regla that had a license to import material for costumes.

The bags were about the size of an Apple cell phone, made of beige canvas with a pull string, and printed with the shop's 1791 logo. Oscar hired women who worked at home to insert the strings. One of those women was Cary's friend Lili Durand Hernández. When a deadline loomed, Lili stayed up until three or four in the morning cutting pieces of cord to length and pulling them through loops to have them ready for Oscar when he came by to get them.

IT WAS ALMOST A YEAR after he'd returned from Florida, and Oscar slowly came up the stairs and entered the Procle workshop in Vedado, his cell phone pressed to his ear and worry scrawled over his face. The sewing machines in his mother's shop were idle, not because the electricity was shut off, the way it had been just a few days before, but because of the eviction notice that Cary had received ordering her to vacate the space.

Oscar looked around the showroom at the colorful dresses Cary had designed and that her seamstresses had sewn. Across the floor were T-shirts printed with his artwork, including his line drawing of the John Lennon statue across the street. Tourists who wandered in from the park liked them. And on a peg in the corner were a few canvas shopping bags also bearing Lennon's image. He cared most about them because they represented his future, a future that suddenly had been thrown into doubt because of the illogical way that business was done in Cuba. After her first two years in Vedado, Cary had signed a lease extension for at least five more years. But here it was, just a few months later, and the women of the federation were demanding the space back because they said somebody else needed it more. They promised to find her new space for her business, and they even offered to help her and Pipo find an apartment closer to central Havana so they wouldn't have to continue making the tortuous commute from Guanabacoa. Trust us, they said, we'll take care of you. But we need you to move out right away.

The federation's change of heart reminded Cary of how the state housing agency had taken back her mother's microbrigade apartment in San Agustín because somebody needed it more, but eventually settled her in something better. Oscar was too young to make that connection. To him, the eviction was a clear violation of their legal rights. Even though he had his own workshop in central Havana, the arbitrariness of the eviction gave him one more reason to think that, despite what his mother often said, his future lay outside of Cuba.

Cary didn't like the idea of moving her shop, but she did not want to antagonize the federation, which planned to convert the space into an apartment. They offered her the ground floor of a building a block in from the Malecón in central Havana, and an apartment nearby. Cary didn't think it was a good location for a business and turned it down. But she had been thinking for a while about giving up the house in Guanabacoa for something more centrally located. Traveling to and from Guanabacoa was a nightmare. The apartment the federation had in mind for them would be convenient, but it needed so much plumbing and electrical work that Pipo—who had poured countless hours into repairing their house in Guanabacoa—refused to even consider it.

Oscar took Cary to lunch that day. Walking the streets of Vedado, they argued about the proposed swap. He was dead set against her giving up the space.

"We have a signed lease for it, with years to go," he said. "That's the only legal right we have in all this. If you give that up, all we'll have is their word that they'll give us something else, and that can change really fast."

"I met with them privately and they assured me it would work out," Cary said. "I believe them."

She had far more business experience than he did, but he saw the world with different eyes. "It's a trap," he said. Like other young Cubans, he could see past the triumphalist rhetoric splashed over the pages of *Granma* every day. His Florida stay had multiplied his doubts about Cuba's shortcomings. Where Cary saw nothing wrong with the federation's offer to give them space, he was less trusting. The government's real goal, he truly believed, was to keep people dependent on it for everything.

After lunch, he was so upset by the eviction and by changes in the United States that he decided to line up a different future for himself. He took one hundred dollars from his savings, converted it to five twenty-dollar bills dated 2013 or later as the Jamaican embassy in Havana required. After the flurry of excitement in the wake of Obama's visit and the changes he brought in, the United States had a new president, and suddenly some of the old worries about relations between the two countries began to creep back in. Donald Trump was a businessman who was said to have been interested in building in Cuba, but in the middle of his campaign he had started to side with the Cuban old guard in Miami, whose vote could be decisive. Then, in January 2017, just before leaving office, President Obama had pulled the plug on the wet foot, dry foot policy that had been established in the wake of the chaotic summer of 1994. Under that policy, Cubans who set foot on U.S. soil without a visa were put on a fast track to receive permanent residency.

Once the wet foot, dry foot policy ended, Cuban migration to the United States suddenly became much more complicated. Worried about what the Trump administration might do next, Oscar felt that it made sense to look south rather than just focusing on the United States for his future. He was the son of Cubans, but his roots went back to Jamaica, where his great-grandmother Sarah had been born. He decided to apply for Jamaican citizenship. Just in case. He wasn't looking for a new identity, but Cubans had such a troublesome reputation as prospective immigrants in the rest of the world that getting a visa for anywhere but Russia or Haiti and a few other countries was difficult. He believed that a Jamaican passport would make it easier to travel, and to open a bank account or rent a car in other countries, if that's what he decided to do.

The next day, they began moving the supplies and sewing machines from Vedado to the workshop that Oscar rented in central Havana. They'd run both businesses from there, as long as Oscar remained in Cuba.

CHAPTER 24

GUANABACOA

2017

Lili's life had dovetailed with Cary's since they both worked at the aluminum plant on Vía Blanca, Cary in the administrative office and Lili doing security at the front desk or inside one of the buildings. That also was when Lili met a Navy veteran named Carlos Castaño, who had been born in Guanabacoa and who owned an apartment a few blocks from Novalum. He'd come of age with the revolution, defending his country after the Bay of Pigs invasion and turning his back on his middle-class family's bourgeois roots. He committed himself mind and body to the socialist cause, continuing with the navy as an electrician after his military service ended. He joined the Communist Party and was a proud member for more than two decades, eventually taking on duties as a regional CDR director. For many years, he even wore a long, bushy beard like Fidel's.

After living together in his apartment for years, Lili and Carlos signed papers in 2010 to be legally married in a civil ceremony at the government-run wedding palace in Guanabacoa. Lili rented a white gown and asked Cary to be her maid of honor. Soon after, Carlos encouraged Lili to take over as president of the local CDR, covering the neighborhood where both she and Cary lived. Prepared to give her all to the revolution, she'd tried to join the Communist Party, but after taking the required classes in communist ideology and studying the required texts, she was turned down, most likely because of some lingering accusation—true or not—by an unfriendly neighbor at some time in her past. She was disappointed, but not embittered. She'd simply serve the revolution in other ways.

Lili's house, the one with the sign declaring PRESIDENTE DEL CDR on the steel front door, was originally a single-family home built around the same time as Cary's during development of the Habana Nueva subdivision. After the revolution, the house had been divided into several apartments. A few years after they were married, Carlos agreed to split his ground-floor apartment in two to make room for Lili's son, Joseíto, and his family, and that ushered in tensions that she hadn't confronted before. Stark differences between generations had become common in Cuba. Cary and Oscar held contrary views of Cuba and the future it held for them, but their incongruities were minor compared with the gap between Lili and Joseíto.

Lili had watched so many people of her generation grow weary of the complications of life in Cuba and leave for La Yuma, the name—taken from an American Western movie—she and others gave to the United States. Although her faith in the revolution remained rock solid, making the trip to Yuma was on her bucket list. She never thought of living there, but she was eager to visit, she often said, "just to see what it is that makes so many people want to go there." If that somehow happened and she got to the United States, she figured she'd stay for a week or two and then come right back. She'd heard how hard life could be in the north, where you had to pay for everything and nobody cared whether you lived or died. That's what she read in *Granma*, and as the newspaper itself proclaimed, "*Granma* nunca miente"—*Granma* never lies.

On the other side of the cinder-block wall running through the middle of Carlos's apartment, Joseíto took it as a point of pride that he never read *Granma* because "nothing in it is true" or resembled in the slightest way the Cuba that he lived in. He didn't pay attention to TV news either, filled with government public relations passed off as news. He had made up his mind about all that and more many years ago, concluding that there was no future for him in Cuba. And even less did he want his two young daughters, Arianne and Adrianet, stuck there.

"I'm almost forty years old, and I have practically nothing of my own," he groused, expressing the same lament as María del Carmen, although he was a generation younger. He smoked Criollo cigarettes, about as many each day as his mother and Carlos smoked combined. He complained that he couldn't go out for a drink with friends because if he did, there wouldn't be enough money left for his girls to eat. To buy a pair of jeans for himself would cost four months' income. Food was becoming more expensive all the time, and the groceries that came with the *libreta* usually ran out after just a few days. He complained that he spent "every day just resolving problems." Like *inventar* and *luchar*, the Spanish verb *resolver* had taken on new meaning in Cuba since the special period. Every day, on practically every street, Cubans like him were trying to figure out a way past the next set of problems, using dodges and feints to get around oppressive laws and burdensome restrictions, relying on their imagination, and a sliding scale of expectations, to get through the day. For many, the only way to keep from losing all faith was to measure current hardships against the bad times of the special period. By that comparison, some things had gotten better. Not good but better. And better only because they used to be so damn bad.

In Cuba, to resolve was to survive.

Joseíto stopped believing in the promise of the revolution when he was still a boy, and in truth he wasn't certain that he'd ever believed in it. Living in Casablanca, where the streets were never paved, electricity was hijacked from power lines, and water was an intermittent luxury, his revolutionary Cuba was grim. He was only twelve when the special period began, and it dampened his expectations even before he'd had a chance to dream. He didn't do well in school and never went past the ninth grade. A short stint in a bakery proved to him that he could never hold that kind of a mundane day-to-day job. He tried living with his grandfather in Santiago, but two years there was all he could take before heading back to Casablanca in 1994, the year of the tugboat sinking and the disturbance on the Malecón. Although he lived close enough to the waters of Havana Harbor that crabs crawled around his yard, he knew little about those incidents or the profound impact they had on Cuba. Nothing that summer touched his life, which then was limited to the hardscrabble patch of dirt known as Casablanca.

Without planning or authorization, Casablanca had grown haphazardly since the revolution, going from a small town to a sprawling, almost lawless harborside slum. Joseíto was arrested after he threatened to kill a neighbor who was building his own shack and tried to tap into a water pipe that supplied Joseíto's house and his grandmother's nearby home. Once he had a criminal record, hard luck seemed to follow him like a shadow until he married a young woman from East Havana named Adriana. That was when he put aside the tough-guy act and set out in earnest to *luchar*. Many, even most Cubans, resorted to *luchando* in one way or another, living by a single defining commandment: keep the big rule—the one that prohibits you from doing anything that threatens the regime—but break every small one if it helps keep you alive.

He was hustling in Havana when he met a man from Guantánamo province who repaired chairs and sofas using rubber strips harvested from old tires. The man was doing enough business to need a helper. He let Joseíto in on the secrets of his unique trade, showing him how to use a long, sharp knife to cut into the rim of an old tire from a car or a truck, pulling the knife through the rubber in widening circles so one-inch-wide strips curled off. Then, like filleting a fish, he separated the tire's steel belt layer from the flexible rubber, producing strips he used as lattice under seat bottoms for the chairs and sofas he reupholstered.

When he had mastered handling the knife without losing a finger, Joseíto decided to take a chance and launch his own furniture business. On the list of self-employment opportunities that Raúl's government had released in 2011 was one for making and selling rubber trim for trucks and automobiles. It had nothing to do with repairing furniture, but because he used rubber, he thought it was close enough to make his business legal. He paid about four dollars a month for the license, plus another ten dollars every three months and 10 percent of whatever he earned for taxes.

A friend with a truck drove him to the highway, where he gathered discarded tires. He worked in the patio outside his house in Casablanca, trying to stay in the shade as he chased away the crabs. Through word of mouth he became known in the neighborhood as the go-to person to fix sagging sofas or bottomless chairs. Money finally started coming in. But soon he learned the same lesson as Cary—with capitalism comes competition and market forces. Dozens of people had learned how to strip rubber. Old tires suddenly became scarce. Everything else he needed to make and repair furniture, from nails to fabric, also was in short supply. And few people had enough money to pay for his kind of work.

He gave up the license and threw himself once more into *luchando* mode. He climbed the hills around Guanabacoa, picking *mamoncillos* to sell for a few centavos, doing what Arturo Montoto and his brothers had done in Pinar del Río half a century earlier. He washed cars, did house repairs, cut grass—whatever he could to make money. By then, Carlos had grown fond of Joseíto's daughter, who called him Grandpa, and agreed that it would be nice to have them all living closer. He split his apartment in two so that Joseíto could bring his family there from Casablanca. Joseíto set up his hand-me-down table saw and other tools in the carport where Carlos used to keep his Moscovich sedan until he became too deaf to drive.

Joseíto went back to repairing furniture, but money remained tight. He and Adriana had a second daughter, and they routinely skipped meals so the girls had enough to eat. He worked when he had orders and spent a lot of time walking the streets, looking for discarded items he could reuse. He often came back empty-handed and, without anything to do, plopped on the sofa in the front room, the only one with a window, watching TV or listening to music on his cell phone, the one luxury he considered a necessity. He adored the Cuban American singer Willy Chirino. A line in one of Chirino's ballads had special meaning for him. The song "La Jinetera" told the story of a prostitute who meets her boyfriend on the Malecón. It was banned in Cuba for a long time, but he had found a pirated copy. Sometimes, when nothing was going right for him, he listened to it. The line he liked so much that he memorized it was *"el partido que parte a quien no lo alababa,"* the party—referring to the Communist Party of Cuba—that cut off those who didn't praise it.

That's what he says happened to him.

At the other end of Guanabacoa, on the corner of Aguacate and San Sebastián, Jorge García's son had carried in lots of green plants to transform the old house into a reserve of tranquility. Jorge Félix used the video camera his father paid for to record weddings and birthday parties, and the business was strong enough for him to bring in his son, called Jorgito, to help.

Jorgito had been only five years old when the *13 de Marzo* sank. He grew up hearing whispered references to the tragedy and had only vague memories of his grandparents and aunt María Victoria, who moved to the United States when he was ten. Ever since his parents had converted to Methodism in the early 1990s, his life too had revolved around the Methodist church in Guanabacoa. Politics and revolution were as foreign to him as the Sierra Maestra.

Jorgito grew up in the house on San Sebastián and attended school in Guanabacoa. Because of a skin condition, he was excused from military service. He attended a technical school for computer science, but he was more interested in helping grow his father's business and remaining active in the church. Music was a big part of Sunday services, with upward of two hundred people clapping and dancing through the aisles for hours. One Sunday the pastor told him that the regular pianist was leaving Cuba, and he asked Jorgito to take his place. He had taught himself to play and, like his father, had also learned English by listening to American radio stations. When American Methodists came to Cuba to help expand the capacity of the church in Guanabacoa, he translated for them.

The church became the center of his life. He met his future wife, Isbel, at the church, and in 2008 they were married there. When Isbel became pregnant, they moved into the house on San Sebastián. Selling off things they had inherited from elderly relatives on both sides of the family, they planned to use the proceeds to add a bedroom, kitchen, and living room on the roof of the San Sebastián house, where Jorge García used to drag mattresses during the special period. Jorgito thought that if he ever decided to leave Cuba, his parents would be able to bring in extra income by renting the upstairs apartment.

But it turned out that it was his parents who left first, not him. In 2014, his father, Jorge Félix, wasn't entirely convinced that it made sense to go, but he realized that his chances of someday getting out were diminishing. His father in Miami was the only one who could legally bring him to the United States, and he had turned seventy. If Jorge Félix ever thought about leaving, now was the time to act. After praying on it, he and his wife agreed that it made sense to begin taking legal steps for all of them—including Jorgito and his twelve-year-old brother Joel, along with Jorgito's wife and their two boys—to leave. But consular officials at the American Interests Section told them that as an adult, with his own family, Jorgito could not be claimed by his grandfather.

Jorge Félix didn't want to leave his son behind, but Jorgito encouraged him to go. "I'm an adult, I can make my own way," Jorgito told his father. Reluctantly, Jorge Félix agreed. He signed over the San Sebastián house to him and left the video equipment so he could keep their business going. Then, while Jorgito's two young sons were sleeping, Jorge Félix kissed their foreheads and gave Jorgito a long, silent hug. He and María flew to Miami and moved into Jorge García's house near the boatyard.

Now Jorgito and his family had the big house in Guanabacoa to themselves. They tried to keep the video business going, but more Cubans had smartphones now and could record their own parties. A friend told him about a job at the San José craft market in Old Havana, a vast waterfront warehouse filled with souvenirs. It was just after the Obama opening, and plenty of American tourists wanted to bring something back from Cuba. Because he spoke English, Jorgito could get them to stop at his stall instead of the others. "Hey, sir, good afternoon," he'd say in accented English that was passable enough to make tourists comfortable. "Come in and take a look at my business."

He worked at the market for a year and a half, making enough money selling refrigerator magnets and souvenir plates to cover household expenses while Isbel, who had been trained as a dentist, stayed at home with the boys. But with the long trip from Guanabacoa to Havana, he was spending twelve hours a day away from home, sometimes not coming back until after his sons were already asleep. Something had to change.

They drew up plans to join the family in Florida. By now they could legally sell the house on San Sebastián and use the money to fly from Cuba to Mexico. Friends told him that for around eight thousand dollars, there were people who could get them safely through Mexico to the U.S. border. Once they reached the other side, they could ask for asylum. They sold the house, but the end of the wet foot, dry foot law early in 2017 scuttled their plans. Jorgito and Isbel saw it as a sign they were not meant to leave, at least not yet. They took some of the money from the sale of the house and bought an apartment in Villa Panamericana, near Cojímar. It was much farther from the church in Guanabacoa than the San Sebastián house, but a free bus would take them to Sunday services. And if they ever decided to try again to leave Cuba, they trusted that it would be easier to sell an apartment there than one in Guanabacoa.

MARÍA DEL CARMEN ALSO HAD WORRIED about her son leaving Cuba, though his destination never was the United States, and he wasn't trying to get away from the government. Virgilio was sent to Venezuela as part of an international medical mission. The Cuban government contracted with Venezuela, Brazil, and other countries to provide doctors, dentists, and a range of medical personnel. In exchange, the Cuban government split the salaries the missionaries received from the foreign governments, taking 75 percent or more of what the doctors and dentists earned. Since 1959, more than 600,000 Cuban health professionals had been sent to 160 different countries. In turn, the Cuban government took in as much as $8 billion a year before Brazil's new president in 2018 called it a form of slavery and demanded the doctors receive their full salaries. An indignant Cuba responded by pulling out all of its medical staffers from Brazil.

The Cuban medics who were sent to Venezuela strengthened the bonds between the two countries at a critical time for Cuba. Besides paying for their services, Venezuela sent Cuba enough oil to keep electric generating stations running without interruptions, as well as additional oil that Cuba sold for a profit. Virgilio had been working in Caracas, Venezuela, when President Hugo Chávez died in 2013.

Sitting at home, watching TV reports of Chávez's death, Mari shuddered at the huge crowds that thronged the streets of Caracas and other Venezuelan cities. It reminded her of the Malecón in 1994, and that made her right hand turn blotchy red, just as it had when Román died.

The rash didn't go away until Virgilio came back home.

CHAPTER 25

With several hours to go before sunrise, the steel door marked PRESI-DENTE swung open, and Lili Durand Hernández stepped out, ready to walk the half mile down the hill to the Regla cemetery where she'd catch a free bus to the Plaza de la Revolución. She'd been going to May Day parades there since she arrived in Havana as a teenager, and there was no way in the world that she was going to miss this one, the first since *el comandante* died.

When she heard the news that night she cried harder than she'd cried since she heard that Chávez had died. Many Cubans had thought the day would never come, that Fidel would never leave them. Even those who did not love him were left breathless when they heard Raúl's somber announcement about his brother's death. It's not that it wasn't expected. Fidel had turned ninety just three months before he died, and in his last public appearance at the party congress in April 2016 he confessed that he wasn't long for this world. Nonetheless, many Cubans—including Cary—convinced themselves that he'd always be with them.

"It's a lie," Cary said on the Friday in November when a friend called to tell her that Fidel was gone. "If you don't believe me," he told her, "just turn on the television."

Unlike the summer of 1994, when the images of the unrest on the Malecón upset her because she thought they were staged, this time turning on the television calmed her. Cary took in the news with the same composure that Raúl showed in his brief message announcing that Fidel was dead. She was sad, but as much as Fidel had been a larger-than-life figure, Zenaida had influenced her more, and somehow she'd managed to keep going after she'd lost her.

Cary and Pipo were in Artemisa that night, visiting friends. She called Oscar, who was by himself at home, working on the computer.

"Are you okay?" he asked before she'd said anything. Since her health scare, unexpected calls from her made him nervous.

"I'm fine. Listen, it's important. Turn on the television. The comandante has died."

"What comandante?"

Fidel's death meant little to him. He had learned the history of the revolution when he was in school, but it might as well have been the history of the Spanish conquest for all it meant to a teenager with ideas of playing drums in a band. He'd been force-fed the history of the revolution through textbooks and countless black-and-white films from the 1950s, but Fidel's hoary mythology—the beards and the guns, the not-so-subtle suggestion of sex and promiscuity of young men and women fighting in the mountains and then taking over an entire country—had lost its glory. Oscar had grown up not in the bright promise of revolution, but in the dingy hardship of the special period, and he, like many young Cubans, had turned his back on it all.

Cary and Pipo returned to Guanabacoa the next morning. Cubans love to talk, and when they do, they tend to shout. But on this day there was barely a sound. No talking. No music. Nothing. They saw plenty of police on the highway and on the street corners, and the tight security continued for the nine days of official national mourning, capped by a ceremony at the Plaza de la Revolución to honor Fidel's ashes.

Lili made it to the plaza that day, but the lines to pass in front of the box containing Fidel's ashes at the base of the memorial tower to José Martí were too long, and she didn't get in. It didn't matter to her. It was enough to simply have been a part of the ceremonies, just as she wanted to be part of the first May Day parade without Fidel. She had learned over the years that arriving at the plaza way before dawn made it possible to get to the front of the marchers and be among the first to pass the reviewing stand when the parade finally began.

Lili had managed to reach the front lines as martial music started up and the huge throng inched forward, but she wasn't in position to see a curious sight. A man waving an American flag had started to sprint across the plaza. State security agents quickly tackled him in front of the reviewing stand, where Raúl and other high-ranking officials watched. *Granma* later identified the man as a dissident with a subversive history: He had welcomed the first U.S. cruise ship to Havana while draped in an American flag. *Granma* called him an "*anexionista*." Within seconds, agents seized his flag, beat him severely, and dragged him away.

Unaware of what had happened, Lili and hundreds of thousands of others marched across the plaza shouting, "*¡Viva Fidel! ¡Viva Raúl! ¡Viva la Revolución!*"

JORGE GARCÍA NEITHER MOURNED FIDEL nor celebrated the first May Day after his demise. Just one date meant anything special to him. All the others that were hallowed by the revolution—January 1, July 26, August 13—he ignored. But the *13 de Marzo* never left his thoughts. As Lili was marching and shouting "*¡Viva!*" for the dead Fidel, Jorge was busy preparing to renew his demand for justice for his son and grandson and all the others who had perished. In a few weeks he was scheduled to appear at Miami City Hall to testify before a new commission that promised to take his claim for justice to the international courts.

On that day in Miami, Jorge wasn't nervous. Most of his adult life, both in Cuba and in Florida, he'd lived off the power of his voice and the passion of his words. The challenge as he stood before the commissioners would be to keep his emotions under control. The new group comprised internationally recognized advocates for justice from around the world. Although the commission had no power to hear a criminal case, it hoped to amass enough evidence to convince an international tribunal to bring charges against the regime. As he opened the hearing, Rene Bolio, a Mexican jurist who headed the commission, described the group's goal as "not revenge, but justice."

Only a few months earlier Jorge had been watching *El espejo* (*The Mirror*), a television news program in Miami, when a report came on about the formation of the International Commission for the Prosecution of Crimes Against Humanity of the Castro Regime. Seeing a way to fulfill his vow to get justice for his son and the other victims, he checked the backgrounds of the panelists and concluded that they were serious about seeking justice, not revenge. He was relieved that not one of them was Cuban, making their stated mission more believable. He reached out to them and was invited to speak at their first public session in Miami.

As that meeting began, the commission watched video testimony from a Cuban dissident who spent seventeen years in prison for opposing the Castro regime. He had recorded his accusations on a thumb drive that was smuggled into the United States. Another witness took the podium in Miami and testified about religious persecution in Cuba. A former professor from the Superior Institute of Art described being accosted by a mob when he tried to leave Cuba in the 1980s. Then it was Jorge's turn to retell the sad history of that Wednesday morning nearly twenty-three years to the day before.

Jorge approached the stand confidently, dressed in a brown sports jacket over a black T-shirt, his mane of white hair creeping over the collar of the jacket, his white goatee and glasses making him look like a Latino history professor. It was a moment for which he had been preparing for decades, and it was clear from the outset how often he must have relived the horrific scene in his own mind. In Spanish, he began, "The sinking of the tugboat *13 de Marzo* occurred at a point seven miles off the coast of Cuba at three-fifty in the morning on July 13, 1994," sounding like the opening of one of the video presentations he had made since arriving in Miami. Despite the calm in his voice, his ire lay just below the surface. In no time, it broke through that thin veneer of restraint.

He accused the Castro government of setting up the disaster, claiming that Cuban intelligence officers knew all about the group's plans and could have prevented the tug from leaving. Instead, they decided to send a message to other Cubans who considered abandoning the country.

Within four minutes of beginning his testimony, Jorge was fully venting his emotions. His voice rose angrily; his right hand pointed accusingly. He condemned the Cuban Coast Guard for hiding in the shadows until a Greek tanker came by and shamed the crew into throwing lifelines to the survivors. He charged Castro's government with continuing to persecute his family after the tug was wrecked. He said his daughter had been drugged while in custody, and the Rapid Response Brigades besieged their corner of San Sebastián and Aguacate, harassing and intimidating them for months. He read out the names of government officials and crew members of the pursuing tugboats he claimed were guilty of murder. And he added the name of the editor of *Granma* who had authorized the articles that portrayed the sinking as an accident.

"In this crime I lost fourteen members of my family," Jorge bellowed, chopping his arm forcefully, his face blood red. By this point he was shouting. "And for this genocide I accuse Fidel Castro Ruz, postmortem, and Raúl Castro." He also named General Senén Casas Regueiro, who headed the Ministry of Transportation in 1994, as the man who gave the order to sink the tugboat.

A few minutes after Jorge finished his impassioned testimony, the commission heard from his nephew Iván Prieto Suárez. He was twenty-seven when he survived the sinking and endured the ferry hijacking. In 2000, he had come to Florida as a political refugee. Now fifty, Prieto Suárez, looking a little dazed by the formal proceedings, gave what sounded like a rehearsed account of that day, repeating some of the same words he evidently had used many times before. But the confusion he experienced that night, the abrupt change from an escape to a death trap, seemed to haunt him still. He described how he had lost track of his father and then managed to swim away from the bridge as the tug was sinking. During questioning, Bolio asked him whether the crews of the pursuing tugs had said anything during the confrontation.

"The *13 de Marzo* was a big boat but not that big. From where I was I could see and hear them," Prieto Suárez responded. "To me, it seemed that they were enjoying what they were doing."

—◆—

María del Carmen didn't know about the commission's work or Jorge's accusations. Cuban state media did not carry a word about it, and she had her own issues to deal with. She hadn't gone to mass at Los Escolapios for a few Sundays since her left arm and shoulder had been wrapped in a cast.

She was a victim of Cuba's crumbling infrastructure. The trucking company she worked for had sent her to a meeting in Vedado, and to get there she had to take a different bus on the other side of town. She didn't mind. She had agreed to hold a package for a friend who lived on Castanedo Street in Guanabacoa, about a mile away. The 25 bus to Vedado passed right by there.

She left her house at about six-thirty that morning. On the long walk to Castanedo, she watched Guanabacoa waking up. The air was fresh, the streets not yet blistering under the August sun. She walked slowly but with purpose, her friend's package under her left arm, Eustoquia's ring on her left hand, and a single peso coin for the bus fare clutched in her right hand. To get around a section of cracked concrete sidewalk, she stepped into the street just as a passing car blasted its horn. Startled, she leaped back onto the sidewalk, stepped into a hole, and lunged forward.

She fell, hard. Much too hard for a sixty-three-year-old woman to simply get up and continue on her way. She sat there, bleeding from her head, until a passing car stopped to help. She asked to be taken to the local clinic on Cruz Verde Street, not far from her home. The doctors there knew her. She walked into the clinic still clutching the peso in her right hand.

X-rays showed that she had fractured her clavicle, bruised her skull, banged up her knee, and quite possibly suffered a concussion. The doctor put her in a cast, taping her left arm to her chest and ordering her to keep it dry for six weeks. She couldn't do most of her chores and she found it impossible to bathe without wetting the bandages. Her friend the historian Armando González offered to help her to mass across the street at Los Escolapios, or a few blocks away to La Milagrosa, but she couldn't sit through a mass knowing she hadn't bathed.

However, she did invite Armando for coffee. They had struck up a friendship several years before based on their shared interest in both religion and history. He was thirty-two, a historian by training, and the archivist at Guanabacoa's municipal museum. His father had worked as an electrician at Novalum in 1994 when Cary was director. Like most Cubans, Armando had been baptized in the Catholic Church, but his religious training ended there until, as an adult, he wanted to receive the other sacraments. That brought him to Los Escolapios, where he got to know Mari.

Savoring their tiny cups of coffee, they sat in the stiff wooden rockers in the antique house on Corralfalso, complaining about the condition of the sidewalks in Guanabacoa. For both, the crumbling streets were sad symbols of what the town they revered had become. The houses of those who fled after 1959 were falling apart, the businesses they operated with such dedication had been reduced to forgotten names embedded in busted sidewalks, the trees and gardens they lovingly cared for now grossly overgrown or dead. There was a time when Guanabacoa had its own newspapers and magazines that worked with civic associations to improve water quality or reduce the number of accidents at train crossings. Now that there was only the ineffectual Attention to the Public office, Guanabacoa limped along, a ghost town filled with spirits of lost generations. The last movie theater had closed years before, and the only place the community regularly gathered was at Viondi Park, where the old town's only wi-fi hot spot was crowded day and night.

Mari felt the civic loss intensely. When she last attended the 5:30 P.M. Sunday mass at Los Escolapios before her fall, she was horrified by the gaping hole in the roof. Even more disturbing was the utter abandonment of the Casa de las Cadenas (House of Chains), behind Guanabacoa's Central Park. Armando considered the Casa de las Cadenas one of the most significant structures in Cuba. It was one of only three remaining examples in all of Latin America of the merciful concept of the chains, which dates back centuries. According to the town's own records, after a hurricane tore the roof off Guanabacoa's main church, La Parroquia, in 1730, a wealthy resident allowed mass to be held inside his mansion a block away. In recognition, King Felipe V of Spain granted the owner the power to pardon individuals accused of crimes provided they touched the chains coiled around the mansion's front columns.

The chains disappeared soon after 1959, and the once-grand structure was carved up into apartments. Over time, it fell into disrepair. The roof developed a leak, and when it was no longer safe, the building was boarded up. Mari and Armando filed complaints at the Attention to the Public office. They were luckier than Arturo because they got to speak to someone who agreed to pass along their concerns to Miguel Barnet, Guanabacoa's representative in the National Assembly. For years, Barnet was the powerful president of the National Union of Writers and Artists of Cuba, the group that Arturo had reluctantly joined. Barnet had close ties to the artistic community and to Eusebio Leal, the historian of Havana. But he had never lived in Guanabacoa, and he never spent much time there. After their complaints were filed, a sign was posted on the building saying the historic structure was part of Cuba's national heritage and would be protected.

"They put it there just to placate us," Mari said. "It's absurd to think they'll actually do what the sign said."

Armando told her that officials in Guanabacoa had already decided to demolish the building, "but when Leal heard about it he stepped in and said it needs to be preserved because it's part of the country's patrimony." As a historian, Armando understood the difference between saying a unique building ought to be preserved and taking the difficult steps required to protect it from vandals and scavengers. "Leal has done a great job preserving and restoring Old Havana, that's for sure," Armando said. "But he's historian for the whole of Havana, and sometimes he seems to have forgotten that Guanabacoa is part of Havana." He agreed that the sign had been put up to appease people like Mari, but once the complaints quieted down, nothing more was done.

In the year after the sign was posted, the remaining ironwork on the Casa de las Cadenas was stolen, and sections of the outer walls collapsed. Thieves stole the tumbledown bricks, tiles, and wooden beams—anything that could be resold and reused. And after all that was hauled away, scavengers scooped up the remaining rubble, ground it into dust, packed it in sacks, and sold it to people who were making mortar to repair their own homes.

Mari bristled at the degradation not only of the physical resources of the town but also of the civility that once characterized it. Her family had lived in, and loved, the same house for more than one hundred years. Culture and history meant a lot to her, and she believed that it was just as important for Guanabacoa.

"I think I've heard it from my mother and father since I was a girl growing up," she said. "When a community loses its cultural identity, the community dies."

"And when a people lose their historic memory," Armando added, "they lose everything."

ARMANDO ATTENDED MASS REGULARLY, sometimes at Los Escolapios and at other times at La Ermita, the oldest chapel in all of Cuba, which sits on one of the highest points in Guanabacoa. There, at the 8:30 A.M. Sunday mass, he could hear distinct worlds overlap. While he was listening to centuries-old hymns and prayers that welled up from the silver-haired faithful in the pews, the heavy beat of African drumming sometimes drifted through the open doors.

One Sunday he decided to find out where the music was coming from. After mass ended, he walked past the adjoining cemetery to B Street and turned left at the garbage dump. The street ran along a deep ravine, making it a kind of urban frontier. He walked past forlorn shacks and shaky little houses made from old bricks, rocks, and tin sheets. Emaciated street dogs picked through piles of trash, and he heard a hog squeal, though he couldn't tell which of the tumbledown structures he passed was its home.

He was less than a half mile from La Ermita when he saw a parked police car surrounded by five uniformed officers. He knew he had found the source of the drumming—an Abacuá religious ceremony that police were monitoring because it sometimes leached out into street violence. Catholic churches abounded in Guanabacoa, but other religions were also weaved into the texture of the community. There were several Protestant congregations, a few

evangelical upstarts, and two Jewish cemeteries. But the old town was best
known as a seat of Santería and other belief systems like Abacuá that had
been brought to Cuba by African slaves. No one stares at the men and women,
and even the children and infants in carriages, who dress in pure white from
head to toe during the year-long initiation rite for Santería. And the beaded
bracelets and tattoos of the other Afro-Cuban cults that thrive there are displayed prominently both to impress and to frighten.

Armando peered up a steep staircase clinging precariously to the hillside
and saw that a crowd had already gathered around the sound of the drumming. At the top of the stairs, he opened a flimsy metal gate and entered the
courtyard of Efi Nurobia, an Abacuá society. He was familiar with Abacuá
because it was one of the sects featured in displays at the municipal museum.
Belonging to the society promised members influence and power over enemies and competitors, advantages similar to those promised the faithful in
voodoo. Past the gate, about one hundred people, most of them young black
men, were drinking rum or beer as they stood in front of a squat cinder-block
building painted in bright colors. When the doors opened, several men danced
out, dressed in the bizarre costumes of Abacuá. One was covered head to toe
in blue-and-white horizontal stripes, cuffs, and sleeves fringed with straw.
Another was dressed in green and yellow, and a third in multicolored plaid.
Their faces were covered by burlap masks with sewn-on eyes but no mouths.
As they marched out of the inner sanctum, they addressed one another by
shaking cowbells around their waists. A man who appeared to be a chief or a
priest rolled out a freshly butchered goat skin on the ground and sang an in-
cantation in a language that Armando did not recognize. The rum and beer
that flowed freely that morning continued throughout the day, keeping the
police on guard until the ceremony ended in late afternoon.

The different belief systems in Guanabacoa coexisted warily. Whenever the
Catholic priest at La Ermita distributed communion during mass, he insisted
on placing the eucharistic wafer directly on the tongues of those receiving it,
fearing that if he gave people the option of receiving the host in their hands,
the custom for Catholics around the world, he might give it to someone who
would defile it in a Santería ceremony. Priests at La Milagrosa had the same

concern on Palm Sunday, when Armando and Mari watched as the usually small congregation swelled to fill the chapel to standing room. It was obvious from the colored beads on their wrists that many Santeros had filled the pews and were there just to snatch a piece of sacred palm they needed for their own rituals.

Because the chapel of La Ermita sat at the top of one of Guanabacoa's many steep hills, Mari didn't attend mass there often. But she sometimes went to the ancient cemetery surrounding the chapel to visit old family graves. Her cousin Alberto had asked her several times to help him with the unpleasant task of removing the remains of his mother from the family tomb, as tradition required, but she put him off again and again, worried that he would be devastated when the tomb was opened. The old cemetery was routinely vandalized, and Armando had told her that some Abacuá rituals made use of human skeletal remains. Mari was afraid that if they opened her aunt's tomb, they'd find that her skull was missing.

As THE SUMMER OF 2017 reached its end, Cary had completed the move out of Procle's workshop near Lennon Park and relocated her sewing machines and remaining stock to the space she had rented for Oscar above a shoemakers' shop on Neptuno Street in central Havana. They planned to run both businesses there until the Federation of Cuban Women offered Cary a suitable space for Procle to move into. Despite the setbacks they'd suffered and the shadow of decay all around them, she felt things were moving in the right direction. They were Cubans after all, and their sense of relativism constantly reminded them that things were far better than they had been during the special period. The business course in Florida had filled Oscar with fresh ideas he was eager to try as he decided whether to stay in Cuba or make his life elsewhere. And Cary felt her optimism in Cuba's future growing stronger with Oscar working by her side, even if only temporarily. Fidel had passed from the scene, but Cuba had not collapsed, and the enemy had not invaded, though the new American president had started sounding more and more belligerent toward Cuba.

On the nightly news, they watched the early reports of a big storm heading their way. At first, they took little notice. It was hurricane season, and storms came and went. But over the next few days the advisories became more serious, and as the storm picked up strength, it was given a name.

Irma.

PART FOUR

RECONCILIATION

CHAPTER 26

GUANABACOA

September 10, 2017

Most Guanabacoa mornings began with noise, lots of noise. Trucks growled down Vía Blanca, roosters kept crowing long after sunrise, and scrawny street dogs seemed to fall in love with the sound of their own barking. But on the morning after Irma, the old town was unsettlingly quiet, noiseless in the same way that the air clears seconds after a crash. Exhausted from her night of terror, and with the clocks in her house still dead, Cary wasn't sure what time it was when she finally ventured outside to check on the damage Irma had done to her street. In the gray light of after-storm, she saw that several trees had been destroyed, including the lemon tree next door that she liked so much. She walked to her gate, and from there it galled her to see that garbage from the wretched corner dump had scattered everywhere, with scraps of paper and plastic embedded in her own chain-link fence. Palm trees nearby still stood tall, but the fierce winds had stripped them nearly bald. The metal roof of the warehouse across the street was peeled back like a can of tuna.

Her first thought: *It could have been so much worse.*

"Are you okay?" she asked her next-door neighbor Mara, whose yard was dense with the broken branches of the downed lemon tree. "How did you make out?" a passerby wanted to know. Taking another look around, Cary understood that they had made out quite well. Their house was intact; not even a single pane of glass had cracked. All three of them were safe. Even Faru wagged his tail after he was let out onto the street to pee. At around ten in the morning the Hopeful fan whirred back into action. When they turned on the television, they found out just how lucky they were. At the last minute, Irma had switched direction, headed due north, and turned its wrath on Florida, sparing Guanabacoa major pain but leaving Cuba with a $13 billion bill for hurricane damage, 156,000 homes that needed to be repaired, huge swathes of the tourist coast torn apart, and—hardest of all for some to accept—a two-month delay in Raúl Castro's promised departure from the office of president of Cuba in early 2018.

When the phone was working again, Cary called Cuka and found out that Tacajó also had been mostly spared. But in central Havana, whole neighborhoods had been flooded when Irma channeled sea swells six blocks in from the Malecón, leaving pools of water deep enough for people to swim in outside their front doors. Had she accepted the Federation of Cuban Women's offer of commercial space, her new shop would have been under several feet of dirty water. *Granma* reported ten hurricane-related deaths, including two young women in central Havana who were crushed when a portion of a dilapidated building collapsed on them.

Back in Guanabacoa, Lili Hernández had lost the lights during the hurricane, but she managed to keep track of her father. And Jorge García heard from his grandson Jorgito that, although he had lost all the food in his refrigerator when the electricity went out, he and his family had survived Irma without any problem more serious than the rare cancellation of Sunday services at the Methodist Church in Guanabacoa.

On Máximo Gómez Street, Arturo Montoto ran out to his courtyard as soon as it was light. He was greatly relieved to find his gigantic baseball safe and mostly dry in the corner where it had been protected from the worst of the wind and rain. But when he tried to inspect his garden, he first had to hack through a giant bougainvillea vine that had been blown down by the storm and was blocking the gate. Inside, broken branches and downed fruit were everywhere, but none of his cherished trees had been uprooted.

A block away, María del Carmen's precious old house had weathered the storm just as her father had always predicted it would. In truth, the house was in better shape than she was. Her shoulder and arm were still wrapped in bandages, so she had to ask Virgilio to lift Caesar and Raphael back onto their pedestals in the parlor. Water again flowed in the kitchen, the electricity had been restored, and she had put away enough food to keep them going until the stores reopened. Best of all, she did not have to worry about the nightmare . that traveling around Havana would become following the hurricane. Her injuries would keep her out of work for several weeks more.

But Cary and Pipo needed to get to their workshop as soon as they heard that electricity had been restored. Getting there wouldn't be easy. Even without a hurricane, commuting from their house to the old city could take an hour, and sometimes much more. Pipo, like most Cubans his age, had never owned a car. So few Cubans had cars that, compared with 1958, Havana's streets usually weren't congested. Havana was one of the few capital cities anywhere not clogged with cars, and it may have been the only one that didn't need to have a local traffic reporter. The problem was a mass transportation system that, under the best of circumstances, was incapable of transporting even a small portion of the people who depended on the tired herd of over-crowded buses, dilapidated taxis, and privately owned American cars to get around. With Cuba struggling back to its feet following the hurricane, taking one of the municipal buses had become hopeless. Even squeezing into the jalopies that functioned like Uber in reverse—instead of going where you wanted them to go, you went where they went—had become a test of patience. The major tunnel beneath the mouth of Havana Bay had filled with several feet of seawater, and traffic had been diverted onto Vía Blanca. By the time cars and buses got to Guanabacoa, people were hanging out of the doors.

Cary and Pipo were too far from Neptuno Street to walk, and neither they, nor any of their neighbors, owned a bicycle anymore. The sour memories of the special period made even the most desperate turn up their noses at pedaling. They had waited two days after Irma passed for things to calm down, but they couldn't wait any longer. They called their friend Oswaldo, who drove a state taxi. His mother, Juanita, had been Cary's secretary at Novalum, and they'd remained close ever since. The cab ride to the workshop cost them the equivalent of four dollars—more than a third of Cary's monthly pension. It was a fortune, but they had to get there.

Irma hadn't done major damage to Neptuno Street, though at first glance it looked like it had. The street was lined with dilapidated state stores with dusty display windows so barren that the shops seemed to have gone out of business long before. Tiny private stores like the one Cary's friend recently opened to sell piñatas and other party favors bravely stood their ground inside the shells of once-grand apartment buildings that looked abandoned, though many families lived in them. Most store windows were cracked, broken, or missing—and they'd been that way for years before Irma hit.

It was 10:15 A.M. when Oswaldo stopped his Lada in the middle of the block. Cary started to stress out before she'd even opened the car door. "Uh oh," Pipo said, peering out the car window. "The lights are out." Gustavo, one of the stoop-shouldered shoemakers who worked in the ground-floor space below Oscar's workshop, was standing on the sidewalk trimming a sheet of ribbed rubber to fit the sole of an old sneaker. He greeted them warmly, then broke the bad news.

"The electricity came back on this morning, but then it went out again at eight-thirty." Gustavo smiled at Cary and shrugged, as if to say, *What can you do? This is Cuba!*

Cobblers can cut and glue and stitch by hand, but without electricity Procle was paralyzed. Cary and Oscar shared the same five heavy-duty sewing machines and an ancient Singer treadle to produce her clothing and his canvas bags. Cary wished the cobblers luck, then she and Pipo ventured inside. They walked past the darkened counter where the four shoemakers usually worked, then squeezed by the mountain of old shoes and cheap sneakers too worn out to wear yet too valuable to throw away. The place reeked of rubber, glue, and dirty feet. Just past the idle burnishing machines at the rear of the shop, they climbed a steeply curved set of concrete stairs to their own space, a jerry-built loft, the kind that Cubans call a *barbacoa*, that was added to the five-story building after the triumph of the revolution to gain more space.

Cary pushed open the metal grating that doubled as a door. "We're here," she called out, her positivity infiltrating the deep shadows. As she scanned the work area, she saw Enna Reyes, one of her seamstresses, hovering in front of an open window like a hen in a hot coop gasping for air. The workshop was about twenty-five feet wide by thirty-five feet long, with crisp white walls and, when the electricity was on, fluorescent lighting bright enough for the seamstresses to see their stitches.

Cary was relieved to see Enna. She had worried about her during the storm and wasn't sure she'd be able to get to the shop. Instead of working at her sewing machine, she was fanning herself in front of the window, sweat beading on her upper lip. That the power hadn't been fully restored by then Cary took as a sign that Irma had caused more destruction than *Granma* and state TV were reporting. Esperanza had told her that in the 10 de Octubre neighborhood where she lived there had been near-riots as crowds swarmed through the streets demanding water and electricity. Cary was certain that lingering damage from the storm would make it nearly impossible for them to find the basic materials they needed to keep their business going.

Shortly after noon, the lights flickered on, and Enna rushed back to her sewing machine. A few minutes later, Oscar bounded up the stairs. He'd been delivering partially finished bags to several seamstresses who worked from home. Cary called him over to an old wooden desk at the far end of the shop. They put their heads together briefly before she leaned over Enna's shoulder and told her they'd be back soon. They left Pipo in charge of the shop and walked a few blocks through the chaos of central Havana, at times holding hands and moving slowly. In a few minutes, they arrived at Confecciones Model (Model Textile Creations), a state-sponsored cooperative that the Cuban government had organized a few years earlier as an experiment in collective entrepreneurship. It may have lacked authentic capitalist spirit, but it enjoyed real advantages that Cary envied. As a state co-op, Model had access to material that Cary, as a private entrepreneur, did not have, especially after a disruptive hurricane. But Model had its own challenges, and covering members' salaries was a big one. Cary was unwilling to simply wait until the supply chain opened up. In a brief meeting, she introduced Oscar to Nancy Varela, the co-op's president, and hinted that if Nancy was interested, there might be a way to give both their businesses a better chance at success. She promised to return in a week with a written plan. For a few moments, she felt like she was back behind her director's desk at Puntex, making plans and taking charge.

Cary and Oscar returned to the workshop to find that the lights were out yet again. Enna apologized, telling them that with all the interruptions that morning, she had been able to sew only about half her daily output of small perfume bags. She promised to try to catch up when, and if, the electricity was restored.

By this time, without the big fans to chase away the heat, Cary felt her energy draining. Somebody had to stay with Enna, so she put Oscar in charge while she and Pipo headed out to search for fabric as they made their way home. "Things are going to get worse, much worse," she warned Oscar.

Walking slowly was not easy for Pipo, with all of his pent-up energy, but he had to put the brakes on because Cary had lost some of her balance since her surgeries. Sticking close to buildings for the slightest shade, they strolled down Neptuno, occasionally popping into a store to check prices. They never shopped at these places because the selection was small and the prices were high, but she was worried they'd be left with nothing. They found some bolts of canvas suitable for Oscar's bags and a few cones of thread Cary needed for her alterations, but not enough of either to make a difference, especially not at those prices. They continued along Neptuno until it opened up to Prado, the wide boulevard built where the old wall around Havana once stood. Entering prime tourist territory, they passed a few of the big hotels and the city's Central Park, where garishly painted Detroit classics lined up, waiting for goggle-eyed American tourists to pay more than a few months of a typical Cuban's salary to revive youthful fantasies. They passed the Floridita, with its bronze Ernest Hemingway bending an elbow at the bar, and headed down Obispo Street, crowded with tourists and lined with state restaurants and souvenir shops.

Cary was in familiar territory. This was where she had worked when she came back from Kiev and where her offices were located throughout many of the years she was climbing the regime's hierarchy. She and Pipo stopped at two stores that had an array of fabric in their windows, but they took only a quick glance at the prices before they continued on their way. A few blocks later, they came to the elegant storefront windows of Quitrín and stepped into the air-conditioned showroom. They were immediately greeted by a sales-woman who embraced Cary, kissed her cheek, and said she couldn't get over how well she looked. Cary returned the compliment and then got right down to business: Yes, our shop lost power. No, we didn't get water inside. Do you have any material you could spare?

The saleswoman smiled, shaking her head no. But she promised that if she came across anything, she'd give Cary a call.

The heat and humidity of Havana in September took a toll on them, and by late afternoon, Cary insisted that they head home. They had gone too far to turn back to El Curita, the trash-covered park that served as an informal transit hub. There they might have been able to squeeze into an old Chevy with three or four others for a sweaty ten-peso shared ride to Guanabacoa. But from where they were at the foot of Obispo, it made more sense to head to the water's edge to catch a ferry across the bay.

The waterfront that Cary remembered from when she departed for Kiev had all but disappeared. Since the Obama opening, gigantic cruise ships tied up where the smelly *Kazakhstan* once was moored. The old piers where Cu-ba's tuna boats docked while María del Carmen and Román worked there had been cleared away, and a new floating dock bobbed next to the brew pub that President Obama had visited. The historic harbor that once had been home to Spain's treasure fleet, that had lured pirates and buccaneers in search of gold, was being cleaned up and transformed into a touristy promenade. What re-mained of Havana's maritime industry was being shunted thirty-eight miles west to the new billion-dollar free-trade zone that Brazil was building at Mariel.

The ferry terminal was a glassy new steel box, but the clumsy routine for getting on the ferry was old and distressingly familiar. Cary stood before a bored security guard as he fingered through her handbag. The hateful ritual always reminded her of the summer of 1994, the guards' pale green uniforms stirring up foul memories of that frightening time when Cuba seemed to be coming apart. Once they made it through security, they rushed onto the dock, where Pipo paid the ten-centavo fare, less than a U.S. penny, a bargain despite the inconvenience. For people in Regla and Guanabacoa, the ferry had long been a lifeline linking them to the capital. For young families, it was a cheap ticket to Sundays in the city. For young lovers, a refuge from crowded homes. And for believers in Santería, dropping a flower, a doll, or a coin wrapped with a written message into the water from the ferry's deck was a sacred ritual.

The handful of seats on the ferry called *Cuarto Congreso* already were taken, so they stood shoulder to shoulder with everyone else for the short ride across the fabled bay of corsairs, sea dogs, and privateers, lifting their chins so the sea breezes that slipped through the open sides caressed and cooled them. The *Cuarto Congreso* docked in Regla just six minutes after it had pulled away from Old Havana. They waited for most of the other passengers to leave before Pipo helped Cary to the concrete landing. They hurried through the turnstiles and past the immaculate white church of the black Virgin of Regla, hoping to get to the corner before the next bus left for Guanabacoa. Behind them, an attendant on the dock gassed up the *Cuarto Congreso*. It didn't take long; it never does. The pump was rigged to discharge no more than ten liters of diesel fuel, just over 2.6 gallons.

Enough to get the little ferry across the stinking waters of the old bay, and back, just once.

JUST AS SHE HAD PROMISED, Cary returned to Model a week later with her ambitious business plan. "That's such a nice dress," she said as she followed Nancy Varela to her windowless office. "Did you make it here?"

The office was a small, overheated space at the rear of the large, mostly empty showroom. A huge photo of Che Guevara playing chess looked down on them, making the cramped space feel like a fishbowl. "It's such a shame that your showroom is so big and so elegant, but your office back here is so small and dark," Cary said.

Nancy tilted her head and pursed her lips as she took up position behind her old-fashioned gray metal desk, a heavy curtain draping the wall behind her. Courtesy clashed with suspicion as she watched Cary arrange herself on a leather sofa along the far wall, facing both Nancy and Che, ready to do business.

The contrast between the two women could hardly have been greater: Cary wore dark slacks and a black-and-white blouse that fit her loosely, her dark skin looking cool and confident despite the September mugginess that enveloped the office as powerfully as cheap perfume in an elevator. Two of the scars on her chest were as visible as medals. Nancy had squeezed herself into a tight guayabera dress buttoned almost to her neck, the dress's yellow cotton washing out her pale skin, already misted with sweat.

Cary gave a printed copy of her business proposal to Nancy. Her "Optimization Project for the Financial Recuperation of Model" laid out Cary's vision for turning around the cooperative while protecting and advancing Procle in those trying posthurricane times. "By any chance do you have any material right here that you can spare?" Cary asked, eager as always to snatch up any supplies.

"Here? Nothing," Nancy replied.

"How about thread?"

"I'm not sure. Let me check the warehouse." Nancy took out an old notebook and started flipping through pages of handwritten names and telephone numbers. "You know what? Just give me a minute." She excused herself and rushed out of her office to find an assistant. The moment she was gone Cary jumped off the couch and settled in behind the desk, looking far more comfortable there than Nancy had a few moments earlier. She picked up the telephone while taking her cell phone out of her pocketbook and opening her digital directory. Her painted gold fingernails swiped across the cell phone screen until she found the number she was looking for. She dialed it on the landline, keeping the conversation short and hanging up before Nancy returned. Cell phones in Cuba had limited talking time, and calls were expensive. Whenever possible—even in someone else's office—Cubans preferred to use a landline.

Nancy stepped back into the office looking more frazzled than before. "They're checking on the thread for me." This time she sat on the sofa beside Cary. Both women had spent their professional lives in textiles and fashion, and both realized that hard times were about to become harder. But the similarities ended there. Cary was about ten years older than Nancy, and her work in Puntex as well as her years on the economic commission of the provincial party had sharpened her political savvy, leaving her with a shrewd sense of the ways in which politics and commerce overlapped in the emerging Cuba. No one at Model, including Nancy, had the drive or confidence to go into business on their own, and nobody had any real experience running a company that did not take orders from a central government office.

Nancy told Cary that once the cooperative had been established in 2013, the government essentially abandoned it. "We have no one backing us or providing support," she said. Cary listened politely. Housed in the former showroom and factory of one of prerevolution Cuba's big furniture companies, Model was known for producing guayaberas and uniforms. The co-op currently had a contract to produce short-sleeved cotton shirts for drivers of Taxis Cuba, the state-run enterprise where Cary's friend Oswaldo worked. "We've got pretty good demand for the shirts right now," Nancy said. But they didn't have the light cotton they needed to make the uniforms. That meant there wasn't enough work for all forty-two co-op members. And when they didn't work, they didn't get paid.

Cary sympathized, then she offered Nancy a lesson in entrepreneurship, Cuban style.

"Let's say I have a license as a seamstress, and I'm going to make sheets, but there's no fabric for making sheets—what do I do? I make bedspreads, but then there's no material for making bedspreads either, so I decide to make dish towels. If there's no material to make dish towels, I'm going to buy hand-me-down clothes and remodel them. Do you understand what I'm saying? You need to do whatever you can to survive."

Cary suggested that Nancy needed to rethink what it meant to be a cooperative and not an arm of the government. She had to consider both what she was required to do and what she had the possibility of doing. Maybe she didn't have cotton, but she had canvas hidden away somewhere, didn't she? Procle needed canvas and had the money to pay for it. Sounding like one of her professors at Cuba Emprende, Cary said that Model's resources were the property it occupied, the machinery it already had inside the building, and its forty-two individual members, each with her own set of marketable skills.

"You have to think about moving in another direction, pursuing other businesses that can provide income." She kept the tone of her voice friendly so Nancy wouldn't feel she was being lectured, although that clearly was happening. Alternatives probably wouldn't bubble up from among the co-op's members, Cary said. They should come from the top down. She'd have to present the ideas to her members and do it in such a positive way that they'd agree on the new direction.

Nancy, Cary said, you need to act like a leader.

In her "optimization" plan, Cary outlined an immediate diversification of Model that she thought could be accomplished without state approval. She suggested reshaping Model along the lines of Quitrín. Model's large showroom building could be divided into several smaller incubator workspaces and rented to ten entrepreneurs. In addition, she proposed capitalizing on the skills of the co-op members by offering courses in tailoring, sewing, design, and modeling, charging students for classes like the one that had gotten her started after she quit government. A conference room on the premises could be rented out for meetings, and Model could take its guayaberas and uniforms to factories and workplaces for pop-up sales that would bring in additional revenue. Lastly, she proposed that Model rent space to Procle to display and sell Cary's own creations.

In all, Cary told Nancy that she could bring in more than $1000 a month, enough to cover the salaries of her forty-two members. Add to that the revenue from regular sales, and the cooperative could eliminate its debt and, at some point, even expand.

Nancy liked Cary's plan, but her worried expression showed how much she doubted it could work. She told Cary that changes like the ones she was proposing had to go before the entire co-op. "That means that there are forty-two members who have to understand the proposals and vote in favor of them," Nancy said. "It's difficult to get forty-two women to agree on anything."

They sat barely a foot apart on the couch, two strong Cuban women peering into the future and seeing two different worlds. "You don't need all forty-two to support every decision," Cary said, explaining that Nancy and her executive board could present a new business plan to the members, who would go along with the idea if they trusted her. She wanted her to believe that although Model had many resources, she, Nancy Varela, was the most important one of all.

"I'm telling you this from my own modest experience in such things, Nancy. It's critically important that your members have confidence in you and in your board. In these times we're living in, it's important to make dynamic decisions."

"But I don't know . . ."

"Easy, friend." Cary used her most sympathetic voice. "You'll find a way out of these problems."

After the meeting ended, Cary walked back to her own workshop with Nancy's whimpering voice echoing in her head. If she was running Model, Cary thought, she wouldn't wait for permission from anyone. All forty-two seamstresses would be at their machines sewing, assuming there was electricity. She knew that despite Nancy's good intentions, she was in way over her head. She tried to remain optimistic about her plan because if it was adopted, it would help Procle as much as or more than it would Model, but she had serious doubts about Nancy's ability to get her members to go along with such a radical change.

A few days later, she learned from friends in the industry that Nancy had been ousted by her own board. The optimization plan never had a chance to be presented, let alone implemented.

AFTER THEIR LONG, UNCOMFORTABLE NIGHT waiting for Irma, Cary decided it was time she and Pipo had another fan besides Hopeful. They called Oswaldo again and had him drive them to the TRD store on Vía Blanca. It was as close as Guanabacoa got to having a department store. There was no rationing at TRD stores, which Cary and most other Cubans simply called "shopping." Whatever they had for sale was priced in dollar-equivalent convertible pesos. Without access to online shopping, supermarkets, or malls, a visit to the TRD on Vía Blanca was Cary's version of going on a shopping spree.

Cary and Pipo walked the length of the building's exterior to a garage where housewares were located. A young man straddled a motor scooter just outside the big garage door. "Whatever you're going to buy inside," he muttered, just loud enough for her to hear, "I can get for you, and cheaper."

She turned toward the man, looked him over, then gave Pipo a skeptical glance. "No thanks," she said as they kept on walking. The garage door led to a dim warehouse space. No overhead lights were on, making it hard for them to see. Boxes were stacked haphazardly, and there were no signs to show where things might be located. Cary asked a man sitting at the entrance where to find fans. "What kind of fan?" he said, showing no interest. She said she was thinking of a stand-up fan.

"We haven't had a delivery for a long time. Whatever's left is over there," he said, pointing to the other end of the room.

They found one model, three and a half feet tall, made of flimsy plastic that looked like it would tip over as soon as it started to circulate. It was priced at ninety-three dollars, about seven months of her pension.

One look was enough. "Let's go," she told Pipo.

The young man was still on his motor scooter. When they drew near, Cary took out her smart phone and pulled up a photo of the kind of fan she was looking for, a black one with a metal stand that was heavier, and less likely to topple over, than the one they'd seen inside.

"Can you get this?" she asked.

He took the phone from her.

"Give me your number," the young man said. "I'll call when I have it."

"For less than in the store?"

"Of course."

She punched her number into his phone.

Cary still didn't like the idea of buying something that most likely had been stolen, but she realized that times had changed and fighting it was hopeless. Almost all business was done that way now. She was convinced that since the special period, Cuban morality had been so disfigured by necessity that what was once considered wrong had become widely acceptable. She thought of it this way: The store manager justified selling fans to the man on the scooter to supplement his own miserly salary. He reported to his bosses that he'd moved his entire inventory while keeping the illicit profit so he could live the way he thought a store manager should live. The young man on the scooter justified paying off the manager and reselling the fans at a profit because his future would be bleak unless he could bring in more money. He was *luchando*. Everybody in Cuba was *luchando*.

After buying some cones of thread from a seamstress in Villa Panamericana, they finished the day in a fresh-food market at the Virgen del Camino traffic circle. Walking to the entrance, they passed a man selling white plastic bags, and Pipo bought two for one peso. Merchants inside were supposed to give away the bags with purchases, but Pipo knew they'd all been sold under the table to the hawkers. A crowd had gathered at the front door, where a large man in a striped shirt tried to shut the metal gates from the inside.

"We've got to close early because of the hurricane," the man was shouting. "We have to clean up."

"And we need to get something to eat," someone shouted back at him. "Let us in."

It was only two in the afternoon, hours before the store's normal closing time. About twenty-five people were pushing against the gate, trying to get in. When the man in the striped shirt opened the gate just enough to let in a friend, the others rushed forward. He held them back for a few seconds, then threw up his hands and stepped back to let everyone in.

Pipo raced through the rows of wooden stands covered with calabaza, scallions, yucca, black beans, and watermelon. Green oranges—apparently knocked off trees by Irma—were piled high, and Pipo bought a few pounds of them. He dashed from stand to stand, filling his bags with calabaza, a can of tomato puree, a bottle of cooking wine, and a small bottle of lemon juice. Farmers at agro markets like this brought in what they grew, and prices were capped by the government. In all, Pipo spent around three dollars, a quarter of Cary's monthly pension. He was glad he had purchased the plastic bags outside because, as he'd expected, none of the merchants had any. That left at least one shopper wandering around the market with hunks of raw pork in his hand.

Oswaldo drove them back to Guanabacoa. It had been a frustrating day, filled with disappointments and reminders of how limited their lives were. To cheer up Cary, Pipo made orangeade. The green oranges needed lots of sugar to counter the bitterness, but as Cary sipped the cool drink, she smiled and told him it was good.

It was a Monday in November, two months after Irma, and Oscar realized that his mother had been right all along. He had contracts to fill, but no canvas to sew. The lessons he had learned at FIU were a universe apart from the reality of his Cuba. The government seemed intent on holding down the private sector it had authorized. Licenses were tightly controlled, tax laws were complex and burdensome, and most frustrating of all: How was he supposed to work without a wholesale market?

He still dreamed of starting a business outside Cuba, but the United States under President Trump seemed more distant than ever, and his application for Jamaican citizenship, along with those of his cousins, had stalled. The three of them had hired a fixer in Jamaica who, for a fee, promised to get the documents that proved their Jamaican ancestry. While the fixer poked around government archives in Kingston, the cousins gathered their great-grandmother's passport and other family documents. They even sat for their own passport pictures, having their headshots Photoshopped onto the same suit-and-tie-wearing torso. After several months, the fixer discovered a copy of their great-grandmother Sarah Ewen's birth certificate, but the Jamaican embassy rejected the document because it was a handwritten copy, not an original. They had wasted precious money and time, and they were disappointed.

So, on this day without either canvas to sew or a clear path to the future, Oscar was hustling. He had hired Jesús, a neighbor who drove a three-wheeled Piaggio Ape van, to help him through a long to-do list that he kept on his iPhone. The first stop was just a few blocks from the house, near Guanabacoa's only traffic light. A friend who lived there designed and printed plastic decals and banners. After passing one young man who was applying bright green and yellow decals to an electric scooter, and another who was attempting to attach pin stripes to an old Ford, Oscar walked into his friend's office to review a design he had drawn for a client. A new bar and restaurant called Tatagua that had just opened on the Prado in Old Havana had ordered a large banner with Oscar's distinctive butterfly design to be displayed on the facade of the building.

There was a problem. The drawing that Oscar had done on his iPad was not compatible with the shop's software. It was early in the day, and he took the setback in stride, telling his friend he'd redo the drawing and have it back to him as soon as possible. He folded himself into the tiny van, and Jesús drove to the workshop on Neptuno. Oscar hustled past the shoemakers and up the curving staircase to the sewing machine where Enna was working on a prototype for a bigger canvas bag he hoped to sell to the 1791 perfume shop once he had enough material. He wanted Enna to sew in a flat bottom so the bag could stand on its own. They discussed ways to minimize the number of production steps, and he left.

Jesús drove the twenty-year-old Piaggio, with its rusted-through floor and windows that could be opened only with a pair of locking pliers, across the city and parked in a residential neighborhood. Oscar had been dreading this stop, and as he walked up to the open doorway of a small house, the uncomfortable feeling he'd had all morning intensified. He stepped inside to a chorus of shrill barks. A young woman with painted nails stepped over a gate that held back nine yapping Chihuahuas.

Tatiana was one of Oscar's piecework seamstresses. The dreary front room of her apartment, no more than one hundred square feet, doubled as a living room and workshop. Against one wall was a well-worn sofa. On the opposite wall, by the only window, an old, industrial sewing machine. Next to it was a large duffel bag filled with the totes she had sewn for Oscar with some of the last canvas he had in stock.

He left home that morning thinking he might have to fire Tatiana. He'd already warned her that her stitching was sloppy and that she had to do better. He pulled a tote bag out of the duffel, turned it inside out, and frowned.

"This isn't the way I showed you." He held out the critical point where the handle was stitched to the bag. It was supposed to be flat. The bag Oscar held had an ugly lump there.

"You fold it once this way and then put in the handle. Do it like that, and it will lie flat the way it's supposed to."

"I can't do it that way," she said. "It won't pass through the machine, not with this needle."

He asked to see the needle. "No, that one's too small. You need a bigger one."

"That's the only one I have."

This was business in Cuba, something his instructors at FIU wouldn't understand. They'd have told him that if Tatiana hadn't changed her attitude and improved her sewing after receiving her first warning, she should be fired. But he couldn't ignore her obvious desperation. The moldy sofa, the dirty walls. The nasty dogs yapping in the kitchen. The pathetic ceramic knickknack of an angel perched on the TV stand.

"You need a stronger needle to get through this material," he told her calmly. "I'll bring one next time."

Oscar took two more totes out of the duffel. They were badly wrinkled. He chided Tatiana for not folding them flat. He also told her he didn't like the ragged seams. "You need to clip off all these loose threads."

She took the bag from him and looked at it as if seeing it for the first time. "I tried, but the scissors I have are no good."

He pursed his lips. "I'll bring you a new pair next week."

Their next stop was the printshop of Osvaldo Hernández Naranjo and his brothers. They began as artists years ago and had grown into a large five-color printing operation. They had the equipment to print on many different surfaces, but their primary business was T-shirts. Oscar hauled in the 150 canvas bags that he had taken from Tatiana's house and dropped them at Osvaldo's feet. In exchange for the bags on which Osvaldo planned to print his own design, he was silk-screening a more upscale bag for another one of Oscar's jobs.

Jesús then drove to a dusty workshop and showroom on Havana's outskirts in Marianao and parked the little truck on the sidewalk. Oscar strode in, rushing past racks lined with dresses and light blouses and entering a back room where two women were bent over sewing machines. Another woman greeted him warmly. "And your mother? How is Cary?" she asked.

Cary had found out through friends that the shop had more bolts of canvas in its inventory than it could use. She also knew that, like Nancy Varela's co-op, this workshop needed cash to pay its workers more than it needed the canvas. In less than five minutes, the little van was loaded to capacity with seven large bolts of canvas that Oscar had paid for. It was early afternoon, the sidewalks were crowded, and Oscar was intent on completing the pickup before anyone realized what he was doing.

After unloading the canvas at home, he wolfed down a bowl of soup, then walked three blocks to Vía Blanca to wave down an old car to take him back to Havana. The car was on a regular route, from Guanabacoa to El Curita Park. From there, he walked half a mile through the colonnaded walkways of Old Havana to the Prado, near the cross street called Refugio. Back in Havana's colonial past, the main gate to the city was barred at night to protect against pirates. Those who weren't able to get inside before the gates closed took refuge in this area until the gates reopened the next morning. The wall was torn down long ago, but a cannon is still shot off at nine each night to mark the symbolic closing of the gate. And the name of the street remains Refugio.

Oscar was supposed to meet the owner of Tatagua to review last-minute plans for the banner as well as for the business cards he had designed. Working with the new restaurant was an exciting opportunity for him to collaborate with people investing real money in Cuba. It was just a few minutes after five when he reached Tatagua. The doors were locked. He was sure that they had said Monday at five, but he realized he ought to have called to confirm. He was disappointed, but not upset. He'd come too far and put up with too many obstacles to let a blown appointment bother him. He'd come back another day. But next time, he'd call ahead.

Oscar was juggling a lot of different projects at once, hoping for a lucky break. He got the break when his aunt Esperanza gave him and his cousins enough money to continue the search in Jamaica for Sarah Ewen's original birth certificate. If the document could be found, Esperanza reasoned, it would make up for some of the guilt she felt about the way she'd earned the money. Relying on her own multiple-entry U.S. visa, she had spent a few months working in South Florida nursing homes, bathing and feeding residents, the kind of work that her mother had done in Tacajó before the revolution. She knew that Zenaida would have hated the idea of one of her daughters doing domestic work after all she had sacrificed to give them both a better life.

But to Esperanza, working in the nursing homes was the best chance she had in her Cuba to give her sons and nephew the better life that her mother had worked so hard to provide. It was a difficult time for her. While she was gone, her former husband Miguel had died suddenly, and the mediocre care he had received in the hospital contrasted greatly with the way Zenaida and Cary had been treated. Her sons had to bring sheets and towels to the hospital, and for as long as he was conscious, Cary and Pipo had to bring him something to eat. When he died, Cary made sure that socks were put on his hands as well as on his feet.

Esperanza came back from Florida after Miguel was buried in the Masons' Tomb in Havana's Colón cemetery. She had more money in her pocket than she would receive from her pension as an architect over several years. With the money Esperanza gave him, her eldest son, Leonardo, had hired another investigator in Jamaica. The price for his service was steep—$500 up front and another $500 when he found the documents they needed. With that proof of Jamaican ancestry, and Sarah's timeworn Jamaican passport, all of them—Leonardo, Leandro, Oscar, and Esperanza too—would be well on the way to becoming Jamaican citizens.

Cary had watched them skeptically, no more in favor of abandoning Cuba than she was of approving her sister's work as a washerwoman in the United States.

But neither did she rule out following in her footsteps.

CHAPTER 27

GUANABACOA

August 2018

Lili was still sleeping when her husband pulled on a pair of baggy gray shorts, dropped an oversize black tank top over his scarred chest and bulging belly, and walked half a block to the local bakery, where he picked up the small rolls— about the size of a hamburger bun—that the Cuban government sells, for almost nothing, to every Cuban every day. "*El pan*" was what Cubans called it, the article before the noun distinguishing the tasteless daily bread from regular *pan* that could be purchased at higher prices if the bakery had enough flour to make it. Carlos then set out on foot to deliver *el pan* door to door around his neighborhood.

His first stop was a squat single-family house half a block away. A white plastic bag tied to the front doorknob let him know the residents had already gone to work. He stuffed several rolls, one for each member of the family, into the bag and then retied it to the door. Then he walked to the corner, passing the *libreta* grocery store, the *libreta* butcher shop, and the stand that distributed tanks of cooking gas, and turned right, stopping a few doors down at the front gate of a well-cared-for single-family house, where he knocked on the front door. "*Hola.*" The owner greeted him with a big smile, asking how he was on this Monday morning.

"No complaints," Carlos said, handing the woman several rolls. He lingered for just a few seconds of small talk, then turned to continue his deliveries. *"Gracias,"* she said, watching him leave. He stayed on the shady side of the street, stopping in front of a five-story microbrigade apartment building like the one Pipo had built in Regla. An older woman waiting on a third-floor balcony lowered a canvas bag on a long rope. Carlos put her two rolls in the bag, and she slowly hauled it back up. *"Gracias,"* she shouted. "And how is the family?"

He walked slowly through the rutted streets and small hills of the neighborhood, trying to avoid the gaping potholes he'd tripped over before. It wasn't yet nine in the morning, but he was already sweating. In another microbrigade building a few blocks away, he delivered a single roll to an older woman who lived alone. He knocked on her door and when she didn't answer he wedged her roll into the iron gate, knowing that she wouldn't worry about flies because she usually fed it to her dog.

Carlos continued down Seventh Street, stopping at yet another microbrigade building where he shouted, "Noriega!" and then sat down on a ledge to smoke a Criollo. In a few minutes, a middle-aged man in a T-shirt and sunglasses came down the stairs. Noriega took five rolls for his family and another two for a neighbor. Carlos ended his route at Casa Loma, a private house with a large pool and a thatched hut that hosted parties. The owner, Aleida Bericomo, had coffee ready for him. As he smoked another Criollo, they chatted briefly about her business and her late husband, who had been Carlos's friend.

"He was a tremendous businessman. Tremendous," Carlos said.

"True." She smiled. "But even he would have trouble doing business now. It's impossible."

"It's difficult, that's for sure. But we survive. Listen, I have to go. Thanks for the coffee."

Because he delivered only *el pan* this morning, Carlos completed his route in less than an hour, not bad for a seventy-six-year-old who'd suffered four heart attacks and was trying to manage his diabetes. It took him much longer when he loaded his cart with the once-a-month beans, rice, cooking oil, and other staples available through the *libreta*. The old communist was a licensed self-employed entrepreneur. His was a business of pennies, but the pennies added up. His forty-nine customers paid between one and two dollars a month for the convenience of not having to stand at the *libreta* store's fly-covered counter, or enter the *libreta* butcher shop where, most days, little was available but hunks of fatty processed meat Cubans call *mortadella*, or a block of farmer's cheese under a plastic covering black with flies. In a month he'd make twice his ten-dollar pension.

Delivering groceries wasn't what Carlos had imagined retirement would be like. He'd been a true believer in the Cuban system since he was a teenager, and when he retired at fifty-five, he planned to spend time fishing at Cojímar. But the special period ruined his plans. Simply getting to Cojímar was a chore, and after buying food and other necessities, he never had enough money left over for a fishing pole. Instead of relaxing by the sea, he'd been delivering other people's groceries six days a week—*el pan* was doubled on Saturdays— every week for more than twenty years. He had no idea how long he'd continue doing it, just as no one knew how long the *libreta* itself would last.

The system of rationing staples had been introduced as a temporary measure at the outset of the revolution, but over decades it became an iconic aspect of Cuban life, the subject of innumerable criticisms and jokes. Cubans roared whenever Pánfilo, the main character of the popular TV comedy *Vivir del cuento,* prayed to an oversize copy of the *libreta* hanging on the wall of his home. The independent Cuban news site *14ymedio* included the *libreta* on its list of the three essentials for surviving in Cuba, along with remittances from abroad and stealing from the state.

For some Cubans, especially the elderly and the handicapped, the *libreta* was a last redoubt against hunger. Others with access to extra cash bought additional food at dollar markets, but they too had grown accustomed to the *libreta,* although they often complained about the quantity and quality of what they received. For the few dollars a month that Pipo and Cary normally spent in the *libreta* store, they got fifteen pounds of rice for the family, a few pounds of chicken, beans, salt, oil, and a quarter pound of what's labeled coffee but actually is a grisly mixture of equal parts coffee and dried peas that they used only when they had no choice. One of Cary's seamstresses fed the ground tofu called *picadillo de soya* to her cats.

For Carlos and Lili, the *libreta* was an almost sacred symbol of the Cuban system, a dependable demonstration of the Cuban government's concern for its people. But even they conceded that the booklet no longer helped them the way it used to. Over the years, the number of items available at below-market prices declined substantially. Milk, beef, and fish often were available only for families with young children or adults with serious health issues. Potatoes could go missing for so long that when they finally were delivered, people lined Vía Blanca shouting, "*¡Hay papas!*" (There are potatoes!) as the open-bed trucks rolled in from the countryside. Some months, Cubans could buy *pollo por pescado*, an additional ration of frozen chicken—usually from the United States—in place of nonexistent fish fillets. Eggs were the primary source of protein for some Cubans. *Libreta* stores usually sold them for fifteen centavos apiece, with a limit of five a month per person. Another five eggs sometimes could be purchased at a higher price of around a nickel apiece. In the rare times when eggs were available without restrictions, they were called "liberated" and cost twice that much. For a full year after Hurricane Irma, Carlos told his customers that so many hens had been killed by the storm, and so many others remained spooked long after the sky cleared, that they weren't laying as many eggs as they used to.

Eggs remained limited for many months, which was a real disadvantage for María del Carmen, whose favorite meal consisted of two hard-boiled eggs. It had been Román's favorite too, and Virgilio inherited the same hankering. Mari's local butcher shop knew about the family's obsession with eggs and allowed her to buy extras in exchange for some of the frozen chicken she didn't care for anyway because it had bones.

The three generations of Cubans who lived with the Castros and the *libreta* grew accustomed to shortages. Even though Raúl promised, in 2007, that Cuba would soon produce so much milk that "anyone who wants to can drink a glass," a full glass of fresh cold milk was only a distant memory for many. Steaks were available in tourist hotels, but rarely in neighborhood stores. Occasionally some found its way onto the black market, where its street name was "Moo."

Cuba's hens weren't the only part of the economy derailed by Hurricane

Irma. Sugarcane fields were so devastated by the storm that Cuba couldn't satisfy the domestic market while also meeting export obligations. The 2017–2018 sugar harvest yielded just over a puny one million tons, about equal to the yield in 1894. Cuba itself consumed seven hundred thousand tons a year and had a standing contract to sell China four hundred thousand tons. To meet its needs after Irma, Cuba—once the mightiest sugar producer on the planet—had to import beet sugar from France. Pipo didn't even realize that he was buying imported sugar at the *libreta* store until he noticed that it was very white, very fine, and very sweet. When Carlos found out that he was delivering French sugar to his customers, he did not consider it a sign of Cuba's economic weakness. Rather, he attributed the move to the cleverness of Cuban managers, figuring they must have paid less for the imported sugar than they received for the sugar they exported.

Every day, when he finished his rounds, Carlos bought copies of *Granma* and *Juventud rebelde* at the kiosk near the Vía Blanca traffic light. He read books like *Paraíso perdido,* about the decline of the Soviet Union, with sympathy and a measure of anger. He tried to catch every baseball game on TV, and when there wasn't a game on, he watched Cuban news broadcasts or the news channel from Venezuela, which is where he picked up his sometimes scrambled interpretation of the rest of the world, including the United States. He was disappointed that President Trump tried to reverse the Obama opening. And when Washington pulled out most of its staff from the embassy in Havana, claiming that mysterious "acoustical attacks" had caused serious injuries to its diplomats, he suspected that President Trump had been looking for an excuse to punish Cuba, a suspicion that he thought was confirmed when the State Department warned travelers that going to Cuba might not be safe, killing off much of what remained of the American tourist trade.

Still, Carlos was hopeful that the two countries at some point could develop a friendlier relationship. He drew a distinction between the American people, for whom he and most Cubans had affection, and the United States government, in particular the administration of President Trump, for which he had no patience. "For the few years of life that I have left, I only wish that he would let us live in peace," he often said. It was a wish held by many Cubans who'd lived under a barrage of actual and perceived American threats, inflated by their own government, for sixty years. The United States had proved to be a most useful scapegoat for whatever went wrong in Cuba. Carlos admired the industriousness of American workers, and he appreciated the breadth of American culture, but based on what he knew about it, he had no desire to live there, or to visit, "even if they offered me a million pesos."

Carlos had attended school at Los Escolapios for a few years when he was a boy growing up in Guanabacoa. But religion drained out of his life, and he considered himself an atheist, albeit an understanding and respectful atheist. It didn't bother him when Lili erected a Santería altar in her bedroom, or when Joseíto's wife, a Jehovah's Witness, put her daughters in long, modest dresses and walked them to the Kingdom Hall in Guanabacoa. But he struggled with the idea that his granddaughters were not allowed to salute the Cuban flag. "That's where you live," he said. "That's who you are. If you don't recognize your own flag, you become a person without a country."

He understood what it meant to turn your back on your own country. In the awful summer of 1994, after the tugboat sank, his son from an earlier marriage, Carlos Jr., climbed into a homemade raft in Cojímar with several other people and set sail for Florida. Carlos didn't know about it until after his son was gone, and he felt betrayed. His own son, fleeing into the arms of the enemy! He heard that his son's raft had been picked up in the open sea by the U.S. Coast Guard and brought to Guantanamo, and from there he eventually was allowed to enter the United States, where he settled in Florida and married an American woman.

As far as Carlos was concerned, he no longer had a son.

But after Joseíto moved in next door with his wife and their two little girls, Carlos did have a new family. He gave up the backyard where he had raised chickens and pigs to build a kitchen and bathroom for them. When the girls started calling him *abuelo* and didn't shy away from his scars, he had no regrets about losing his yard. Then one day Lili received a call from her own father's caregiver in Santiago telling her that the "Gallego," which was how everyone knew her father, had trouble remembering anything, even when to eat. He was losing weight and spent much of the day, and night, wandering. Looking after him and keeping him safe had become more than the caregiver could handle. You need to move him, she told Lili, and Lili convinced Carlos that she couldn't leave her father alone.

José Durand was eighty, a few years older than Carlos, and his dementia grew worse after Lili brought him to Guanabacoa. He'd sit on a bench outside the house for hours, dressed in a wrinkled striped pullover and shapeless pants, wearing a shoe on one foot and a sandal on the other. If no one was watching, he'd pull open the steel door and wander off. One time, he was gone for hours, and no one knew where he was until one of his great-granddaughters came home from her preschool and said she'd seen him loitering nearby. Then, just days after Irma, he slipped out and was gone overnight. Cary and Pipo discovered him on the street miles away. Lili had to constantly remind her granddaughters to keep the steel door locked. Joseíto had agreed to have his grandfather live on his side of the house, but the old man insisted on getting up in the middle of the night and stumbling around without any clothes on, frightening the girls. Lili went to the municipal building in Guanabacoa to ask for help, but she was told that as his daughter, responsibility for taking care of her father fell squarely on her shoulders.

As a committed revolutionary, Lili knew that her faith in the system was being tested, just as Cary's faith had been challenged when first her mother, then she herself, had to rely on Cuba's health care system. That experience had left Cary disillusioned both morally and politically because the treatment she and Zenaida received was so much better than it should have been in an egalitarian society. Now that Lili needed help for her father, she struggled to understand why the system she supported so completely seemed to have turned its back on her.

"I am very proud of my country, proud of my revolution, of my communism," she said many times. "I was born in 1962, basically the same time as the revolution, and it created me. I studied it, and I am grateful to it. But I'm now passing through a time in my life, one of those passages in every life . . . I feel very, very bad."

She confided in Cary, describing her disappointment with the way she was being treated. Cary tried to console her, assuring her that everything would work out, even though she was worried that it wouldn't.

Besides being turned down when she sought space in a nursing home for her father, Lili had been pleading for years for wheelchairs for her mother, Cristina, and her handicapped sister, María Isabel, who continued to live in their squatters' shack in Casablanca. You'll have to wait, she was told again and again. "By the time we get the wheelchair, my mother could be dead," she told the government office. When she quit her job as a Coraza security guard to care for her parents, Lili went to the local office of the Ministry of Work and Social Security looking for help, but the response she got was insulting. The government worker at the office asked her if she'd ever considered taking out a self-employed worker's license to sell candy or *duro frío*—homemade popsicles made with condensed milk—from the doorway of her home the way some people did.

The money Carlos earned making deliveries became more important than ever. Cary also pitched in to help her friend whenever she could, dropping off clothes or a packet of the 50/50 blend of coffee and dried peas as she passed by on the way to the workshop, and making sure Oscar kept sending her bags to sew. As her father's condition worsened, Lili grew more frustrated. He became incontinent, but a box of twenty disposable adult diapers cost ten dollars. "How could I afford that," she asked the government workers, "when I don't have forty centavos to take the bus?"

Finally, at her wit's end, Lili made one of the most difficult decisions of her life. It became obvious that her father required round-the-clock care. He often burrowed so deeply into his dementia that there was no reasoning with him. His naked wanderings repulsed Joseíto's wife and scared his daughters. Something had to be done to restrain the old man and, Lili thought, keep him safe. Not knowing what else to do, she asked Joseíto to wall off a corner of his workshop, creating a three-by-six-foot closet with a small window that opened onto an alleyway. There was just enough room inside the closet for a narrow cot but nothing else. Lili took her father's hand and led him into the space and then locked him in there to keep him from wandering and to allow her family to finally get some rest. She brought him meals and washed his clothes when he soiled them.

She knew that keeping her father penned in a room that small was inhumane, but she didn't know what else to do. She refused to ask for help from the Catholic charities operating in Cuba because that would be a betrayal of her faith in the communist system. For her, the revolution was tantamount to religion—with education and health care sacraments that Fidel and Raúl bestowed on all Cubans. Her trials with her father, the collision of ideology and reality, left her shaken and uncertain, and at one point pushed her close to blasphemy. "And to think," she'd say, "they keep telling us that Cuba is a medical powerhouse in the world." Cornered by her party loyalty, she spent part of each day cleaning feces off the floor and walls of her father's cell, and resentment surged in her. There was no prayer to help her through her ordeal, no song like "Pregúntale a las estrellas" to keep her calm the way it did Cary when she was in a difficult place. Her indignation built and built until it tumbled over into rage against the injustice of being abandoned by the system she believed in when she most needed its help.

When Cary found out what Lili was doing to her father, she was appalled. She couldn't walk past the house without cringing at the thought of the old man imprisoned in the box they had made for him, sweltering during the day, shivering throughout the cool of the night. Despite the long years they'd been friends, her opinion of Lili changed. *If that's the way she treats her father,* Cary thought, *what would she do to me if I needed help?*

The tragedy hurtled toward its inevitable end. The old man refused to eat. Lili ground up chicken and tried feeding it to him on the tip of a spoon. She prepared a hearty broth and, with coaxing, got him to taste it, but when she tried to feed him again later that day, he turned his head away. When she tried to give him water, he refused to drink. It continued that way for several days. Then one evening a little after six, she entered the stinking, sweltering cage and found him stone dead.

LIVING IN CUBA WAS EXHAUSTING, and dying was no easy task. When Lili told Carlos what happened, they carried the old man from the closet to her sofa, where she washed her father's body and dressed him in clean clothes.

They needed a doctor to write out a death certificate because he had died at home. Joseíto went to the neighborhood clinic to bring back the local doctor, but she wasn't there. He tried several other clinics and finally came back with a doctor who wrote that the old man had died of natural causes in Lili's house, without mentioning the closet in which he'd spent his last days.

Cary had already heard what happened when Lili called to tell her. She hid her disgust at the way the old man had been treated.

"This is the way life is, Lili," Cary said. "It happens to all of us."

Lili called the funeral parlor in Regla and gave directions to the house, but the driver got lost. It was after ten at night when the funeral car finally pulled up. The driver apologized for being late. Then he apologized again because they'd run out of sheets and had nothing to cover the body with. Lili took it in stride. There were shortages everywhere; no one was to blame. But she was not going to let her father be taken out of the house without being covered. She rushed to her own bedroom and came back with a white sheet.

"My father is going to leave here the way all the dead leave their homes," she told the hearse driver, handing him the sheet. He thanked her. "And keep it so you'll have something to use next time."

They wrapped the body carefully and carried it to the hearse. Lili rode with them to the funeral home. While she'd waited for the hearse to arrive, she'd had time to change into a new blouse, clean tights, and a new pair of black sneakers in preparation for the long night ahead. According to tradition, she was expected to sit with the body at the funeral home until eight the next morning, when they'd leave for the cemetery.

Joseíto joined her at the funeral home and sat with her until Carlos came by after making his deliveries. They accompanied the body to the cemetery in Regla, where the director checked the records for an available tomb connected to a family that no longer lived in Cuba.

In two years, Lili would have another challenge to face. She had not put socks on her father's hands.

The old man hadn't left much. He had signed away his house in Santiago to the young woman who cooked and cleaned for him. It could not have gone to Lili anyway because she and Carlos already had their apartment, and the law prohibited them in most instances from owning more than one property. There was one aspect of her father's modest legacy that she hoped to save. Even though it wasn't much—about ten dollars a month—she wanted his pension to go to her mother and sister in Casablanca.

Lili was told that she'd have to provide proof of her sister's infirmity and when it began in order to transfer the pension to her. Doing so wouldn't be easy. She'd have to bring her sister in to be evaluated by a panel of psychiatrists, but that meant controlling María Isabel on the crowded buses they'd have to take to get to the medical offices in Havana. Several months after José Durand died, Lili's lobbying got his pension assigned to her mother and sister.

TRAGIC AS WERE THE FINAL DAYS of her father's life, the ordeal left Lili's faith in the revolution bruised but not broken. In March 2018, a few weeks after he died, single-candidate elections were held for provincial delegates and National Assembly members. Lili enthusiastically handled her responsibilities as president of the CDR and member of the neighborhood electoral commission. The elections—though criticized outside Cuba as largely ceremonial and nonrepresentative—were too important for Lili to let any personal issue, no matter how intense, stand in the way.

The March vote was the culmination of an elaborate electoral process that had been delayed by Hurricane Irma six months earlier and that eventually would play a role in replacing Raúl Castro as president. That first phase had been pushed back to November 26, one year to the day after Fidel had died. To honor *el comandante*'s memory, the members of the electoral committee had worn red T-shirts that day. Lili had asked Cary for one.

Now the 605 seats in the rubber-stamp National Assembly would be filled. Based on its official population of around 120,000, Guanabacoa was allotted six seats. Miguel Barnet, the head of the National Union of Writers and Artists, had held one of them since 2008, and his name was on the ballot again. Lili considered the national election this time to be much more important than usual because once the assembly members were affirmed (605 candidates for 605 assembly seats), they'd select one among them who, in another month, would replace Raúl Castro as president. Raúl would still be pulling strings from behind the scenes, but there wouldn't be a Castro nominally in charge of Cuba for the first time since the triumph of the revolution.

On election day, a Sunday, Lili woke at five in the morning, thrilled to cast her vote and play a role in the process even though elections remained a sore spot in her family. When the polls opened at seven, Carlos was among the first to vote at the medical post a half block from their house. Joseíto stayed in bed. He never voted in any election, and he had no intention of making this one an exception. "Elections are supposed to be about change," he'd told his mother countless times, "but here nothing changes, ever." Other Cubans worried about reprisals if the local CDR found out that they hadn't voted. But not him.

Ballot boxes at every polling place were ceremonially guarded by two student *pioneros*. Dressed in their red, white, and blue uniforms, they gave the *pioneros por el comunismo* salute as voters deposited their paper ballots. Lili's dream of having her granddaughters stand guard on election day were dashed because, as Jehovah's Witnesses, they were taught to abstain from elections. Despite his mother's obvious disappointment, Joseíto never forced the issue. Since he didn't see the point of elections, he reasoned, why should his daughters take part?

Cary and Pipo walked the half block to the clinic and cast their votes before heading to church. Oscar came by a few hours later, filled with optimism, but not about the election. He and his cousins had just received good news from the investigator they'd hired in Jamaica. He had found their great-grandmother's original birth certificate. Oscar still wasn't sure how he'd use the Jamaican citizenship that was now within reach, but the security of having that option gave him peace of mind.

In his studio across town, Arturo Montoto spent election day working without the least intention of voting. He was busy finishing a number of large sculptures for an upcoming gallery show. It would be his first exhibit in several years. Besides the giant black baseball he'd protected from Irma, he was making a huge basket and a monumental egg, along with an eggplant and a slice of watermelon, all on the same gigantic scale. Each piece was rendered in a single color: black.

Jorge García's grandson Jorgito and his wife, Isbel, got their sons ready for Sunday service at the Methodist church, without giving any more thought to casting a vote in this election than they had in any other. And María del Carmen had already made it clear in her neighborhood that she had no interest in voting in the one-sided contest. In previous elections, party faithful went door to door on election day, making sure everyone voted, presenting an image to the rest of the world that Cuban elections were a participatory process. But this time, no one had knocked on the door of the small house on Corralfalso, and Mari preferred it that way.

CHAPTER 28

GUANABACOA
April 19, 2018

When the day finally came for Raúl Castro to fulfill the promise he'd made five years earlier that nobody, not even a man named Castro, should stay in office for more than a decade, Cary was ready. She brewed a pot of coffee and made herself comfortable in a wooden rocking chair in front of the TV, putting her bare feet up on a stool and turning on Hopeful to keep her cool. She was excited and also worried as she watched the newly affirmed members of the National Assembly cast votes for a new president, a man who would mark a generational change in Cuba's leaders from the age of those who remembered, and cursed, Batista to those—like her—who had known only the Castros' Cuba.

As she sipped her coffee, she saw little that surprised her. It was not an election in any real sense. Rather, it was a succession, one deftly choreographed by Raúl. A commission made up of his allies had announced the day before that the first vice president, Miguel Díaz-Canel Bermúdez, a bull-chested, silver-haired, fifty-seven-year-old apparatchik from the center of the country, was the sole candidate for president of the council of state and the council of ministers, two separate titles that had been reserved for either Fidel or Raúl since they were created. The members of the newly reconstituted National Assembly then voted to affirm the commission's choice of Díaz-Canel to replace Raúl.

The deputies waited a day to announce the results, as if they needed time to count votes about which there hadn't been the slightest doubt. The transition to the post-Castro generation went off as smoothly as a Silvio Rodríguez ballad, and without either criticism in the Cuban media or input from the Cuban people. As Cary finished her first cup of coffee, the election commission announced that three of the five new vice presidents were black, and two were women. Cary smiled. Clearly these were good signs for Cuba. Her smile disappeared when Ramiro Valdés, the eighty-six-year-old general who had headed Cuba's security forces for years, was confirmed as one of the vice presidents. And the name of Gladys María Bejerano Portela, a stone-faced seventy-one-year-old who earned a fearful reputation in her years as comptroller general of the nation, made her grimace.

Then came the announcement that she had been waiting for: Díaz-Canel had been affirmed by a vote of 603 out of the 604 members present. Cary assumed that Díaz-Canel, in a show of public humility, had not voted for himself.

All 604 delegates, including Díaz-Canel and Raúl Castro, rose to their feet as if on command and applauded. Cary watched intently, recalling the euphoria she experienced when she had attended the Fifth Communist Party Congress years before. But now she knew better. She was no longer blinded by revolutionary zeal. Six hundred individuals all believing that this one man, whom most did not know, was the best person to lead Cuba for the next decade? This was neither democracy nor revolution.

Oscar poked his head into the living room to see what was going on. When every deputy raised a hand to confirm the vote for Díaz-Canel, without a single no vote or abstention, he jeered. The whole proceeding was nothing more than a sham. Cary turned away from the TV screen to try to convince him that they were witnessing something important, a step along the path that for years she had been telling him Cuba would follow. He didn't buy it. "Nothing's going to change," he said, still smirking. "It'll all be the same." He watched for a few minutes more as Díaz-Canel was called up to the dais. The new president walked briskly, his expensive suit jacket unbuttoned. When he casually slapped the hands of the first-row delegates as though they were opponents at the end of a friendly baseball game, Oscar yelled, "Hey, look at that!" This new guy's politics might not be any different from the others, but at least he had a sense of style.

It hurt Cary to see him sneer at the transition.

"In twenty years, you'll be looking back and thinking that this moment was actually the beginning of an important change in Cuba."

"In twenty years?" Oscar shook his head. "In twenty years I'll be what? Forty-seven years old? I'm not going to be thinking about this moment. No way." He kissed his mother on the cheek and finished getting ready for work.

There was no formal ceremony as Díaz-Canel took office. Like all the other deputies in the National Assembly, he had signed a form the previous day vowing to fulfill his duties as deputy. That was all. He wore no ceremonial sash with the national colors. He did not take an oath of office. No trumpets blared to intensify the spirit of the moment. When he spoke, he directed his words at his fellow deputies, not the Cuban people. And his fundamental message quickly became clear. In other countries, incoming officials promised change. In Cuba, they promised that nothing would change. Díaz-Canel offered a firm commitment to follow the path Cuba had been on for as long as most people could remember—in fact, longer than he'd been alive. To prove his loyalty, Díaz-Canel paid elaborate homage to Raúl and Fidel and the rest of the historic generation, including eighty-seven-year-old José Ramón Machado Ventura, who was sitting at Raúl's side. Both men, who had fought with Fidel in the mountains and had run Cuba with him since the triumph of the revolution, had just been elected to new terms as deputies.

The old generation of the Sierra had not yet faded into the shadows. But the next generation of Castros was not continuing the dynasty, at least not now. Raúl's daughter Mariela Castro Espín was a high-profile member of the National Assembly, but she had not been given a leadership position. Raúl's son Alejandro was not an assemblyman and therefore couldn't constitutionally ascend to the presidency, although he had been a significant player in the secret negotiations with the Obama administration. And Fidel's eldest son, sixty-eight-year-old Fidelito, had committed suicide just weeks before the handover.

As he wrapped up his speech, Díaz-Canel repeated the basic message that state-run media had delivered nonstop for weeks: faces might be different, but there would be no disruption. The revolution would continue. The new president ended with one of Fidel's old rallying cries: "*¡Patria o muerte! ¡Socialismo o muerte! ¡Venceremos!*" (Homeland or death! Socialism or death! We will be victorious!).

Cary looked pleased. She knew that Oscar thought of her as a dreamer whenever she mentioned that changes were coming, though she hoped that one day he'd see things differently. Díaz-Canel surely represented a new generation, her generation, and she probably knew him better than did many of the legislators who'd just voted for him. She'd worked with him when she was vice minister and he was head of the party in his home province of Villa Clara, but she never imagined that one day she'd watch him take over as president. Based on her experiences in and out of the system, she saw through his rhetoric about continuity and was certain his ideas would someday conflict with those of the old guard he was replacing. Even though Raúl had groomed him to take over, there were bound to be differences. His reluctance to make specific promises was a sign that he realized he had not been given a magic wand that he could wave to create housing and food. Making promises he couldn't keep would be far worse than not making any promises at all. She saw definite signs of hope. Small signs, but real hope. This was the end of an era and the beginning of a new day when Cuba could maintain what it had already achieved and change what needed to be changed. She was sure of it.

Cary listened intently as Raúl, in his long and sometimes rambling final address, sent the same message of continuity as his successor. She nodded when, in a brief summary of the revolution's critical moments, he referred to July 1994, the summer of tugboats and protests, as the "peak of the most desperate part" of the special period. He didn't specifically mention the sinking of the *13 de Marzo*, the hijacking of the ferries, or the disturbances on the Malecón, but his mention of July 1994 reminded Cary and everyone else listening of how bad things had been then and how much better everything seemed now—a comparison that Cubans routinely made to take the sting out of daily life. He made it clear that although he was stepping down as president, he was

continuing as supreme leader of the party for three more years. He then laid
out his vision for the future—calling for a substantial rewrite of the constitution to set term limits and age restrictions on all political leaders. He said he'd
like to see Díaz-Canel replace him as leader of the party in 2021 and then begin
a second term as president in 2023. He admitted that he had not done a very
good job of preparing the next generation to take over, and he described how
hubris and scandal had eliminated many potential leaders. Cary understood
the cryptic reference to the 2009 purge of Carlos Lage, Felipe Pérez Roque,
Roberto Robaina, and other rising stars who were said to have celebrated with
drinks at the Ambos Mundos Hotel the news that Fidel Castro was seriously ill.
The government even claimed to have videotapes proving that, in Fidel's own
words, the disgraced officials had succumbed to "the honey of power."

Cary perked up when Raúl mentioned that the process of "neoliberal
privatizations" of nonstrategic sectors in the economy would continue, but
she was disappointed when he failed to address the creation of a wholesale
market or the unification of the dual currencies that made doing business a
nightmare. Just then the doorbell rang, and Faru started barking. Cary looked
out the window. "How much?" she shouted. An elderly woman stood outside
the front gate holding a big transparent plastic bag filled with crackers. It
weighed several pounds.

"Six dollars," the woman said. That was half of her pension, but just a minuscule share of what she, Pipo, and Oscar were making at Procle. Cary shuf-
fled to the kitchen for her purse. She knew without asking that the crackers
came from a state-owned bakery on Vía Blanca, just past the Guanabacoa
traffic light. The woman was *luchando*—hustling—but Cary bought the crackers anyway. Someone was always coming to their door selling something this
way. That's how she'd bought the Hopeful fan. A few pounds of unsliced mortadella imported from Spain? Stolen, but Pipo bought it. Fresh snapper from
Pinar del Río, with the spear hole in its side? Illegal catch, but Pipo bought it.
Several weeks after Cary purchased the looted crackers, she saw a news report
about the cracker factory, and she had to laugh. The plant manager was praised
for exceeding quotas in *tiempo récord*, but there was no mention of what everyone in Guanabacoa knew—that innumerable bags of crackers illicitly taken

from the plant had ended up being sold door to door. The thieves made money, the buyers found food, and the factory manager was praised for meeting production goals. *Luchando.*

Cary returned to her rocker to watch the end of the inaugural ceremonies. For her, the significance of the handover was undeniable, despite the assurances of continuity from Díaz-Canel and Raúl. Cuba would not be transformed overnight; she knew that, and she harbored no illusions about Díaz-Canel turning out to be Cuba's Gorbachev. But she sensed that the chains had been moved, steps had been taken, and as one era receded, a new one had dawned.

IN HIS STUDIO THAT NIGHT, Arturo Montoto forced himself to watch the rebroadcast of the speeches, another act in what he considered the tragicomedy that was Cuba. He had more than politics on his mind. In the outdoor section of his workshop, just beyond the lush garden with all his trees and plants, Arturo was spending most of every day overseeing the finishing touches to *Dividendo*, his gigantic watermelon sculpture. He and his assistants had built a scaffolding to get up high enough to finish the work that never seemed to end. First the challenge had been finding enough of the foam Arturo needed to complete the basic shape of the six-foot-tall melon slice. He had to rely on friends bringing in cans of spray foam, the kind used to insulate around windows. Once the foam hardened, he applied resin, which he purchased locally, but on this day, he was cursing the manufacturer—the Cuban state—because the resin hadn't held up the way he expected. Alfredo, one of his young assistants, was scraping off layers of the resin with a wire brush and a hand broom to create the texture Arturo envisioned. It was tedious, backbreaking work.

"With a power washer we would have this done in a few minutes," Arturo told Alfredo, who raised his eyebrows but did not stop scraping. Arturo had invented this time-consuming alternative, which had taken days, delaying the project yet again. His life seemed to be conforming to his art. The concept that unified the melon slice with much of the rest of the work he'd been wrestling with for four years was darkness, which he readily admitted probably reflected his view of life in Cuba.

"I'm not at all interested in who is chosen president because I know that they have not been elected by the people," he said as his assistants waited for instructions. Nothing in Díaz-Canel's speech had given him hope for the future, and he remained deeply pessimistic. "For the last sixty years all that I have seen here is demagoguery. I've lived practically all my life under this demagoguery, and I know that everything is a lie. When changes appear to take place in Cuban politics, they are not real changes. Everything stays the same, and we all know that everything will stay the same."

A block away in her house on Corralfalso, María del Carmen had not bothered watching any of the assembly proceedings. Díaz-Canel's promise of continuity, designed to appease hardliners in the government, had the opposite effect on her. In Villa Panamericana, Jorge García's grandson Jorgito had scoffed at the notion of wasting time with elections that in point of fact were selections. And Miriam Díaz, alone in her one-room apartment perched above a filthy stream in Guanabacoa, had recently retired from her job at the municipal social security office and had nothing better to do. But even at the risk of boredom, she refused to watch.

Change was what people like Cary hoped for while it was what people like Lili and Carlos feared. They had the TV on throughout the entire handover, and they watched it again during the rebroadcast later that same day to make sure they caught every word. Lili knew that many people outside Cuba had predicted that without a Castro in charge, the revolution would flame out. "But on the contrary," she said after she had watched Díaz-Canel take Raúl's place. "Everything is moving forward. The legacy will continue."

Next door, Joseíto had not bothered to watch any part of the proceedings. Old music videos were more interesting.

As THE HANDOVER WAS UNDER WAY in Cuba, Jorge García was in Miami settling back into his regular routine after an extraordinary few days at the eighth Summit of the Americas in Lima, Peru, where he again denounced the Castro regime for its role in the sinking of the *13 de Marzo*. The International Commission for the Prosecution of Crimes Against Humanity of the Castro

Regime was one of several human rights groups that had participated in the civil-society meetings that led up to the Summit. As he had done in Miami in July, and then again at hearings the commission held in November in Washington, DC, Jorge poured out his impassioned memory of that day in 1994. In Peru, the commission's activities were highlighted by the unveiling of billboards around Lima showing a photograph of Raúl Castro with the words WANTED FOR CRIMES AGAINST HUMANITY. The commission formally requested that the Trump administration bring charges against Raúl since he was no longer protected by international laws shielding national leaders. Jorge knew that the commission's chances of getting any international court to prosecute Castro were slim. The commission had decided that its strongest case for prosecution was not the tugboat sinking but the 1996 downing of the Brothers to the Rescue plane. Nonetheless, the commission's persistence on such an international stage fortified Jorge's own commitment to finding justice for the victims, and he was willing to continue being patient. When the commission presented its findings to the Organization of American States (OAS) in Washington at the end of 2018, he left home once more to spill out his painful memories and continue his crusade.

"In front of you today, I renew my yearning for justice," he told the commissioners as he wrapped up his allotted ten minutes. Although they had heard his emotional testimony before, they listened with rapt attention, and in the audience, people with stone faces shook their heads in anger and disbelief at the carnage that Jorge described.

Then, with his face red with emotion, he peered at the commission members sitting at their long table in the elegant headquarters of the OAS. It was a long way from the humble house he had built with his own hands on San Sebastián Street in Guanabacoa, and nearly a quarter century had gone by since he had told his son Joel that he would see him in eternity.

"I know that your work will bring vindication for my dead." The anger had dropped out of his voice as he rededicated himself to those who perished. "And permit me here, in front of you, to renew my promise to continue denouncing these atrocities for as long as I am alive."

CHAPTER 29

REGLA
2018

For as long as anyone in Guanabacoa could remember, whenever the refinery on the shore of Havana Harbor processed sulfurous Cuban oil, the night sky blushed red with fire. Few here doubted that the diabolical glow was proof of a world turned upside down, but why, they wondered, if flames of hell roared in the clouds above, why in the name of Pepe Antonio were they living so far from heaven on the ground below?

Cary stood practically below those twenty-five-foot-high flames, surprised at how easy it had been to get into the Ñico López refinery. People still talked about the time in 1958 when Fidel's men blew up what was then an American-owned facility. She thought such a strategic target surely would still be heavily guarded, but when she and her friend Anabel rolled up to the refinery's front gate, security wasn't much tighter than it was to get on the Regla ferry. They showed their ID cards and allowed the guards to poke through the back of Jesús's three-wheeled mini-truck, and they were in.

It was payday at the refinery, and Cary was trying to sell Procle's clothing and Oscar's canvas totes to the workers, the same pop-up concept she had encouraged Nancy Varela to try with Model. They set up a table with canvas bags, cotton blouses, flowery housedresses, straw hats, and pullovers that she'd taken from the storeroom at home. If they did well, she'd have a new market to help move inventory until they could find material and restart production.

Within a few hours, Cary realized she'd hit pay dirt. They sold almost all the inventory they'd brought, raking in about seventy-three dollars. Oscar's canvas bags were a big hit. At two dollars each, the ones with the outline of Cuba or the profile of Che had sold out. When she packed up to leave, about all she had left were John Lennon T-shirts. She felt encouraged. Finally, they might be able to recover from the hurricane. Opportunities were all around, if she looked in the right places. Life in Cuba wasn't hopeless. Things could get done.

But her optimism didn't last long.

A few days later, someone stole the wheels off the garbage containers on her street corner. Five of them were lying on their sides, cannibalized and useless. Plantain skins, coffee grounds, plastic bottles, and every other kind of stinking household rubbish spilled over the street, all but blocking traffic. And the flies! She had to keep every window in the house shuttered. Cary had had just about all she could take. Greater Havana's 2.1 million people relied on the large plastic containers, about the size of household freezers, that were placed on random corners to collect the 700,000 cubic feet of household trash, yard waste, and construction debris that was thrown out every day. In Guanabacoa, there might be just one or two containers for dozens of families living along a few city blocks, and the containers filled quickly. Three or four weeks might go by before the city came to empty them, and by then, the containers would be overflowing, the garbage knee deep and spreading into sidewalks, streets, even the many streams that once made Guanabacoa famous.

The problem, officials told Cary and anyone else who complained, was that there weren't enough heavy trucks and front loaders to collect the trash. The equipment was old and kept breaking down. The embargo made spare parts hard to come by.

But Cary knew that the real cause was something else: the system was failing.

She had tried several times to resolve the problem on her own. She drafted a simple contract to have a local man with a horse and wagon pick up the trash in her neighborhood. She and her neighbors agreed to share the cost, but the municipal government shot down the idea. Trash pickup was not one of the private businesses approved by Raúl's government; only the state could collect garbage. In response to Cary's complaint, the city had delivered the five new plastic trash bins and positioned them on the corner near her house. But it took only a week or so for each one to be tipped over in the middle of the night and stripped of its wheels. Self-employed vendors used the wheels to build pushcarts for the vegetables or candy they sold on the street. In time, the containers themselves also would disappear. When no one was watching, they would be hauled off to clandestine workshops where they'd be chopped up, melted down, and recast into brooms, dust pans, and cheap plastic toys that were sold at the La Cuevita flea market, along with everything else that the black market offered but state-run stores did not.

At the Procle workshop that same week, Cary told Enna and another seamstress, Zademys Estrada, that she was going to write to the new president about the trash problem. Both of them told her she was wasting her time. They didn't share Cary's approval of the new president's reluctance to promise change. "Yeah, sure," Zademys had said, bent over the old treadle sewing machine, "all it means is that nothing is going to change, even though we all know that almost everything needs to change." Zademys never voted, and she hadn't seen a minute of the transition on TV. Even if she had been curious about the process, she couldn't have watched it because she didn't have an antenna. She watched only programs she paid to have loaded onto a thumb drive. It was a widespread illegal business that Cubans called *el paquete*. People in the United States recorded *Game of Thrones* and other popular shows and then charged to download them onto buyers' individual flash drives in Cuba. The Cuban government tolerated the illicit business, which operated openly in many cities although it didn't fit into any of the officially recognized categories of legal businesses.

This government will never take care of things, Zademys told Cary, unless the people force it to. But after sixty interminable years, Cubans were burned out and far too focused on just surviving to organize themselves into an opposition the way the disaffected did in Venezuela. "What if I go outside in the street and start shouting 'Down with Castro,' or 'Freedom,' and when I turn around I find out that I'm all alone?" Enna asked. She had been listening quietly from her sewing machine. "Then what happens to me?" She told them how, in her hometown of Bayamo at the eastern end of Cuba, a man who identified himself as being part of the opposition had started publicly calling for change. The local CDR called a meeting and told all his neighbors that they needed to show this man what happens to those who oppose the revolution, "and show him with sticks and stones if necessary." This is the logic based on fear that, combined with their adaptability, keeps the vast majority of Cubans from having anything to do with dissidents and the opposition groups they lead. And it is why the protests on the Malecón in 1994 have never been repeated, despite the continuing misery of so many lives. They have so little—and that's too much to risk losing. In the privacy of the Procle workshop, Zademys let her grievances pour out. "People are unhappy," she said, "but they are afraid to complain publicly. You say something, and then what? Then the little bit you have, they take it away."

It dismayed Cary to hear her friends talk this way. She scolded them for being much too pessimistic and, frankly, for giving up hope. Then she did something that took the other women by surprise. She stood in front of Zademys's old-fashioned sewing machine and began to recite a patriotic song that she had learned as a girl, ending with a phrase that left Zademys wrinkling her brow. "Comandante," Cary sang out, taking a few steps as though she were once again marching in the youth wing of Cuba's Territorial Troops Militia. She was taunting her friends, reminding them of the past they shared, the sublimation to expectations none of them could have escaped. "¡Ordene!" (At your command!) "Here, no one surrenders!"

Zademys bowed her head over the arm of her sewing machine, and Cary could hardly hear her laughing.

DESPITE HER INITIAL OPTIMISM about Díaz-Canel, Cary was disappointed by some of the first steps his government took. Instead of dealing with major problems, like the absence of a wholesale market or the troublesome dual currencies, the administration seemed to focus on absurdities. Within weeks of the transition, a special edition of the *Official Gazette* contained a reduced list of approved private-sector businesses, which had been whittled down from more than 200 to just 123 in part by consolidating similar categories. It included one—bathroom attendant—that was outlined in such detail that it embarrassed her. The regulations set license fees for attendants based on the condition of the public bathroom, ranging from very high quality to hard-to-accept, very low quality. She was certain that the officials who drew up the regulations had never used a very low-quality public restroom like the one in the center of Guanabacoa, which consisted of a row of three lidless toilets, each filled with a splash of bleach. The regulations set at one Cuban peso the maximum fee bathroom caretakers could charge for using their restrooms, although they were allowed to add whatever the market would bear for "additional services," like handing out toilet paper or soap.

After reading those new regulations, Cary realized that looking for government help with the illegal garbage dump on her corner was clearly futile. She called several neighbors and tried to convince them that together they could get the problem resolved. Some of the women weren't comfortable taking power into their own hands. You're overreacting, they told Cary. It's the fault of the careless people who tossed trash in the streets. Cary switched tactics, telling them the illegal dump was a sign of a breakdown of civic culture as well as a failure of political leadership. The people who put their garbage on her corner were only partly to blame. It was the government's fault that the containers weren't picked up often enough. It was the government's fault that there weren't enough containers in the right spots. It was the government's fault that there was nowhere for a would-be entrepreneur to get the wheels to build a pushcart except to steal them from the trash bins. It was the absence of accountability that allowed local, provincial, and national leaders to ignore citizen complaints. Cary got her neighbors fired up enough to haul the vandalized trash bins to a corner away from her house, but the people who lived on that block dragged them right back and warned Cary and her coconspirators not to try that again. A few days after that, the containers simply vanished.

The women realized they had few options left. They had done all they could on their own and needed help. So together they marched down the street to confront the one person they believed had the power to do something: Lili.

A community meeting was already scheduled for that day, and it seemed like the right moment to press Lili on the garbage issue. CDR presidents no longer were the principal spymasters of the Cuban government, but they still had the power to denounce, and they maintained close contacts with the governing Communist Party. Cary remained deeply disappointed in the way Lili had handled her father's last days, but she agreed with her neighbors that it was worth complaining to her about the garbage. They found her down the street from the *libreta* store, at the nameless vest-pocket park where they held their nominating sessions. But when they saw that a troupe of young girls was performing a dance in honor of the birthday of Raúl's late wife, Vilma, the angry ladies of Guanabacoa stood down. They waited for the performance to end before they pulled Lili aside and vented to her about the trash. Lili listened politely.

"I'll give you the names and phone numbers of the people you need to talk to," she told them. "I'll call them myself, but it helps if you call them too." Wistfully, she acknowledged that the CDR no longer had the power it once possessed. And yet despite her disappointment with the system for its failure to help her with her dying father, she believed that her Cuba was greater than any single tragedy, bigger than the life of any one man, even her own father. Moreover, her own recent experience told her that sometimes the system worked in mysterious ways.

Only days before the confrontation over trash, Lili had heard from Lourdes, the local ward leader who had been reelected in November. She was too ill to continue, and she wanted Lili to take her place. Lili saw it as a chance to do for her neighborhood what she hadn't been able to do for her father. It was her duty to say yes, to agree to become a candidate in a special election, to give even more of herself to the system that had cradled her since birth.

But she had other responsibilities: To her mother, who was struggling with dementia and Parkinson's in her Casablanca slum. To Carlos, who, though he kept making his deliveries every morning, was growing fatter, less healthy, and so deaf that they had to wire a speaker behind his chair to help him hear the TV. To Joseíto, who had taken apart the closet where his grandfather died and was working again in the carport but did not have any true spirit of socialism to guide him.

She was considering her options as May Day approached again. It was another reminder of how times had changed. She no longer had to rouse neighbors to attend the parade, keeping tabs on those who stayed home. Workplaces now kept that list, though she couldn't understand why anyone wouldn't want to be there this year when, for the first time, neither Raúl nor Fidel was president.

With the streets of Guanabacoa dark and still mostly quiet on May 1, Lili came out of her house at 3:30 A.M. and swung open the metal door with the PRESIDENTE sticker on it. Pipo was already standing outside waiting for her, carrying a frozen bottle of water. They were going to have to walk a lot, and once they got to the Plaza de la Revolución, they'd have to wait until after sunrise for the march to begin. It was too strenuous for Cary, who'd only recently been told by her doctors that the batteries in her pacemaker were wearing down and she should prepare herself for more surgery. She told Pipo she'd watch for him on TV. Carlos also wasn't well enough to walk. Joseíto? He planned to sleep through it.

Lili wore her red election-day T-shirt, along with capri pants with bedazzled pockets, and the new black sneakers she'd worn the day her father died. Her lips were flush with red lipstick, and large earrings framed her face that was still puffy with sleep. By the time she and Pipo rushed past the Novalum offices on Vía Blanca, she already had a lit Criollo between her lips. Behind the factory's central workshop where Cary had, decades earlier, warned her employees not to sell aluminum sheets to the rafters, a few workers had gathered. "Are you going?" someone shouted. It was Juanita, Cary's former secretary, who still worked there. Pipo waved at her and shouted, "Sí, ¡a la plaza!"

When they reached the Regla cemetery, Lili and Pipo hopped on an almost empty bus that would take them, free of charge, close to the plaza. By the time the bus pulled away from the curb at four in the morning, Pipo was surprised that only a dozen people were on board. In years past, the bus would have been filled. It didn't take long to reach Twenty-third Street in Vedado, where, a few blocks past the Coppelia ice cream park, the bus could go no farther and let them off. Pipo told Lili he knew a shortcut through the medical complex off Avenue of the Presidents. "Are you sure?" she asked as she rushed to keep up with him. He cut through side streets, went down an alleyway, and came out on a street leading directly into the plaza. She was impressed.

It wasn't yet 4:30 A.M., but the street was already jammed with people. Some had started partying the night before and apparently had not slept at all. They huddled against fences or hunched down on the curbs, little cardboard boxes of rum at their feet. Lili changed places with Pipo and took the lead. She weaved around the knots of young men with fade haircuts and swooped past the nests of little kids sleeping on the asphalt. She glided along a fence, and as the crowd grew thicker, Pipo tried to tell her they had gone far enough. She pressed on, squeezing closer to the front, until she found a vacant spot about twenty rows from the starting line.

In a few minutes they found out why that space had been left vacant. Two dozen young girls who belonged to a dance group were using a sewer grating there as a makeshift toilet. A woman who was in charge held up a blanket as the girls squatted nervously over the grating, giggling as they peed. It didn't bother Lili. Each time another girl approached, she stepped off the sewer. When the girl had finished, she reclaimed her spot.

The hours passed slowly. People who were drinking got drunker and sang off-key. Those who were not drinking stood until they were ready to drop. Lili held on to a barricade, at times closing her eyes and dozing as Pipo kept looking around at the crowd building behind them. The huge plaza itself remained empty but for a bank of gigantic speakers and TV screens. The famous multistory profiles of Che Guevara and Camilo Cienfuegos shone brightly through the night, staring across at the towering monument honoring José Martí. The windows in the government office buildings surrounding the plaza were dark but for one room, where somebody had forgotten to turn off the lights.

At 6:30 A.M. the sky brightened and, with a gush of excitement, the crowd surged forward until security guards stopped them. At 7:00 A.M. another trill of anticipation ran through the crowd, but it came to nothing. Finally, at

7:30 A.M., with the first day of May fully unwrapped, the lights behind Che and Camilo went out, and with the air not yet scorched by tropical heat, martial music blared out of the loudspeakers. Security guards gave a signal, and the crowd—officials later estimated it at an unrealistic one million—swelled forward. There was no repeat of the previous year when the lone protester ran ahead of the crowd waving an American flag; the man with the flag was still being held in a psychiatric hospital, and security made sure there were no copycats. The TV screens showed Raúl at the base of the Martí memorial, Díaz-Canel standing stiffly by his side, but neither one spoke. The head of the country's sole workers' union repeated platitudes about the valor of the Cuban worker. He bashed the U.S. embargo and voiced optimism for the future well-being of the hundreds of thousands amassed before him.

Similar marches took place around the world, but in almost every one of them, official speeches were countered by the angry shouts of workers demanding higher wages and more generous benefits. In Cuba, workers who did not have the right to strike listened tranquilly to the official speeches about workers' rights. Workers who earned on average less than a dollar a day did not raise an arm in protest as they marched in front of the country's leaders. Workers denied the right to form independent unions listened to the leader of the only union in Cuba tell them they were the envy of the world. Workers in a country that got poorer every year, with a population about the size of Ohio but producing less than 20 percent of that state's economic activity, raised their arms high, waved their flags, and shouted, ¡Viva el primero de mayo!

Pipo marched quickly, shouting, ¡Viva! without much enthusiasm. Once Lili let go of the barricade and turned away from the urine-soaked grating, she came alive, waving her cap and shouting, ¡Viva Cuba libre! ¡Viva Cuba libre! She pointed to the reviewing stand where she believed Raúl and Díaz-Canel were standing, and then she waved at the journalists from around the world who were recording the march. In less than ten minutes, she and Pipo made it across the plaza. They kept walking toward Ayestarán Street and down to Carlos III Avenue, where they searched for one of the free buses that would take them back to Guanabacoa.

They were home by 9:30 A.M.

Although she hadn't seen anyone besides Pipo from the neighborhood board the bus to the parade, Lili came back energized and ready to assume additional civic responsibilities. Over the next few days, she spent hours in the office of Attention to the Public complaining about the garbage and yet another neighborhood problem that had been brought to her attention. Their little corner park had been invaded by giant African snails that someone had released in a Santería ceremony. She had been told that just touching one of the snails could cause kidney damage or blindness. Officials from the Ministry of Agriculture couldn't say with certainty what danger the snails represented, but they dispatched a crew of men with machetes to clip the grass in the park and throughout the neighborhood.

One morning, not long after the park had been manicured, a bulldozer appeared on the corner of Cary's house. It scooped up the bulk of the garbage and dumped it into a huge open-bed truck. Cary and Pipo swept the remaining trash off the corner, and Lili came by to help. Even Joseíto was willing to lead a hand, bending low to cut overgrown grass with a machete. When the corner was cleaner than it had been for years, they posted signs pleading DON'T THROW TRASH HERE.

Cary was impressed with the way Lili was getting things done, and she told her so. Then, after talking it over with Carlos and weighing her family responsibilities, Lili decided to accept Lourdes's invitation to run for *delegada*. Like Cary, she saw the neighborhood's need to take care of its own problems as a metaphor for Cuba. "Everybody blames everything on the embargo, the embargo, the embargo," she started telling her neighbors. "Well sure, the embargo is a problem, but the streets here need to be repaired, and the garbage has to be taken care of. What does the embargo have to do with those things? Nothing. The real problem is organization."

She called Cary, whispered her decision, and asked for her support. "You can count on me," Cary replied, trying to be courteous to her old friend despite the tension that had grown between them. For the second time in less than a year, neighbors were called to the little park, which some had christened *el parque de los caracoles* (Snail Park). It was a Monday night, just before a popular telenovela started, and about seventy neighbors showed up. They began with the national anthem but sang without enthusiasm, still confused by the unusual nature of the meeting. Most remained standing because four of the eight concrete benches around the perimeter of the park were broken. The CDR coordinator in Guanabacoa, a woman also named Caridad, explained to the group that Lourdes was sick and that a new delegate needed to be selected to replace her. She proposed two candidates, both men, and described them as loyal members of the party. One was in the military, and the other owned a motorcycle, a material advantage that could benefit all of them because he could easily get to government offices to represent their interests. She then also nominated herself.

Cary knew then that the cards were being stacked against Lili. Nonetheless, she was ready to put aside her disgust with the way Lili had treated her father and do what she could to help get her elected. What Lili had done was cold-blooded, that's for sure, but Cary reasoned that your blood has to be cold to sit in an office for hours to complain about poisonous snails and garbage. Lili had taken care of the snail problem, and she got the trash on the corner removed, even though a week later, the garbage was back. The snails, however, were nowhere to be seen. Cary had already convinced several of her neighbors to join her in backing Lili.

She raised her hand and asked for the floor.

"I propose María Luisa Durand Hernández, and I'm going to tell you why."

Cary laid out as strong a case for Lili's election as she honestly could. "I've lived in this community for twenty years, and I've never seen it so run-down. The streets are destroyed, there's garbage on almost every corner, and fleas are everywhere because of all the rats."

Cary's history in the Communist Party left her with a keen political sense of how to complain about the other candidates while at the same time praising them. "The others who have been nominated are solid revolutionaries, and I have nothing against them, but they are working men and they don't have the time to go to the municipal government to take care of these things. Everybody already knows that Lili's spent the time to resolve some of our problems. For that reason, I ask everyone to support her nomination."

On election Sunday, Lili's biography was taped to the wall along with those of the three other candidates. Carlos again was one of the first in line to cast his ballot. Poll workers were surprised when Joseíto actually showed up to vote. Lili voted too, but only after she had been convinced that it was okay for a candidate to vote. "The comandante always voted," she was told.

Once again, Cary and Pipo walked down the street to vote before going to church. When Pipo saw that there was a pencil at the table where they were to mark their ballots, he considered it a sure sign that the votes were going to be tampered with. When the ballots were tallied that night, the top two candidates were tied. The two men would face each other in a second round. Lili and the coordinator had been eliminated.

Lili was disappointed but not disillusioned. She doubted the vote had been rigged against her. It wasn't so much that she had been defeated. Somebody else—not necessarily a better candidate, just someone else—had won. She was determined to continue helping her community, and in the weeks after the election, neighbors continued knocking on her door to ask for help, thinking she'd won.

"There are times in life when you think you'd like to do something, something good, but if you can't, you can't," she'd tell them. When the garbage dump on the corner again nearly blocked the street, she helped organize a petition to the local government to get it cleaned up and to propose that a guard shack be put there to prevent any more dumping.

Lili admired Cary and believed that her willingness to always help others was evidence of her true socialist colors. She called her "the most revolutionary" person in the neighborhood, even if she had turned into something of a capitalist. Lili repeatedly asked her when Oscar would be restarting production of the perfume bags, hoping he'd have work for her.

CHAPTER 30

GUANABACOA

July 26, 2018

It was the start of one of the most important revolutionary holidays in Cuba, and the big Novalum building on Vía Blanca was draped with two huge flags. On one side the red, white, and blue Cuban flag hung straight and tall. Beside it, the red and black banner of Fidel's 26th of July movement sagged limply after one of the ropes holding it up gave way and no one bothered to fix it. It was a graphic sign that even with a new president, Guanabacoa wasn't in much of a mood for celebrating. The cutting machines and stamping presses of the aluminum factory had been silent for months since Cuba had run out of money to import aluminum. Uncertainty about Díaz-Canel, shortages of everything from potatoes to ibuprofen, and an exceptionally warm late July kept the streets mostly empty even on July 26, the day that marked the beginning of Fidel's revolution. Raúl was in faraway Santiago making an angry speech, but he could have gone to the moon for all that María del Carmen cared. She was busy preparing for one of the biggest days in her year, and it had nothing to do with the revolution. It was the graduation ceremony for the Spanish dance classes given by her good friend Tamara Rodríguez, with whom she'd shared a passion for dance since they were as young as the girls she was teaching.

At nine that morning, Mari showed up at the entrance to what she still called Los Escolapios even though its name officially had been changed to

Jesús Garay fifty years earlier. Her cast had been removed, but her head still was not right. The bump she got when she fell had disappeared, but the persistent headaches and dizziness had not, and she seemed to always be in a bad mood as the day wore on. But it was early, and the excitement of finally getting to see Tamara's girls dance brightened her morning considerably. She had put on a long pink sundress and pulled her hair into a tight bun. The tan arms of her eyeglasses contrasted with the gray in her hair. And on her left hand was Eustoquia's enameled ring.

She was glad the graduation was being held for the first time in the auditorium at Los Escolapios, and that it had been scheduled for the morning, the time of day when she was at her best. But where were the girls? She checked the time—9:15, 9:27, 9:45 A.M.—and grew increasingly nervous. The performance was scheduled to start at 10:00 A.M. But there were no girls.

"The bus is late," she muttered to an attendant. Most likely, the girls hadn't shown up when they were supposed to and the bus driver had had to wait for them. Every year it seemed the girls who enrolled in the class were less disciplined, less willing to put in the hard work that Spanish dance required and, frankly, deserved. It was the age-old complaint of every society about the young. When she was their age, she couldn't wait to dance. She'd change her shoes and put on her makeup—careful not to spill anything—while she was still in her father's Ford. She'd get agitated if he insisted on obeying speed limits. "But, Papi, can't you hurry? I'll be late!" she'd yell at him. As soon as they arrived, she'd bolt from the car, throw on her costume, and be ready to dance the moment the instructor entered the room.

"It's all the same to these girls if they arrive at nine-thirty or if they show up at ten-thirty," she told the attendant. "It just doesn't matter to them."

Too nervous to keep waiting outside, she decided to let the staff inside know they'd probably be late starting the performance. She crossed the large courtyard of what used to be a convent and marveled once again at the life-size statue of Christ standing with outstretched arms in the center of the patio, surrounded by tropical plants. Every time she saw the statue, Mari thought it was a miracle that it had never been pulled down the way the

Virgin's statue had been banished from the red patio at La Milagrosa school after the government took it over.

She walked stiffly through the courtyard, then entered the former seminary and what had been the dreary dining room of the priests and seminarians when they lived there. Next to it was the part of the complex that had been the school that Jorge García attended and later directed. Half of the building was shuttered. The other half was in ruins but was still being used as a school.

Mari breathed a sigh of relief as she heard the bus finally pull up. Girls began to trickle in with their parents, their costumes on hangers. Controlled chaos had been a part of the shows that Mari and Tamara put on for more than twenty years, and she did not see any reason to think this year would be different. Passing along their love for flamenco, jota, and the other traditional dances of Spain got harder every year because most of the girls dreamed of getting into a professional dance troupe like the National Ballet of Cuba but weren't willing to do even a small percentage of the work it would take to get there.

"Hurry, hurry. Go right in. Don't waste time." Mari gently prodded them toward the back room, where they changed into their costumes. While their mothers and big sisters helped them dress, their fathers and brothers lingered along the shaky railings overlooking a concrete courtyard, smoking or just staring ahead. A man with a change box under his arm set up a table to sell five-peso tickets. When the performance was finally ready to begin at around ten-thirty, he forced the visitors to enter one at a time, tearing their tickets in half before allowing them to pass.

The auditorium had seen better days. About a third of the 350 seats were unusable. Seat covers were torn, wooden armrests worn down to little more than splinters. The heavy green curtain with gold trim was well past its prime, and there wasn't a single fan to budge the stale air. The tall windows were opened wide, and the clamor of a scrub soccer game in the courtyard alongside the theater roared in.

At the sound of castanets, the fifteen people in the audience turned around to watch a dozen girls in fluffy white gowns dance down the center aisle, then climb stairs to the well-worn stage. Mari's job was the same as it had been for many years. She was to narrate the program while hidden in the folds of the curtain. In a stern, academic tone, she welcomed the audience and introduced Professor Rodríguez. They'd created an ambitious hour-long program with fourteen costume changes. The youngest of the girls was four, about the same age Mari had been when she started dancing. The most experienced dancers were in their early twenties. Mari read from a handwritten script as she introduced each musical number, beginning with the lively standard called "¡Que viva España!"

The girls danced in groups according to their age and their intimacy with Spanish dance. With the dark-green curtain covering her, Mari watched them intently. "This one doesn't smile for anyone," she whispered, tilting her head toward one of the girls who seemed to be struggling to remember her steps. Music flowed through scratchy speakers that dulled the notes but not the girls' nervous energy. One performance after another, Mari narrated a brief history of the music, then retreated into silence. When the most experienced girls performed "Amor Gitano," she sighed. "I love this one. For me this is the true classic of Spanish dance." The young women swirled and strutted to the exotic music with staccato heel strikes that Mari followed intently. Her eyes focused on one dancer in particular, a slender young woman with reddish-blond hair, glistening red lips, and dark eyebrows that flared across her broad, unlined forehead. She danced with precision and a sharp-edged dignity that suggested the María del Carmen of forty years ago, when she was a young woman immersed in the sounds and sensual movements of Spanish dance. Mari stared as if she were watching herself performing onstage back when she had dreams, when her hopes and visions for the future had not yet been blocked by obstacles that were impossible for her to overcome without denying her true self.

She did not applaud at the end of this performance or any other, remaining singularly focused on her duties as presenter. When the last dancer left the stage at the end of one number, she resumed her narration and introduced the next. Tucked into the curtains, she remained apart from the commotion of the girls preparing to go on. She didn't see how frustrated Tamara was be-

coming with the girls until her friend brusquely pulled back one of her youngest students, who'd nearly popped into the audience's view while she was
staring at the older girls dancing to "Mi Salamanca." Mari slid over and,
without a word, took the young girl's hand from Tamara. "Now, you stay
here," she told the girl, keeping a firm grip on her while motioning for Tamara
to go back to the dressing room to cool off.

Just past the halfway point of the ceremony a crisis erupted: a senior girl
who'd made several mistakes in her first routine was too embarrassed to go
back onstage. She'd begged her mother to leave, and now they were going
home, upsetting Tamara's carefully arranged choreography. When she heard
that the girl had gone, Tamara exploded. "It's the fault of the parents," she
complained to Mari and the other women who were helping backstage. "If
they would only instill some discipline in the girls and tell them no matter
what happens in an individual routine they have to go on. An artist always
continues."

Mari commiserated with her. "That's the way it is now," she said, shielding
the microphone so her words wouldn't slip out over the loudspeaker. "If the
parents don't enforce any discipline, what can you expect from the girls?"

More than an hour after they had started dancing in the molten heat of
the July sun and the broiling stage lights, the girls finished their final medley
and gratefully accepted the applause of their relatives and friends in the audience. Then, beginning with the youngest, Mari read each girl's name as Tamara handed out their diplomas. At the end, the girls presented their frazzled
teacher with a bouquet of three flowers, including one red rose.

"It's a disaster," Tamara said once she was back behind the curtain. "A
total disaster."

Mari tried to calm her down while reminding the girls of what had gone
wrong: one dancer's lack of commitment had affected them all. The girls listened absentmindedly, glad the show was finally over and eager to leave. And
so was their teacher, who had one month of rest to look forward to before
beginning her twenty-fourth year of classes.

Mari helped out in the dressing room as the girls got back into their street
clothes. But she was drained and told Tamara that she needed to go home

before her headaches started up. As they were leaving the old building, one of the attendants overheard her telling Tamara about the school and asked her what it had been like when she was a student there. Although her head was splitting, Mari launched into a detailed history, pointing out where the nuns once lived, where the priests once ate, and where she once was told by a music professor not to run up the grand staircase they were standing by.

"It must have been splendid," the woman said. "Do you think it can ever be restored?"

She had touched a sore point. Mari explained that her family was among the oldest in Guanabacoa, and she'd worked with concerned residents to petition the local government to restore the old complex before it was too late. "Every new priest who comes in makes the same request, but the government's answer is always the same." Municipal officials were willing to let the Church restore the convent, but they reserved the right to control the refurbished building, the kind of deal that was no more acceptable to the priests than it had been to Arturo Montoto.

"Once we were considered the Trinidad of western Cuba," Mari told the woman. It was a familiar lament, sad in its implication of lost opportunity for Guanabacoa and its people. "Now we're known as the land of collapsed buildings."

Mari walked out of the convent and through the courtyard, where she said goodbye to Tamara. Her shoulders stooped, her forehead creased with worry lines, she slowly walked down the curving sidewalk that borders Los Escolapios to Corralfalso, hoping to get back inside her own little house before her head exploded. Virgilio had urged her to see a doctor, but there was so much to do. Maybe now that the recital was over, she'd be able to find out what was wrong.

AT AROUND THE SAME TIME that Mari was lamenting the declining interest in Spanish dance, Arturo Montoto was across the street from Los Escolapios making last-minute preparations for the often-delayed opening of his comeback exhibition, the show he called "Dark."

He had seriously considered showing up to the opening on a horse to make a point about the absurd life of a renowned Cuban artist who couldn't even own a decent car. In the end, he drove his 1988 custard-yellow Moscovich to the Galería-Taller Gorría, which also made a statement to those who happened to see him and understood that a house painter in Florida probably owned a better car than he did. There's a wisecrack about cars in Cuba that lists only three kinds of automobiles: good ones, bad ones, and Moscoviches— underpowered, unreliable econoboxes from the old Soviet Union that might not be considered much of a step up from a horse.

Not many foreign tourists found their way to the rough-edged neighborhood in Old Havana where Galería-Taller Gorría was located. But Havana's cultural elite flocked there. Despite oppressive heat and skies laced with flashes of summer lightning, scores lined up before the doors opened. Arturo wasn't happy that they had to wait. The gallery had pushed back the opening an hour to seven o'clock without notifying anyone. *Bad form,* he thought, *but typical.*

He'd already been forced to postpone the date of the opening several times because he simply couldn't get the material he needed to finish the projects. Sometimes he wondered why he had been so ambitious. It had taken him years to conceive of and execute the pieces, and he knew that critics were likely to see them as a radical departure from his previous work. He considered them merely an evolution. The sculptures depicted the same ordinary objects that he'd painted so often before, but he had expressed them in a new way that suggested his own sense of the world. As the ideas grew in his mind, so did their scale, but because his vision was bigger than what he had to work with, he often had to set the pieces aside until he got his hands on more resin or an additional jar of graphite. The enormous eggplant he worked on had consumed all the resin he had managed to find and still wasn't complete. He decided to leave it out of the show rather than further delay the opening, already five months late.

By the time he was ready to have the pieces moved from Guanabacoa to Havana, it took five men to load them on a truck and then set them up inside the gallery. Besides the four gigantic sculptures, Arturo had created four huge canvases on similar themes for the show.

When the doors of the gallery opened promptly at seven o'clock, more than one hundred people poured inside. Pipo was among them. Cary had planned to attend but wasn't feeling well enough to make the trip across the harbor. The first thing Pipo saw was the word DARK in foot-high letters above Arturo's name. As the crowd spread over the gallery floor, conversation was subdued. There was no shortage of quizzical looks as people posed in front of the king-size objects. Many were drawn to the huge black egg, the size of a bathtub, with its dark shell cracked open to reveal a gleaming yellow yolk that some couldn't resist touching. People marveled at the towering slice of watermelon, with its single white seed, and crowded close to it to take selfies. Something about the large black basket in a corner made it seem less extraordinary than the other pieces, and soon a few people were casually leaning against it, chatting. A video loop at the back of the gallery showed Arturo and his assistants working on the pieces, including the one that Pipo, a baseball fan, thought was the star of the show, the refrigerator-size black baseball.

DARK brought out the stars of Cuban culture. Arturo's old friend Leonardo Padura, one of Cuba's most popular authors, was there, tanned and beaming. Tomás Oliva, a sculptor, showed up, and so did television host Maritza Deschapelles, along with several actresses and actors. When Jorge Perugorría, the actor who owned the gallery, arrived, a frisson of excited chatter coursed through the room. Perugorría, one of Cuba's best-known actors, had starred in the film *Fresa y chocolate*, playing a gay Cuban at a time when homosexuals were being persecuted by Fidel, a period of Cuba's history that Arturo had lived through and despised. Almost unnoticed in the stellar crowd was Daily de la Peña, Arturo's twenty-eight-year-old sweetheart, who scurried around in spiky heels and a slinky white dress as she chased after their toddler, Marcela.

Pipo tried to keep an open mind about the show, even though his own tastes tended to be far more conservative. He and Cary had no original artwork in their house, and their decor tended toward shabby chic. "Interesting" was all he said as he checked out the big sculptures and tried to figure out the meaning of the four large paintings that went with them—collages of images shaded over so darkly that they could have been Guanabacoa during a black-out. He opened up far more when Arturo's sculptor friend Tomás Oliva mentioned that he too had studied in Kiev in the 1970s. They found out that they both had crossed the ocean in the same Russian cruise ship and debated which was worse, the bunks on the ship or the food that was served.

Oliva was impressed by Arturo's sculptures, and he approved of using the English word *dark* as the title of the show. "It is shorter than *oscuro*, and blunter, so it conveys a different sense of the world, one that reflects his vision," he said. But for Arturo, it was more than a title. He knew critics would see DARK as a sixty-five-year-old man's growing obsession with mortality. But by using only black, he hoped to encourage people to look at the items from a purely aesthetic point of view while allowing his trademark irony to rise to the surface. In a country where eggs had to be "liberated" before people had free access to them, what could be more exciting than an egg big enough to bathe in?

At about eight in the evening, Arturo, dressed casually in red pants and a navy-blue short-sleeved shirt, stood in front of the baseball and thanked his assistants for doing the heavy work he couldn't do. Then he took a stab at explaining his art. "To some people this looks like a departure for me, but really, though some aspects are different, it is a continuation of all that I've done before, elements I've used before." The paintings, he said, wiping his chin in his odd way, as if he had dribbled coffee, represented a layering of objects that "conforms with the reality of life in Cuba today." In other words, they showed a world where daily events added up to something more confusing and illogical than the individual elements. The huge black baseball represented Cuba's infatuation with the game. And in its representation of something so fundamental about Cubans, Arturo felt it also stood for *cubanidad*—Cubanness—that hard-to-define sense of what it uniquely meant to be Cuban. Like baseball pitchers who use guile to fool batters, Cubans have to *luchar* and *inventar* in order to survive.

CHAPTER 31

GUANABACOA

August 2018

María del Carmen finally took her son's advice and went to see a neurologist. Since her fall, doctors had focused on her broken bones and had done little more than bandage the bump on her head. Now, nearly a year later, the neurologist sent her to La Benéfica for tests, but the equipment there was out of order, and she'd had to wait for an appointment at the neurological institute in Havana. She wasn't sure exactly what the tests showed, but what she understood was that there had been damage to a part of her brain that controlled emotion, which explained why she hadn't been feeling like herself. The doctors couldn't tell her whether the damage was permanent or her brain simply was slow to heal. They prescribed a drug normally given to epileptics and advised her not to watch TV in the dark or sit in front of a computer for too long.

Depressed, irritable, and exhausted, Mari officially retired at the end of 2018, although she continued working with the refrigerated trucking company in Regla as an independent contractor for a few more months as she trained her replacement. After testing fish and seafood for nearly forty years, her pension came to roughly twenty-eight dollars a month. That was slightly higher than the average salary for a state worker, but without family living abroad to help her, she struggled to keep up with escalating prices for food, clothing, and just about everything else. She already knew that she'd eventually have to cut out her one luxury, buying new eyeglasses.

She planned to devote as much time and energy as she could to her beloved Spanish dance, and who knows? Perhaps one day she'd visit the Spain
of Doña Eustoquia, which she'd never seen. She hoped to stay active, and besides walking whenever possible, she thought about taking up tai chi at the
Arcoíris, a recreation center located a block from the Novalum plant. But she
worried about getting there. The number 50 bus would drop her off right in
front of Novalum, but it was always packed solid. After her fall, she stayed
away from crowded buses.

She isolated herself in the old house on Corralfalso, reading books with a
cup of coffee or tea at her side. She withdrew even further from daily life, re-
fusing to look at one more issue of *Granma* or watch a single additional
nightly news program. When public meetings were scheduled in Guanabacoa
and around the country on the revised constitution that Raúl Castro had announced on the day he stepped down as president, she refused to attend. Nor
did she buy a copy of the proposed constitutional revisions that had been
printed on newspaper stock and sold at newsstands for a peso. "An old dog
with a new collar," she called it. It was inconceivable that a constitution put
together by a group of Communist Party leaders representing the seven hundred thousand members of the party could possibly address the issues that
ordinary Cubans cared about, things like retirement in a country where the
elderly struggled every day just to survive.

At times, the quiet of the old house put her in a reflective mood. She
couldn't help feeling bitter when she thought about the limitations that had
been placed on her because she had chosen to bear witness to her faith. The
injustices had loomed even larger since she learned that the girls who had
been most strident in condemning her lack of revolutionary zeal had left
Cuba years ago while she had stayed behind. And the girl from the Young
Communist League who had been the most ideologically aggressive back
then had turned into a devout Catholic, one who Mari said suffered from
"political amnesia" and never acknowledged the dark side of her past.

Outside the sanctuary of her home, she was not at all comfortable in the
Cuba that had evolved around her. It was a world she hardly recognized. She
couldn't accept the sentiment conveyed by the way the words *luchar* and

inventar had replaced the word *robar*, nor was she willing to go along with the sense of forgiveness it implied. What concerned her far more than a new president who acted the same as the old one, or a revised constitution that offered no more rights than the one it replaced, was the survival of deeply personal traditions that linked her to the Cuba of fine manners and noble intentions that still existed in her memory.

She continued to look forward to helping Tamara with the Spanish dance graduation ceremonies, though how much longer they could go on became less certain as they both grew older and more fragile. Each year brought her disappointment as, one by one, cherished traditions ended. After her fall she missed the reunion for old girls of La Milagrosa for the first time ever. Later, she found out that so few alumnae showed up that the handful of survivors decided having more would be too sad. The same thing had happened with the reunion of the tuna fleet veterans. Not enough people attended to fill a small room, though Mari was sure that their memories could have filled a cathedral.

No tradition meant more to Mari than the holy day of the Assumption of the Virgin Mary on August 15. Guanabacoa had been linked to that Catholic doctrine since soon after its founding in 1554. By 1743, the official name of the town had been changed to the Villa de Nuestra Señora de la Asunción de Guanabacoa. The high point of the year had long been a ten-day festival that combined a colorful street fair with a solemn religious procession. As a child, Mari used to portray one of a flock of petite angels that marched through the streets ahead of the statue of the Virgin that was carried on the shoulders of local men. By the time the procession ended, she'd have a painful red band around her waist where her mother had too tightly secured the belt that held on her wings.

Cities all over the world celebrate the Assumption of Mary with a procession every year, but none do it quite the way Guanabacoa did. The town was unique in having the statue of the Virgin first brought from the church to a private house where it was dressed in fine clothes by a volunteer known as *la camarera*. Generations of women in the same family fulfilled the role of *camarera*, and their fine, large colonial house on Guanabacoa's main street was the place where the statue, which itself dated to 1680, underwent its yearly makeover. When the well-to-do family of the *camarera* fled Cuba soon after the revolution, the government seized their house and eventually converted it into the municipal museum. Nearly all of its collection and displays were devoted to Santería and other Afro-Cuban religions, without a single mention of the *camarera* or the Virgin after whom the town was named.

After the triumph of the revolution, the government prohibited religious processions. But Guanabacoa's Catholics continued to celebrate the Assumption inside the main sanctuary of La Parroquia, the eighteenth-century church dedicated to the Virgin that dominates the main town square. The three huge doors of the church were thrown open after mass ended every year on August 15 as the faithful inside pleaded, "Take her outside." On the street, crowds shouted loud enough for those inside to hear, "Don't let her leave."

For more than thirty-five years, the statue never left the sanctuary. After the visit of Pope John Paul II in 1998, the Castro government lifted many of its religious restrictions. By 2001, the statue of the Virgin was again being carried through town, though without a *camarera* to dress her.

On the feast day in the summer when the new constitution was proposed, Mari's friend Armando delivered a public lecture in the municipal building about the centuries-old connection between the town and the Virgin Mary. The number of devout Catholics in Guanabacoa had dwindled so severely since 1959, and traditional religion had drained out of Cuban life so completely, that only a small number of residents like Mari understood how deeply the procession was linked to Guanabacoa's history and culture.

"We can't talk about local tradition and history without talking first about religion," Armando said at the start of his talk. About two dozen people had crammed into a second-floor meeting room in the town hall. As he began, the sky opened, and an August rainstorm pummeled the old town just as, tradition had it, happened every August 15.

Despite their friendship, Mari had decided to skip Armando's talk, unwilling to be a part of what she considered the government's deliberate attempt to draw attention away from the religious aspect of the day by scheduling it just as mass was starting across the street at La Parroquia.

Armando also was troubled by the timing, but the museum director had picked the date and time, and he had no choice but to comply with his boss's wishes. He projected slides onto a blank wall as he ran through the nearly five-hundred-year history of the town and its patron, touching on its founding as a refuge for colonizers' castoffs, the six months it substituted for Havana as Cuba's capital, the opening of its first Catholic chapel in 1578. When he put up a slide showing the ruins of the Casa de las Cadenas, some people in the room groaned, making the mayor—who had come in to watch—shift uncomfortably in her seat.

At 5:00 P.M., a few people excused themselves and ran across the street to attend mass. Armando wrapped up just before 5:30 P.M., giving the floor to the mayor, who assured the group that she had plans to restore the Casa de las Cadenas and other important sites. Armando managed to conceal his skepticism. He joined Mari at the rear of La Parroquia just minutes before the new bishop of Havana, Juan de la Caridad García Rodríguez, ended the holy day mass. From the pulpit, a priest then asked the people, "Should we take her out or keep her in?" The rain had lightened considerably, but the skies were still threatening, and the streets were soaked. A procession around the interior seemed prudent, but the overwhelming response was "Go out!" The 338-year-old statue, dressed in fine clothes and a wig of human hair, metal rays of grace emanating from her back, was rolled along on a large cart and lowered down the church's main stairs. Mari and Armando had rushed out to be in the park when the statue emerged.

By the time they got there, the rain had stopped.

A local band started to play. The statue, on its rolling throne, was mobbed. Bishop García walked solemnly behind it, wisps of incense lingering around him as the entourage passed. Ambling up José Martí Street toward the museum, Mari put her disappointment behind her. The old streets were not strung with colored lights the way they had been before 1959, and the storefronts weren't decked out with fancy displays. Memories of the feasts of her youth were so strong that she could smell the sweet churros and delectable little hamburgers called *fritas* that were sold at food stands around the park nearly until daybreak, though not one was there this day to tempt her. But for a few moments, as the Virgin swayed through the street, the band played familiar hymns, and a clergyman swung his silver thurible, Guanabacoa again rose to the glory of her past.

The band played joyfully, though slightly off-key, as the procession slowly passed in front of the municipal museum. The Virgin was turned a block later, coming out on Máximo Gómez Street near Arturo Montoto's studio. As it approached Pepe Antonio Street, Mari glimpsed her old friend Caridad Guerra slowly marching along with the procession. Caridad, now seventy-one, was as tiny as she had been when she attended La Milagrosa sixty years earlier, and she walked as if she had borne the weight of the tugboat tragedy on her delicate shoulders for a quarter century.

They grazed each other's dry cheeks with kisses and chatted as they followed the procession back to the church. Bishop García led prayers and took advantage of the moment to gently protest what was quickly becoming the most controversial proposal of the new constitution—a proposition permitting same-sex marriage. The Virgin and her throne then were lifted up the stairs and carried back into the church. No more than half an hour had passed since she'd emerged, a far cry from the two-hour procession through the streets that Mari remembered with such tenderness. Still, the Virgin had come out, the rain had stopped, and the tradition had continued for one more year.

Caridad invited Mari and Armando to her small apartment for coffee, the essential Cuban courtesy. Walking through the old streets still glistening with rain, Mari harangued Armando for having cooperated with municipal officials and not calling them out for failing to preserve Guanabacoa's heritage.

"I wouldn't have sat quietly when the mayor boasted about vague restoration plans that will never come to pass," she huffed.

"Confronting her directly would have achieved nothing," Armando said. But bringing up the Casa de las Cadenas as he did during his lecture forced the mayor to address the issue publicly. Mari was still angry that the officials had tried to placate them with a sign, and he agreed. "All they really did was taunt us," he said. He remained pessimistic about chances the building could be saved, but he felt satisfied that he had done what he could to raise the issue again.

Caridad lived in a cramped two-room alleyway apartment with two small dogs that yapped constantly. "Calm down," she yapped back at them, pushing open the front door. She apologized for the condition of her home. "It's a mess. My son is fixing the back room." She told Mari and Armando to sit on the edge of a small bed by the door as she made the espresso. She weighed no more than seventy-five pounds and lived on the double ration of food she'd been qualified to receive with her *libreta* since she paid the local doctor ten dollars to list her as a diabetic, even though that was one health problem she did not have.

Mari looked up from the bed and was surprised to see hanging on the wall above the table a photo of Caridad's daughter, Lissett, and below that, a picture of four-year-old Giselle, Caridad's first grandchild. On the other side of the same picture frame was a photo of her son-in-law, Lázaro, the stepson of Jorge García's rebel uncle Gustavo, who drove the tourist bus on the night the *13 de Marzo* tried to escape. Below Lázaro was a photo of Caridad's brother Guillermo, who had been so confident about the voyage that he promised to call her from Miami the very next day.

Mari knew that all four had drowned when the *13 de Marzo* sank, but she had always been too timid, too respectful of her friend's grief, to dare ask her about it. On this night, however, she didn't have to ask. Whether it was because of the nostalgia of the procession, or the melancholy of the rain, Caridad opened up voluntarily. As the coffee perked, she said the sinking of the tugboat still haunted her, not only because of the unbearable pain that had not lessened even after nearly a quarter century, but because the government refused to acknowledge what had happened. Just as Jorge García had done, she had been forced to go to Spike's widow to give back the *libretas* of the victims. But the government never issued death certificates for them, saying only that they had left the country. In the crazy quilt of property ownership in Cuba, the lack of death certificates would always obscure the legal title to their house. Back in 1994, Caridad had tried to get some official to listen to her, but when all her efforts fell short, she put a sign on the front door of her house that read IN THIS HOUSE FOUR PEOPLE ARE MISSING. It was an almost unheard-of public protest, but in a country without an independent press or any other forum for people to air grievances, it was the only way to voice her concerns. The government didn't like it. A member of the local Communist Party came to the house and promised to help Caridad if she just took down the sign. She did. A week later she saw the man in Guanabacoa's Central Park and stopped him before he could slip away.

Look, he told her nervously, there are no cadavers. If we have no cadavers, we can't declare them dead. They're just missing.

"It sounds like a bad joke, one that's not funny," Armando said.

Outraged by what she'd been told, Caridad had replaced the sign on her front door and continued demanding a legitimate response. None ever came. After her husband died, she traded that house for another, but she continued to worry that when she died, her surviving son would have trouble legally inheriting the property that was still in his dead sister's name.

Mari listened to her old friend's anguish, pained by how much deeper it cut than she had ever imagined. Caridad told her that she'd gone to the Villa Marista headquarters of state security to demand an accounting of what happened in 1994 and was again told that the government had no proof of the deaths. "They told me that there are no records," Caridad said, close to tears. "No records, as if those people, my family, they never existed."

The only lawyer she ever found who would talk to her about the case turned out to be Spike's son, who still lived in Guanabacoa. He appeared regularly on TV to discuss real estate issues, but he never spoke publicly about his father or the tugboat. His advice to Caridad: just fill out the papers transferring the property to her son now without even mentioning that her daughter was dead.

She said she couldn't bring herself to do that.

Unless they were friends with victims or survivors, most people knew only what they'd read about the tugboat in *Granma*. Inevitably, rumors had spread. Caridad said that many of them had revolved around Jorge García because of his business training Dobermans and German shepherds. Some people—including her own mother—believed he had been an agent of state security.

"She blamed him for not trying to stop the group from leaving," Caridad told them. Others in Guanabacoa had blamed Ramel, but in her mind, there was no doubt who had destroyed her family.

"No one was responsible but the government," she said.

JORGE GARCÍA NEVER LET THE FACT that Caridad Guerra's mother blamed him for the tugboat tragedy interfere with his friendship and respect for Caridad. He held no grudges against her family or anyone in Guanabacoa who repeated the unfounded rumors. Nothing they said could interfere with his quest for justice.

Along with his numerous testimonies before the commission investigating the Castros, he worked with a translator to self-publish an English-language edition of his book on the *13 de Marzo* to coincide with the twenty-fifth anniversary of the sinking in 2019. His nephew, Iván Prieto Suárez, had agreed to pick up the tab. He could afford it. After coming to the United States, Iván had started a trucking company and a real estate business in Miami that made enough money for him to easily cover the few thousand dollars it cost to have the book printed. He was chasing the American dream, but he never let the tragedy of Cuba drift far from his mind. In the front room of his ranch-style house in a marginal Miami neighborhood, on the wall facing the front door where he can see it every time he enters the house, he hung a three-foot-high painting of his father.

Jorge's daughter, María Victoria, also lived in Miami, not far from her father or her cousin Iván. She tried to put her life back together in the United States, marrying a Cuban man from the province of Granma. She never became an advocate like her father, and after arriving in Miami, she rarely spoke publicly about the *13 de Marzo*. In the summer of Díaz-Canel's ascension to power and the introduction of the revised constitution, she took advantage of the temporary resumption of cruise ship service to Havana to quietly pay tribute to her lost family. She and her husband booked a cruise that departed from Key West. On board the ship, she asked the crew to notify her when they were seven miles off the Cuban coast. When they reached that point, María Victoria dropped a floral spray into the water, roughly marking the spot where she had last seen her son, her husband, her brother, and so many other relatives and friends.

The cruise ship docked in Havana and passengers disembarked to tour the city. All but María Victoria and her husband. They believed their names were on some kind of restricted list because a Cuban official who stood at the bottom of the gangplank checking passports refused to let them through. Not wanting to argue with him, they simply turned around and walked back up the gangplank. On the return trip to Florida, when they reached the same spot, seven miles offshore, she tossed another bouquet into the sea.

THOUSANDS OF PUBLIC HEARINGS on Raúl's proposed new constitution were held across Cuba A satirical one was even written into a few episodes of *Vivir del cuento*, with Pánfilo, Luis Silva's curmudgeonly character, wondering why so much fuss was being made over one proposed change—legalizing gay marriage—when so much that cried out for change, like the wretched economy and the straitjacket political system, had been left basically untouched.

Miriam Díaz attended one of the meetings in Guanabacoa, even though she didn't think anything she or anyone else said would matter. "They," she'd say, tapping imaginary epaulettes on her left shoulder to indicate Raúl and his generals, "have already decided." Still, she had a point she felt needed to be made: when you are struggling to get by on a measly state pension of ten dollars a month as she did, "who's worried about gay marriage?" But many Cubans were concerned about the proposal. Signs posted on doorways in Guanabacoa proclaimed I SUPPORT TRADITIONAL FAMILIES. Religious leaders from several faiths across the country opposed it. And even though they knew the same-sex marriage provision was backed by Raúl Castro's daughter Mariela, and that made it almost certain to pass, Jorgito García and most members of his Methodist church in Guanabacoa signed a national petition to preserve marriage as a union between one man and one woman.

At his studio across from Los Escolapios, Arturo forced himself to become familiar with the new constitution, but he called the whole process of consultations "a carnival" orchestrated to give the impression of public participation when the reality was that, like Miriam Díaz, he believed the final version had already been written. It was Raúl Castro's last attempt to prolong the revolution that he and his brother had started more than sixty years earlier. Raúl had assembled the constitutional commission and put himself at its head. The draft proposals had been written, submitted to the National Assembly, and approved unanimously, in less than four months, another initiative accomplished in *tiempo récord*. The consultations led to the final step, a national referendum, early in 2019.

Arturo did not expect anything in the new constitution to affect his life as much as DARK would. The exhibition had been well received. Critics gushed over the monumental pieces. Days before the show closed, Jorge Fernández Torres, director of Cuba's National Museum of Fine Arts, viewed the exhibition and afterward told Arturo that the show was everything the reviewers had said and more. Fernández then took a proposal to his board, which approved his plans to present DARK, and several other Montoto pieces, at the museum, where they'd be seen by thousands every day. Arturo was overjoyed. His comeback was complete.

But until the exhibit opened, he had to find a place to store the gigantic artworks. He had hoped to sell one or two of them, but he'd had no luck. Had he sold any of the pieces, the government would have taken 30 percent off the top, and he'd have had to pay taxes on the remaining 70 percent. But after his prolonged dry spell, any money would have come in handy. An American baseball team he'd been talking to about buying the black baseball lost interest. He had also gotten queries from Cuban teams, but in the end they had shied away, fearing that the black ball could be interpreted as a sign of the decline in Cuban baseball after so many players had defected.

He wrapped the watermelon, the basket, and the egg in cardboard and found space for them inside his studio. But bringing the baseball back to Guanabacoa was out of the question: no matter how they twisted or turned it, it wouldn't fit through the doors from the courtyard to the dry and protected area of the studio itself. When it became impossible to find a place to safely store the baseball, the Museum of Fine Arts agreed to hold it until the exhibit opened at some point in the future.

Arturo immediately went to work on his next project. The simplicity of restricting himself to a single color satisfied his artistic urge, and he wanted to do it again, but this time in white. Given all he'd said and done—and not done—for decades, white did not represent optimism about Cuba's future. He didn't expect anything positive to come from a new president who was just like the old one, or a new constitution whose lofty guarantees were no more likely to be enforced than those of the one it replaced. He was a man in his mid-sixties who was raising a toddler. If white represented anything other than the reduction of objects to their most basic form, it was the hope that for Marcela, his little girl, Cuba would be not a cursed island surrounded by cancerous waters but the land that God graced with the most precious sunlight in the world.

Arturo was starting to feel trapped in Cuba again, trapped in Guanabacoa, trapped in the studio he had worked so hard to build and that sometimes felt like a fortress under siege. Strangers were always congregating on his front step as they waited for a bus, tapping the door knocker for fun and leaving bottles and trash as if the building were still the dumping ground it had been before he rebuilt it. There were days when the electricity was out, when his cook didn't show up for work, when the noise from the cabaret behind him became so unbearable that he was desperate to get away. But then reality set in, and he knew that if he wasn't in Cuba, he couldn't paint.

He was in his workshop late one morning when his cell phone rang. It was Daily telling him that Marcela wasn't feeling well, again. She'd been plagued with sniffles and colds, fevers and congestion almost since she'd been born. They'd taken her to the local clinic, and after some tests the doctors determined that she was allergic to so many things that it might be easier to simply say she was allergic to Cuba. She'd do much better in a cooler northern climate where she'd be isolated from everything that irritated her. Did they have such a place where she could go?

Daily didn't, but Arturo did. He had remained in touch with his daughter Elena in Moscow. He called there regularly and spoke to his faraway family in the Russian he still remembered. *Dochka moia,* he'd tell his daughter. *Vnuchki moi,* he'd call one of his five grandchildren when they got on the phone. He might have to brush up a little on his Russian, but he planned to ask Elena to take in Daily and Marcela, at least until the little girl's allergies could be brought under control.

Arturo told Daily that he had managed to get hold of a few bottles of children's allergy medicine that wasn't available in Cuba. "I'm coming right over," Daily said. There was no time to wait for a taxi. One of her neighbors agreed to carry Marcela to the studio.

A moment after he opened the studio door to wait for her, Daily came rushing around the corner. Then, facing the decomposing walls of Los Escolapios across Máximo Gómez Street, Arturo fetched Marcela from the neighbor who had carried her, took her in his arms in a loving embrace, and squired her into the studio that had become both refuge and prison, a singular place where, despite everything, he believed he had done some of his best work.

A few weeks later, Arturo put Daily and Marcela on a plane to Moscow, secure in the belief that they would be in a better place. On his own again, he tried to get back to his work, and the life he had created in Cuba, but he was having trouble painting. The dirt and pollution from the city streets made it hard to breathe, and the *ta-toom, ta-toom, ta-toom* from the cabaret behind the studio kept him up half the night. Most frustrating of all were the cuts on his fingers and hands from building a cage for quail chicks that he hoped would eventually give him all the eggs he wanted, without having to wait for the government to liberate them. The irony of it could have been the subject of one of his paintings.

"The revolution promised to create the 'new man,'" Arturo said, holding out his bruised hands. "After sixty years, where is that new man we were creating? I've lived through every stage of it and I tell you that I am that new man. But who am I? What do I have? I'm an artist, and I'm cutting up my hands to make a cage so that someday I can have eggs to eat. That's the self-sufficient new Cuban man!"

With a mock salute, he repeated one of Raúl's favorite propaganda slogans with the same irony as when he ordered a "Ha-Ha-Ha" at a bar. "*¡Por un socialismo próspero y sostenible!*"

"For a prosperous and sustainable socialism!"

CHAPTER 32

The five shillings that Cary's grandmother paid for her Jamaican passport in 1922 upended her world just as thoroughly as it would nearly a century later for the Cuban family she never knew. The document, signed by Sir Leslie Probyn, captain general of Jamaica, cleared the way for Sarah Ann Ewen—described in the passport as a twenty-nine-year-old washerwoman, five feet six inches tall, with "round forehead and chin, ordinary nose and mouth, oval face, and black complexion"—"to pass freely without let or hindrance," a privilege she used to begin a new life in Cuba. Nearly a century after Sarah crossed the Caribbean from one island to another, her great-grandsons—Oscar, Leonardo, and Leandro—received their own Jamaican passports. And a few months later, Sarah's granddaughter Esperanza did the same. Esperanza's plans for using her Jamaican citizenship were as vague as her sons'. But she knew one thing: if they ever decided to leave Cuba, she wanted to be able to follow them "without let or hindrance."

Esperanza traveled to Jamaica to pick up her passport in mid-2018, and while there she felt compelled to try to connect with some part of her grandmother's history. She found an old address in one of the papers the researcher had turned up and, with the help of a taxi driver, made her way into Kingston's slums to look for it. Ten Wellington Street had long since been razed. But as she got close to the place where the house once stood, the emotion of what she was doing caught up with her. "I felt it here," she told Cary after she had returned, pressing a fist to her chest. "It was something I can't explain but I felt it physically." She'd been able to stand where the grandmother she knew only through her passport photo had once stood as she dreamed of the life she would have in the land called Cuba. It was the spiritual recentering that Zenaida had foreseen so many years before.

Within a week of Esperanza's return from Jamaica, Cary decided that she too was ready to hedge her own bet on the future of Cuba. It hadn't escaped her attention that many Cubans were looking backward to where their ancestors had come from in order to go where they wanted to go. It was impossible to ignore the long lines outside the Spanish embassy in Havana, where people were determined to prove their linkage to Spain—Cuba's oppressor for half a millennium, against whom three wars of independence had been fought—in order to secure a passport that would give them privileges to travel and do business that other Cubans didn't have. There were crowds in front of the embassies of Jamaica and Mexico too.

Cary filled out her application for Jamaican citizenship, but she harbored no desire to "abandon" Cuba, the terrible phrase that had long been used to vilify those who no longer were willing to live under the Castros' rules. She believed that a Jamaican passport would ensure that she'd always be able to see Oscar wherever he settled. She wouldn't have to worry that her government might change the law and prohibit Cubans from leaving the country without permission, as it had until 2013, or limit them to just one trip per year—the kind of restrictions that had kept some of her friends from seeing their families for a decade or longer. And she wouldn't be captive to American policy changes either, now that Oscar had revived his American dream after realizing that both new presidents were reshaping his world.

Cuba's old American cars can give the impression that time has stopped, but in fact, life for most Cubans was an endless string of surprises, many of them unpleasant. When Cary, Pipo, and Oscar had a chance to read past the silliness of the bathroom attendant rules in the *Official Gazette* published weeks after Díaz-Canel took over, they were appalled. Embedded in those pages were new rules that could choke the life out of businesses like theirs.

Raúl had left it to Díaz-Canel to crack down on the meager accumulation of wealth that so bothered the old socialist guard, the die-hard *castristas* who considered the five hundred thousand self-employed Cubans a mortal danger to the state they had created.

By the end of 2018, the new rules would make it difficult for anyone to hold more than a single business license, advancing the government's goal of prohibiting anyone from becoming wealthy. Oscar had one license as a designer, another as a textile worker, and he'd have to surrender one of them. Taxes were being raised; controls were being tightened. More than half of Oscar's revenue in 2018 came from sales to a single tourism-related state enterprise, but the new regulations limited the amount of business the state could do with any one private company. Entrepreneurs would have to open special bank accounts where they'd be required to keep more than half of their revenue for several months, giving the government both access to and control of the money. Even though there still was no wholesale market, the government was going to crack down on the illicit acquisition of basic material—the *inventando* and *luchando* that kept the private sector alive. If a private business couldn't provide receipts showing that it had acquired material legally, the consequences would be serious.

For Cary and Pipo, it was a reckoning. For Oscar, it was a flashing alarm telling him it was time to leave. Perhaps it had always been inevitable—he was young and ambitious, and he had already tasted life in La Yuma. But this latest round of restrictions pushed him to the edge. And the chance to get out was sitting right on his desk. It was an invitation to participate in a monthlong leadership program in the United States for young entrepreneurs from Latin America. Just as when he had attended Florida International University two years before, he realized that fate was waving a ticket in front of his face. This time, though, he decided to include his parents in the plans.

They held family meetings around the kitchen table that began calmly but soon led to tempers flaring. Oscar's design and promotion business already was more prosperous than 95 percent of all Afro-Cuban enterprises, but it depended on a supply of canvas, thread, and other basic materials that, as Cary had predicted, had become almost impossible to come by legally. The designs, the printing, the delivery, and the accounting for all of it was in Oscar's head, and if he left, who would assume responsibility? Don't worry, Oscar said over and over. But Cary worried. By the time some of these kitchen negotiations ended, she was slipping a pill under her tongue to keep her blood pressure under control. When she thought about her family turning their backs on their homeland and voluntarily adopting another, it hurt as much as it had when her mother first raised that idea of claiming Jamaican citizenship decades before Oscar was born. A passport was made of paper and ink, but homeland was in the blood.

They eventually agreed that he should use the business training course not as a way out, but as a test to see whether the Cuban businesses could run without him. When he arrived in the United States a few weeks later, he was assigned to work with a small start-up company in Louisville that made artisanal leather bags and belts. He was astonished by the freedom the small company's young founders had to pursue their own goals. He returned home in October more convinced than ever that he had to get out, although he couldn't say he'd never return to Cuba.

If he left Cuba for the United States, Oscar knew he was entering a Rubik's Cube of deadlines and calendar dates. His multiple-entry U.S. visa would get him into America legally, but he'd have to stay in the United States at least a year and a day to qualify for the 1966 Cuban Adjustment Act's fast track to permanent residency—an option uniquely available to Cubans—which could take up to another year. That would bring him dangerously close to another deadline. Under one of Raúl Castro's 2013 changes that eliminated the dreaded departure visa, Cubans were no longer considered to be abandoning the country if they left. However, if they stayed away for more than two years, they lost their social benefits as well as any property, like a house, that they owned in Cuba. Cary and Pipo had drawn up a will that left the Guanabacoa house to him.

After he returned from Kentucky, Oscar finished putting his plan into action. He gave up one of his licenses, legally melded his business into his mother's, and signed papers giving Pipo the legal right to represent him and pay his bills. If they needed a new design for a tote bag or a T-shirt, he'd send it from the United States in an email. He prepaid several months' rent on the Neptuno workshop and made advance payments on their business loans, but not too many because that would make government auditors suspicious.

Oscar had watched both his parents work at different jobs and felt he too was flexible enough to try something new. A school friend named Daniel who worked for a home-renovation contractor in the United States had been urging Oscar to come join him. Oscar had never worked for anyone but his mother, and he'd never done manual labor. Even the canvas totes at the heart of his business were made by others. But he was cocky enough to believe that combining his design degree and business know-how with Daniel's contracting experience would enable them to eventually start their own home-renovation company. And with his Jamaican passport, he figured he'd be able to open a bank account, get a credit card, even buy a car. They may have been pipe dreams, but he made up his mind to leave Cuba before year's end.

At the same time, his cousins Leonardo and Leandro finalized their own escape. After they sold their late father's apartment, they discovered that he'd left a bank account. With the modest windfall, they decided to try their luck in Uruguay, where they'd heard that a Cuban community was forming. Cary had been in touch with a former colleague there who agreed to help the brothers once they arrived. They too decided to get out before the end of the year.

Oscar kept going to the workshop on Neptuno Street right up until his last day. That's when he and Cary held a meeting with a young Cuban entrepreneur named Maykal who was interested in selling tote bags that he'd design and that Oscar's company would manufacture. Cary fingered a small yellow tote he'd brought and frowned. "Speaking as a woman I can tell you this won't work," she said, slipping the bag over her shoulder to show him how small it looked. "This might be okay for Cubans, but for European tourists going to the beach, it isn't big enough for their towels and suntan lotion and everything else they carry."

When she asked Maykal how he planned to acquire canvas for the bags, he said that a contract with the state would make it easy to import material from Panama.

"Do you have a contract now?" Cary asked.

"No, not yet."

They promised to stay in touch. As soon as he left, Cary told Oscar, "He has a lot of dreams but no contract and no material."

"Don't worry," Oscar said. "All you have to do is produce the bags when he brings the material and leave the rest to him. If he can't get the canvas, you don't have to do anything."

After the meeting, he left the workshop to take care of a few last-minute errands. He flagged down an old Lada taxi and rode to the Havana Libre Hotel and then walked to a row of ATMs to withdraw $1000. He then stopped in at a state-run company to collect a payment for uniforms that Cary's company had manufactured, but he came out half an hour later empty-handed. The state-run company couldn't pay him because it had run out of paper checks.

He called Jesús to pick him up in his three-wheeled truck and take him to the Carlos III market, one of the biggest stores in Havana. Oscar grabbed a sandwich and a beer, then walked through the crowded two-story indoor mall to the butcher shop at the far end, where a six-foot-high stack of frozen chicken boxes was rapidly melting. Such treasures usually were picked clean by the owners of private restaurants who paid tipsters to tell them when supplies arrived, then bought nearly the entire shipment, leaving little for ordinary Cubans. Oscar had his own informant who told him when the chicken had been delivered. After scanning the boxes, looking for one that was still frozen solid, he bought a thirty-pound box of drumsticks marked "Made in the USA" for twenty-eight dollars. He wanted to make sure that his parents' freezer was full before he left.

They returned to Neptuno to pick up Cary and close the shop. After he said goodbye to the shoemakers downstairs one last time, they all hopped into Jesús's truck—Cary in front, Oscar and Zademys in the windowless back, where they sat on top of the box of frozen chicken. When they reached the 10 de Octubre neighborhood, where Zademys lived, she gave Oscar a big hug and said she expected him to write to her whenever he could.

At home, Oscar, Cary, and Pipo sat around the computer going over last-minute plans. In no time they hit a snag. They couldn't find a contract that Pipo was supposed to deliver to a client the day after Oscar left. "I put it right there, alongside the computer, just a day ago," Pipo said. Both Cary and Oscar looked through the books and folders on the desk but couldn't find it. "Look in your other file, please," Pipo implored. "I don't have it."

Cary thought it was a bad way to start. Agitated, she scolded Oscar and Pipo for being disorganized. "If I was in my office at Puntex, I'd just turn to my secretary and say, 'Find it,' and that's what she'd have to do." Worried that things would probably get worse after Oscar left, she gave both of them a stern warning. "I can't order you around like that, but you need to keep track of where you put things."

That weekend Cary and Pipo hosted a farewell dinner for the whole family. Leonardo came with his two-year-old daughter, Lianna. Leandro and Oscar helped set the table, and Cary's old friend Juanita, her secretary at Novalum, sat alongside Esperanza. They all understood it would be the last time they'd be together, and their mood was solemn.

Esperanza took Juanita's hand and reached over the table for Leonardo's. The others did the same, making a circle as Esperanza asked for blessings on the meal that Pipo had prepared: fried seabream he'd bought at the door from the fisherman from Pinar del Río, along with shredded chicken, rice, and tomatoes. She invoked the graces of a greater power on their family and friends without mentioning the impending departure, the next morning, of her two sons, nor Oscar's plan to leave a day after that. But when she prayed for them to achieve success in their endeavors, her voice cracked, and she started to cry. Across the table, Cary choked up. The moment she had dreaded for so long was upon them. After this last meal, her table would never be the same. Oscar and Pipo were silent, holding back their own tears.

After dinner, they exchanged long, soulful hugs while Faru circled their legs. Then Esperanza and her family walked slowly down the broken asphalt street to Vía Blanca, where they caught the number 50 bus home.

CARY ARRANGED FOR HER FRIEND Tony to drive them to the airport in his red Lada, just as he had taken Leonardo and Leandro the day before. Esperanza had been too distraught to see her sons off, but Cary and Pipo insisted on accompanying Oscar to the airport. He spent the morning filling two hard-shell suitcases with clothes and shoes and threw in a box of Cuban cigars for a friend. He said goodbye to Faru, and the three of them got into the Lada for the thirty-minute drive to José Martí Airport. On the way, Tony did most of the talking.

Oscar's large bag was two pounds overweight, so he removed a knit sweater and stuffed it into his backpack. The line to get through immigration was long, giving him plenty of time to say goodbye. At one point he took Cary's face in his hands and gently kissed her forehead. She whispered, "Be careful there," as they hugged again. "Don't let Daniel control your life. You have two eyes, two ears, and a mouth of your own. He's more experienced than you, and he's got his way of doing things. Remember that you have your own way too."

The line inched past the barrier that Cary and Pipo could not pass. They waited there until Oscar was all the way through immigration. They'd heard stories. Would they hold him back because he never did his social service? Could there be a denunciation on his record from the CDR that they didn't even know about? Would there be a problem with his passports?

Oscar stood erect as the immigration officer took his photograph and ran his Cuban passport through the computer system. Cary and Pipo watched intently, not relaxing until the gate opened and he walked through. They waited for him to be screened by security, then waved one last time before he disappeared into the waiting room.

"He's on his way," Pipo said, giving Cary a big hug.

Just as Jorge García had understood that their farewell might have been final the night his son Joel left the house to board the *13 de Marzo*, they had no idea when, or even if, they would see Oscar again. To a Cuban family, the departure of a son, especially an only son, is devastating, no matter how old he may be or how long he says he will be away.

"Your little boy has grown up," Cary told him.

It took them two hours in three separate buses to return to Guanabacoa. They chatted quietly as the bus crawled through large swathes of Havana, passing close by the Plaza de la Revolución, then stopping at the bus terminal where in 1994 they'd spent the night sleeping on the ground so they could get to their vacation in Varadero the next morning. It was getting dark as they passed through 10 de Octubre. The bus finally rattled up Vía Blanca and stopped opposite the Novalum factory, where they got off.

As soon as Cary entered the house she called her sister.

"He's gone," she said.

The first few days would be filled with work and the new schedule of running Oscar's business without him. Cary hoped she'd be so busy she wouldn't have time to think about how fractured her family had become. But she knew that Nochebuena and the end of the year would be harder. For the first time since 1990, she and Pipo, and probably Esperanza too, would be alone on those special days.

That's when she was sure she'd cry.

But now Cary did what many mothers facing an empty nest for the first time would do: she cleaned the house, starting with the kitchen. It had always been a good place for her, the heart of the house, where she felt most comfortable. They had plowed much of their early profits back into their businesses, but this had been a good year, and they splurged on a kitchen renovation. Pipo and Oscar did some of the work themselves, ripping out cabinets and installing new ones. They hired someone to create the stone counters, and a carpenter finished installing the remaining cabinets and shelves.

As soon as the shelves were in place, Cary displayed the dishes, cups, and saucers she'd purchased in the Soviet Union when she and Pipo had started their life together four decades before. On another shelf she arranged a set of juice glasses printed with the image of Misha, the smiling bear mascot of the 1980 Moscow Olympics, the one the United States had boycotted while she was in Kiev. They'd replaced their old appliances with a new stove and a stainless-steel LG fridge with ice maker that Oscar had bought for them in Panama. Their twenty-year-old Daewoo refrigerator—the first thing they'd purchased after Fidel legalized American dollars—they'd sold to Joseíto, allowing him to pay it off whenever he had the money.

Although they were separated by just a city block, Cary realized more than ever how large a gap there was between her family and Lili's, and that forced her once again to confront the privilege that existed in a country that claimed everyone was equal. She knew that since the turning point of the summer of 1994, and the gradual opening of the economy, some Cubans clearly had become better off than others, not just because they worked harder, but simply because of who they were, who they knew, or where they worked. That realization had forced her to untangle her contradictory feelings about so many things: equality most of all, but also work and incentive and merit, even wealth. She now felt that she could show off her new kitchen without apologizing or feeling guilty. Everyone in her family worked hard. Their businesses helped Lili and the other women who worked for them, along with the drivers, printers, and everyone else they hired. That didn't reflect the spirit of the socialism that Fidel had introduced and that Raúl still promoted. Nor did it conform to the transformation that she thought their revolution had promised. It had been difficult, even painful for her, but the experiences of her life had forced her to see through those promises, and she had found a different way of living.

Lili also had come to a troubling realization that challenged her long-held beliefs. When she needed help for her dying father, the socialist system hadn't treated her the same as it treated generals or vice ministers. She had believed the promise of equality every bit as much as Cary once did, and now it was clear to her that she would never feel the same about it either. "What's happened is not that I don't feel like a revolutionary. I do," she'd say. Both her family and her homeland were passing through a difficult stage, and she didn't expect things to improve any time soon. Her mother's health was failing. In a few years, Carlos would be too old to walk the hills of Guanabacoa delivering bread and groceries. And every day it hurt her to watch Joseíto's family struggling to just get by. Lili knew that the revolution wasn't as significant a factor for him and his girls as it had been for her. And although she hated to admit it, she knew in her heart that if he could choose, her only son would jump at a chance to live in the United States.

"Not just the United States," Joseíto responded from next door where he had been killing time, loafing with one leg over the arm of a chair he had reupholstered. "It could be anywhere else. Spain. Anywhere, but not here." Unlike his mother, he'd never bought into the notion of real equality in Cuba. He had no relatives outside Cuba who could send money to help get his business going or make sure his daughters had the medicine they needed. Cuba's old command economy had failed him, and the new economy, with all its licenses and regulations, hung over him like a dark shadow. He was angered by the thought that his daughters had never tasted a grapefruit or held a pear.

"Those things are only for people who work for the hotels or the government," he said.

"And the generals."

But not his girls.

IT TOOK NO TIME FOR Cary and Pipo to feel the added strain of running their combined businesses without Oscar. The contract that Pipo and Cary had looked for never surfaced. "Oscar had no filing system, and you're just as bad," she lectured Pipo. Cary spent more time at the workshop, making the arduous trip there almost every day until, nearly exhausted, she limited herself to no more than three days a week. As more responsibility fell on her shoulders, she worried that her health would suffer the way it had when she was vice minister. The operation to replace her pacemaker had been delayed first two months, then six, then an entire year because of a shortage of pacemakers and confusion over how long the old one was supposed to last. Every time she went in for a checkup, doctors determined that her battery still had life and would function properly, as long as she didn't get too excited. She took the delays in stride, certain that things would turn out all right for her. Good news can balance out troubles, and a month after Oscar left, the Jamaican embassy called to tell her that her citizenship had been granted. She didn't feel any more Jamaican, or any less Cuban, but she was relieved that she had a backup plan in reserve and that it seemed to be working.

Their house in Guanabacoa had become an empty nest, one of the few in housing-starved Cuba. Although they missed him terribly, Cary, Pipo, and even Faru eventually got used to Oscar's absence. But sometimes, when she was feeling lonely and particularly unsure about Cuba, Cary worried about her far-flung family, and especially the newest member, the baby girl who had been born on the night Hurricane Irma blasted Cuba. Pipo's nephew in Cárdenas and his girlfriend had not named the baby Irma as Cary had feared. Instead, they had given her a sweet name, Celine. But before she had even completed her first year, Celine's life already was in turmoil. José Miguel, Pipo's nephew, and his girlfriend had split up. She took the baby and moved in with another man. Cary knew that Celine would have no memory of living under a Castro government. But unless things changed, she would grow up in a Cuba that was as dysfunctional and unprepared for the future as was her own family.

Every new day seemed to produce more evidence that Díaz-Canel and the historic era he had ushered in was being swallowed by chaos. In response to an angry backlash against gay marriage that took the government by surprise, officials removed the proposal while leaving in most of what Raúl wanted, including term limits, property rights, and the creation of the post of prime minister, as well as an irrevocability clause guaranteeing the continuation, in perpetuity, of the socialist system.

Then, just weeks before the national referendum on the new constitution, an extremely rare tornado struck metropolitan Havana just as the city was entering its five-hundredth year. For superstitious Cubans, it was a terrifying sign of bad things to come. Ferocious winds thrashed poor neighborhoods in the capital, hitting Guanabacoa harder than anywhere else. Scenes of the devastation were quickly uploaded to social media. Cell phones were out in force when Díaz-Canel and his entourage stopped near the Guanabacoa traffic light a few days later to inspect the damage. But instead of the tour showing solidarity, videos appeared to catch frustrated neighbors, who had gone days without electricity, cursing at the president's men as they jumped back into their cars and sped away. Lili claimed that the incident never happened, but Joseíto tapped the cell phone in his pocket and told her, "Mami, if it's on here, it happened." For him and many Cubans, that scene revealed the difference between Díaz-Canel and Fidel. "When there were problems on the Malecón in 1994, Fidel was there, and he wasn't afraid of his own people," Joseíto said, repeating the official version of events. "This one doesn't have the balls."

As everyone expected, the new constitution was overwhelmingly approved, but even though the results were a lopsided victory for the government, there were signs that Cubans were losing some of their fear. In all, 2.5 million eligible voters did not bother to vote, voted no, or submitted ballots that were blank or invalid, an astounding level of defiance for Cuba. Díaz-Canel had already recognized the growing restlessness of the people and, in a rare move, had decided not to enforce some of the drastic economic measures that had so discouraged Oscar, including the prohibition against holding more than one business license. But within a few months, he would have to announce that blackouts, shortages, and hard times were coming.

Oscar wasn't sorry he'd left when he did because just as he was settling into his new life in the United States, Washington was getting tougher on Cuba. The five-year multiple-entry visas that were a critical part of his and Cary's plans for their future were suddenly ended. Once theirs expired, they could not be renewed. Oscar had several years left on his. But Cary's was set to run out in less than a year.

With her family scattered across the hemisphere, Cary felt more than ever that the Cuban revolution had ended, at least for her. The dream she'd been born into had turned into a nightmare that pushed out those she cared about most. On TV and in the official press, they always referred to the "triumph of the revolution," but here they were, sixty years later, and a Castro was still pulling the strings that moved the country, they were poorer than they had been decades earlier, and the socialist utopia she had been promised was crumbling like the Casa de las Cadenas. Cuba boasted of creating a classless society, but she now realized that it had been her own sympathies that kept her from seeing that there had never been true equality. Arturo had always been treated with more respect because of his politically neutral art, just as María del Carmen had always been held down because of her belief in God. Cary's life had been made easier by state cars, vacations in Varadero, the big house in Guanabacoa, and many other privileges that someone like Lili had only ever dreamed of. It was certain that there had been real achievements for women and Afro-Cubans, but the color line still ran deep in the Cuban conscience, something she was reminded of when a customer stopped in the Neptuno workshop soon after Oscar left. She complimented Cary and Zademys on the way they were running the business. "I have to tell you," the customer said, "you all are so professional and courteous that I feel like I'm in a business run by whites."

Perhaps, she thought, the revolution's promises had been too ambitious, too grandiose, even for a small island nation with an ego the size of a continent. Perhaps Cubans, led along by Fidel, had fooled themselves into thinking they were capable of the impossible. Looking back, she realized that the revolution she once venerated had gotten old and tired, "even though they," meaning the regime, "keep adorning it with fancy words."

It hurt her deeply to say it, but she now accepted what she never thought she would.

"The revolution," she said, "is lost."

For decades she had been a true revolutionary, a faithful and loyal *partidista*. She believed wholeheartedly in the revolution and its promises. But they weren't the only things she believed in. She now proudly considered herself to be a true *patriota*, a patriot who loved her bruised and disfigured homeland more than any ideology, or any ideologue.

One afternoon, while she was resting in her newly renovated kitchen, surrounded by the proof of her hard work and unashamed that she had earned more than some of her neighbors, she put into words what Cuba meant to her. She gently took a sheet of paper from a yellow pad, and, falling back on an old habit that she said always helped her think things through, she wrote the word CUBA in block letters.

The *c* in Cuba, she said, stopping for just a second to collect her thoughts, stands for *calor*, heat, "not just the kind of heat that makes you sweat, but the warmth that all Cubans possess."

She smiled.

The *u* represents *única*, the uniqueness that feeds into what Cuban poet Elena Rivero called "the national insanity" of Cubanness, the exceptionalism of a people of intense passions, the pretensions of a big country on a small island, a nation always playing a much bigger role than it had any right to play.

For her, the *b* in Cuba means *buenísima*, not just good but very good despite the austerity, the repression, the lack of freedom, and the excessive government control. "Not everything in my own life has been good, but when I weigh it all, on balance, there has been so much that is good. To have had a mother who taught me so much was a blessing. To see that my son has achieved so much, so soon, but still thinks of buying this refrigerator for us without even asking. I know it's a material thing, but when I look at it and know how it got here, I see how he was raised, and how we now are harvesting what we sowed."

And the *a*, Cary said, is and always will be *amor*, the kind of profound, unlimited, inextinguishable love that she feels for her family, wherever they may be. For her husband, who, despite the odds against it, has remained loyal for more than forty years. For her friends and neighbors and everyone around her, whether or not they see the future the same way she does. And for the country that had changed so much since she'd been born into it, that has delighted and disappointed her in equal measure. The country damned to be surrounded by water that connects it to and isolates it from the rest of the world. Her damaged heart might need help to beat with enough strength to keep her alive, but nothing could ever empty it of the affection she feels for her Cuba, and the hope she keeps alive for its future.

AUTHOR'S NOTE

In the old Kodachrome photograph, a young girl is posing like a starlet be-tween two red-and-white Esso gasoline pumps. In the street behind her, you can see the arched windows and double doors of a grand old house that radi-ates the elegance, dignity, and history of a Cuba that once was, but has been lost.

Years after that photograph was taken, I married that budding show-off, and the street where that picture was taken—the neighborhood in Cuba where Miriam lived until 1960, when she was spirited out by a grandmother who thought Castro would last no more than six months—was in ruins. That photo—among the little she had been permitted to take with her—was for many years the image I had of her Cuba, the Cuba that existed before the revolution. It challenged the other perception I had of Cuba, the one I'd been seeing since I was a boy about the same age as she was in that photo. That came from the black-and-white news footage of Fidel Castro shouting, snarl-ing, and pointing his accusing finger straight at the United States. Later, it was all those news articles I read about "Fidel Castro's Cuba." But that photo of the red-and-white gas pumps proved that there had been another reality before Fidel and his revolution wiped it away.

Cuba is a tiny country, no bigger than the state of Pennsylvania, with a population about equal to Ohio's. But it has had an impact on the world far out of proportion to its modest size. For generations, the world's attention has focused on Fidel and Raúl as if they ruled a superpower. Revolutionary Cuba produced so many outsize characters like Che Guevara, so many terrible events like the Bay of Pigs invasion and the missile crisis that nearly triggered a nuclear holocaust, that it's easy to fall into the trap of thinking about huge events like revolutions on a grand scale and forgetting that real people are involved, that what happens on history-changing levels seeps down to local streets and utterly transforms the lives of not only presidents and generals, but sassy eight-year-old girls.

When I began this project to write about ordinary Cubans and their lives, I had that photograph of Miriam and the Esso pumps in mind. Over the nearly half century I've known her, I've tried many times to imagine Miriam's life in Cuba. What must it have been like for her to watch so many of her classmates fly away that she thought New York was a place in the sky? I was astounded when she explained that she returned to Cuba with her grandma in 1961, just weeks before the Bay of Pigs fiasco that was supposed to remove Castro but instead secured his hold on Cuba, to be with her dying grandpa. A year later, not long before the missile crisis, she was put on a propeller plane by herself and sent off to Miami, and then to New York, where she reunited with her grandma, this time for good. Even after so many decades, she can reveal things about Cuba that she's never mentioned before. Upheaval does that, turning what might otherwise have been an ordinary childhood into an unending series of memories so sharp that their colors and sounds never fade. A missing doll, a phone ringing late at night, drops of blood turning brown on a hot sidewalk—they exist not as simple recollections but as markers on a long, fateful path.

To write about Cuba in a way that would evoke that type of resonance, I felt that I needed to see Cuba from the same level as the street in Guanabacoa where Miriam's uncle Raúl operated his Esso station. I wanted to reach beyond the myths, to show the real Cuba and the real Cubans who live there, to pull back the curtain on Cuba's long-running political theater and concentrate on the people who were living the lives that Miriam might have lived had her grandma not carried her away. Who are the Cubans living there now, and what is their Cuba like? How have they survived inside one of the most controlled, most isolated, most propagandized countries in the world? How do they perceive the reality of their own lives? Of the conditions in which they live? Of the government that controls most aspects of their daily existence, that censors what they read and see, that limits what they eat, what they drink, what they say? And why has there been only that one moment in 1994 when they marched in the streets demanding change?

I've learned that there are two Cubas: one is the largest island in the Caribbean, the place that Columbus described as the most beautiful land human eyes have ever seen. The other is preserved in the hearts of exiles around the world, many who have vowed never to return until Cuba is free. Miriam is one of more than 1.5 million Cubans who have left since 1959. But there now are more than 11 million people on the island, nearly twice as many as there were when Castro rode so confidently into Havana with his rebels and his guns. What is life like in both of those Cubas, and how could I tell that story?

During the two decades that I reported for *The New York Times*, I learned that writing about Cuba can trip lots of land mines. Any story about Cuba, no matter how small, causes some readers to bare their teeth. As Wayne Smith, a U.S. diplomat, has said: Cuba has the same effect on some people "as the full moon has on werewolves." I was subjected to that weird intensity when the obituary I wrote on Fidel Castro was both praised and condemned, and I expect to get the same kind of reaction when the obituary I have prepared for Raúl is eventually published. The conflicts are deeply entrenched, passions aroused by the simplest statements. In many parts of the world, Fidel remains a superhero even after his death, the Cuba he created a socialist utopia that, even in shambles, is worthy of imitation. Elsewhere, he is the embodiment of a power-hungry dictator and 1959 is considered a year not of triumph but of disaster.

I decided that the most valuable approach I could take would be to avoid the holy trinity of Cuban icons—Fidel, Che, and Hemingway—and let the ordinary Cubans who are never heard from tell their own stories. Like a popular quote about teachers, my goal was to show you where to look, but not to tell you what to see. I set out not to bash the Cuban regime but to give voice to individuals whose lives have been overshadowed by those towering historical figures. Through their personal stories I could assemble a more profound truth about Cuba and its people than by focusing yet again on the country's leaders or its politics. To link together the narratives of individual people, I decided to focus on a single place and dig into the way a range of people living there reconciled themselves to the reality of the revolution. I looked for a place neither too deeply entrenched in the system nor too estranged from it. Neither too urban nor too rural. Neither too prosperous (if that could be possible, which I don't believe it is) nor too down on its luck (I could have found many to choose from). I wanted a place touched by recent changes, where individuals were adapting to the Cuba that is taking shape today.

It didn't take long for me to decide that Guanabacoa could be that place. It is a municipality, or borough, of the city of Havana, yet it has its own history, grandly laid out in Gerardo Castellanos's *Relicario histórico: frutos coloniales y de la vieja Guanabacoa* (Editorial Librería Selecta, Havana, 1948), a nine-hundred-page tome I found beautifully preserved in the New York Public Library, as well as battered, stained, and dog-eared in the Guanabacoa Museum. Lying across the famous harbor from the city center, Guanabacoa is close enough to have ties to Havana's businesses, politics, and culture. Yet it operates at its own speed, with its own idiosyncrasies and an overriding sense, as one Cuban told me, of "geographic fatalism" that comes from being so close to the capital, yet so very hard to reach from there.

Guanabacoa also was the right place because of the central role it played in the events of 1994, the low point of the revolution and the beginning of many of the changes that are manifesting themselves in Cuba today.

And, of course, having a personal connection, something that linked me to Guanabacoa not as a writer or as an American, but in essence as a part of the family, allowed me to enter the psyche of the town faster and observe it more intensely.

Miriam doesn't have any family left in Guanabacoa. Her aunt Alicia was the last to leave Máximo Gómez Street, and she too was gone by the early 1970s. They never owned any property there, so their most valuable possessions were their memories. Over several years of intensive research in Guanabacoa, I came across only two people who knew her as a girl. One of them, Bertica, happened to be a classmate of María del Carmen at La Milagrosa. A gynecologist who served three overseas medical missions for Cuba, Bertica had moved from Guanabacoa years ago, and Mari helped arrange for Miriam to finally see her again after more than fifty years apart. I also met Nancy, the daughter of the businessman who owned the house Miriam's family lived in. She still lives in the building that once housed her father's store. The tiny house next door that was Miriam's home still has the same floor tiles that she danced on as a little girl, though since buying and selling houses became legal in Cuba, new owners have renovated the kitchen and bath.

Although Miriam briefly attended La Milagrosa, she never knew María del Carmen. She sometimes attended services at Los Escolapios church, but that was long before Arturo built his studio across the street. Her uncle's gas pumps on José Martí Street were long gone before Arturo took photographs for the municipal museum's architectural survey. The service station is now a public health clinic to fight the spread of the Zika virus.

CUBA'S PLACE IN THE WORLD now is more in keeping with its reality—a Caribbean island nation blessed with endless sun, gorgeous white-sand beaches, and beautiful people, but without petroleum, modern technology, or a commitment to democracy and individual rights. Its leaders no longer are universal symbols of resistance. Fidel and Che are dead, Raúl's tomb in Segundo Frente already has his name on it, and the new president is as unrecognizable around the world as the leader of any small country. The mythology of the revolution means little to Cuban youth, who, with their tattoos, smartphones, and seething nihilism, see the old men of the Sierra as impossibly out of touch with their own reality. The foreign aid Cuba relied on for so long— first from the former Soviet Union, then from Venezuela, and additionally from sympathetic nations around the world—has dried up, and, to quote Margaret Thatcher, Cuba has run out of other people's money. At the bottom of every prescription it now prints the line HEALTH CARE IN CUBA IS FREE, BUT IT COSTS MONEY.

Exporting cigars and rum doesn't bring in enough to keep the system going. The government has its hands in the pockets of the Cuban doctors it sends to Venezuela and other countries, keeping most of what they are paid. It skims 10 percent off every U.S. dollar traded for its worthless Cuban convertible pesos. And it squeezes every peso it can out of its new generation of entrepreneurs.

The long period of economic stagnation under both Castros has come at a terrible cost for ordinary Cubans, and, despite adopting a new constitution, there's no clear path to a future with individual freedoms and basic human rights. Aided by technology, the opposition is growing, but it is splintered into many different groups, led by many headstrong leaders, which makes them easily controlled or ignored by those clinging to power.

My first visit to the island was in 1979 when Fidel and President Jimmy Carter reached an agreement that allowed Cubans like Miriam to finally go back. We three—Miriam and I and her grandmother Elena, who was born the day before the treaty of Paris was signed in 1898 ending the Spanish-American-Cuban War—were on one of the first planes allowed in. The Cuba we saw then was quite different from the country that Miriam left, and a world apart from the Cuba that is evolving today. There were no *paladares* then, no *paquetes,* and no way for most Cubans to connect to the rest of the world except through the distorted pages of *Granma.* The newsmagazines and tape recorder that I brought with me were taken away when I landed in Havana, but I was able to keep my camera to record the moment when Miriam saw her father for the first time in seventeen years. She had left as a little girl and came back as a married woman. For ten days they were together, their shattered world briefly reunited. Then we had to leave.

She never saw him again. In the summer of 1994, as Cuba reached its low point, she had to be there when her father's bones were removed from the tomb in Colón Cemetery and placed in an ossuary.

He hadn't been buried with two pairs of socks.

The separation caused by the rift between Washington and Havana has taken a terrible toll on so many families like hers and made even the simplest tasks impossibly complicated. For years, phone calls were difficult, mailing

letters almost impossible. Traveling to the island is far easier now, but ironi-
cally not for all Cubans. To help me with this project, Miriam tried to renew
her expired Cuban passport. Even though she has been an American citizen
for decades, she cannot enter Cuba the way I do. She was told that the process
of renewing her passport would take about four months. She sent in her original birth certificate from Guanabacoa, her old Cuban passport, and a copy of
her U.S. passport showing she was born in Cuba. As we waited, relations between Havana and Washington soured. Fifteen months after submitting her
application, she received a phone call telling her that the embassy wouldn't
renew her passport because it couldn't prove that she was Cuban. But, she was
told, if she still wanted to visit Cuba, she could apply for an HE-11 visa, one
that is reserved for Cubans. She did apply for and receive the HE-11, and she
returned with me to a Guanabacoa so different from the one in her memory
that she regretted going back.

When I set out on my first research trip for this book after deciding to
focus on Guanabacoa, I had little more than that photo of Miriam and the gas
pumps and a single name in my notebook. My good friend and colleague Tim
Padgett had suggested I get in touch with a woman from Guanabacoa he'd
interviewed in Florida for a report on Cuban entrepreneurs. He cautioned me
to keep in mind that although Caridad Limonta had started her own business, she was still quite revolutionary. Cary can come across that way, but as
I spent time with her, I realized that her story was far more complex. Her
voyage from her beloved sugar-mill town to the office of vice minister of light
industry to a successful career as an entrepreneur, and finally from revolutionary to patriot, encapsulated for me the journey that Cuba itself has taken
over the same half century. The steps of realization, reckoning, reconsidera-
tion, and reconciliation that she has lived through are a remarkable testament
to her intelligence, her passion, and her spirit.

I was also blessed that besides being as fearless as a badger, Cary has a
stereophonic memory and a long list of friends and family. Through her I
eventually met and got to know Pipo, Oscar, and Esperanza, as well as Lili,
Carlos, Joseíto, Miriam Díaz, and many others. As I spent more time in
Guanabacoa, I met Arturo Montoto and María del Carmen Álvarez, living on

either side of Los Escolapios and within a mile or so of Cary's house. And as I learned more about the town, and the role it played in the events of 1994, I reached out to Jorge García in Miami; through him I got to know his grandson, Jorgito, who still is part of the Methodist church in Guanabacoa. Jorge also introduced me to his nephew Iván, who is either the luckiest Cuban I've ever met, or the unluckiest.

During more than three years of work on this book, I traveled from one end of Cuba to the other, tracking down personal histories. Arturo and I walked through his boyhood haunts in Pinar del Río. Pipo showed me around his hometown of Cárdenas and accompanied Cary and me on the sixteen-hour, 485-mile trip from Guanabacoa to Tacajó in a pink 1956 Cadillac. I recorded more than fifty hours of interviews in Spanish, and as many without a recorder as I accompanied them at work, at home, in church, and at events like the May Day parade and the Assumption Day procession in Guanabacoa. Much of the account of what happened on board the *13 de Marzo* is taken, with permission, from Jorge García's *El hundimiento del remolcador 13 de Marzo*. He conducted most of his interviews, including the initial ones with his devastated daughter, María Victoria, within a short time of the tragedy, when emotions were freshest and memories strongest. The sinking of the *13 de Marzo* was thoroughly documented by the U.S. Congress and several NGOs before he published his book, and the Cuban government has never backed away from its initial defense of its actions. As I interviewed Jorge over the course of several months, I was struck by his dedication to the quest for justice. Even a quarter century after the tragedy, narrating the events that stole away his family brought him to tears.

After I completed this manuscript, Jorge presided over a sorrowful act of remembrance at the American Museum of the Cuban Diaspora in Miami, marking twenty-five years since the *13 de Marzo* tragedy, and twenty-five years of impunity for the Castro regime. The International Commission on which he had pinned his hopes hadn't yet managed to bring charges against Raúl or any other Cuban official. Also since this manuscript was completed, President Miguel Díaz-Canel went on television to announce the return of planned blackouts, convincing Miriam Díaz and many others that the new "special period" of shortages and deprivations that they feared had arrived.

Perhaps it was because of that unwelcome reminder of bad times that an infectious restlessness seemed to settle over Guanabacoa. Arturo Montoto longed to abandon his studio and move to Spain, but he stayed put and welcomed back Daily and Marcela after three months in Moscow that helped relieve the child's allergies. He set aside his "white" project to go back to painting, and he gave up on raising quail after cats devoured his chicks. María del Carmen briefly considered moving from her beloved house on Corralfalso to a small apartment down the street, but dropped the idea after her son refused to consider selling the house. Even a staunch Communist like Lili felt the new special period creeping in on her as food and cigarettes grew scarce, and Castaño suffered another heart attack that forced him to give up his delivery service.

And it was the flies that finally became too much for Cary and Pipo. After living in Guanabacoa for more than two decades, they sold their spacious empty nest near the infernal garbage dump and moved to a small house on the other side of Havana, across the street from a well-equipped medical clinic. "A house is just a house," Cary said, "a kitchen just a kitchen." From the rooftop of her new home, she has a fine view stretching all the way down to the Caribbean seacoast. When the battery in her pacemaker had only a few days of power left, she finally was admitted to the hospital and had her surgery to replace it. As she recuperated, she stayed away from the workshop and spent many long hours watching the vast city, leaning on Pipo, missing Oscar, and wondering what was happening to her Cuba.

WHATEVER CUBA BECOMES, I am indebted to Cary, Arturo, Mari, Jorge, and Lili, as well as to all the others included in this story, for the incredible courage they showed in opening their lives to me. They spoke fearlessly, even when they lowered their voices and leaned in close as if someone were listening. Old habits die hard. They understood the risks they were taking by laying out their thoughts so openly, yet they rarely asked me to skip anything they said because they feared reprisal.

I also want to thank Armando González, the erudite young historian in the Guanabacoa Museum who dedicated many hours to helping me understand, and appreciate, how unique Guanabacoa is while repeatedly pointing out how much the triumphs and tragedies that have occurred there are typical of all of Cuba. In Guanabacoa, I stayed at Casa Victoria, a legal *casa particular* near Vía Blanca that María Victoria Hernández had opened after President Obama's visit. I was her first guest, and I watched as she was squeezed between the Cuban government's increasingly burdensome regulations on private businesses and the restrictions placed on American travelers by President Trump. I hope her gamble eventually pays off.

To protect the people I worked with in Cuba as much as I thought possible while still witnessing their lives, I had no contact with any officials of the Cuban government. As far as I know, no one in Guanabacoa was harassed because they talked to me, and I was unencumbered by government minders throughout my travels. The people in the book did not ask me to change their names, and I didn't, trusting that no one would be punished for simply having spoken the truth. I carefully explained to them what I was doing and tried to make them all aware of the possibility of the repercussions they could face for talking to me. They all told me to use any of their words I wanted because, they'd say, usually with a smirk or sideways smile, "What else can they do to me?"

I have not altered any dates and, whenever possible, I have checked personal accounts against official records and printed reports to the extent that is possible in a country without independent news sources or anything resembling a freedom of information law.

Whenever I have used quotation marks, the words are based on the recollections of at least one person who was present to hear them. That includes the words of María Victoria, as recorded by her father and various journalists. She turned down all of my interview requests, still too distraught to relive that terrible day. Descriptions of how individuals feel or think come from repeated interviews with those people or their relatives. As they became more comfortable with me, and I with them, the gaps between us grew smaller until we reached a level of trust that overcame the decades of hostility that span the Straits of Florida. In all my time in Guanabacoa, I never heard a single hostile word directed at me as an American. Boarding the bus was a different story, and it wasn't my passport that caused trouble but my misunderstanding of local transit etiquette. When the bus stops suddenly and the driver jumps out, there's no need to panic. He's just grabbing a little *buchito de café* from the woman sitting on her stoop, or dashing into the bakery to buy *pan con chocolate* before they run out. Nor did I feel that anyone there, not even an ardent communist like Carlos Castaño, considered me *el enemigo*. Most Cubans draw a line between the government of the United States and individual Americans, between Miami and the rest of America, between policy and people.

I did the same with Cuba and the Cubans.

I have chosen to leave out details of small illegalities individuals may have committed while *luchando* because the trouble it could cause them far outweighs any additional illumination the details could provide. I took to heart their own explanation that under their system, every Cuban becomes a criminal to survive.

Although I have focused on individuals, I understood and tried to make clear that every Cuban possesses a measure of *cubanidad*, Cuba's presumptuous national ego. "Cubans are the chosen people" goes a line of an essay published in the *Miami Herald* years ago and repeated unremittingly since, "chosen by themselves." Cuba, the best of the Antilles. The ever-faithful isle. The country with the finest beaches in the world, the classiest rum and cigars, the prettiest women, the most irresistible music, and the baddest rebels. *Cubanidad* is part of every Cuban and an element of every Cuban story. There must be a measure of vanity in a people willing to overlook the fact that it is almost impossible to get ibuprofen or lice shampoo in a Cuban pharmacy while boasting that Cuba is a global medical power. In the engineer who raves about the free university education he received but prefers to wait tables in a Havana restaurant because there he gets tourists' tips. And in true believers like Lili Durand, who remains proud to call herself a communist and a true revolutionary even after putting her father in a closet to die.

José Martí first measured glory in terms of a grain of corn, but it was Fidel who popularized the phrase "All the glory in the world fits in a kernel of corn." The guides at Santa Ifigenia Cemetery in Santiago are quick to point out to bewildered tourists that the boulder where Fidel's ashes are entombed was hauled in from the Sierra Maestra because some architect thought it resembled a gigantic kernel of corn. Despite what Martí wrote in 1893, the reach for glory is an element of *cubanidad*. The Cuban spirit is as complex as the nation's history and as rich as its culture, as indominable as El Morro Castle and as seductive as the waves at Varadero Beach, as easy to recognize as a Cohiba cigar, yet as hard to describe as the sunlight of a Cuban day.

This book wouldn't have been possible without a push from my agent and friend, Stuart Krichevsky, or the agile talents of my editor at Viking, Wendy Wolf. I owe a lot to *The New York Times* and my editors there, particularly Bernie Gwertzman, Bill Keller, Andy Rosenthal, Susan Chira, John Darnton, and Chuck Strum, for giving me the chance to enter Cuba again and again. Several friends agreed to read chapters as I was writing them and made valuable suggestions: Ruth Behar, Benjamin Goldfrank, Andy Gomez, Ted Henken, Tim Padgett, Tony Perrottet, and María Werlau. Chris Wilson, my South African mate, read an early version of the entire manuscript and encouraged me to see it through. Others who offered suggestions and helpful guidance include José Azel, Claire Boobbyer, Jonathan Hansen, and many Cubans whose names must be left out for their own protection, but whose willingness to lend a hand makes me forever grateful. I owe them all what Arturo calls a "Ha-Ha-Ha." I would be remiss in not calling attention to the brave work done by Yoani Sánchez and the independent Cuban journalists at *14ymedio*, *Diario de Cuba*, and other nonstate news sites. Their influence keeps growing, and the need for reliable information in Cuba is greater now than ever.

From the beginning of this four-decade journey of understanding, I have relied on the help, encouragement, and inspiration of one very special green-eyed Cuban. As I wrote in an essay in *The New York Times Magazine* years ago, I owe Fidel an enormous debt because without that improbable history of his, I would not have met Miriam Zebina Rodríguez. Our paths would never have crossed. We would never have married and never have had three incredible children who've now given us four awesome grandchildren, whose DNA contains the seeds of *cubanidad* that, undoubtedly, will take them on their own glorious journeys.

Con todo el agradecimiento del mundo,
Les doy mis gracias eternas a todos.

LO ESCRIBÍ EN MI CELDA DE LUZ Y PAZ

GUANABACOA

MARCH 28, 2019

INDEX

ferry hijackings, to escape Cuba during, 106–8, 153
Fifth Congress of the Communist Party, 140–41
fish, 258
food rationing, 68–69, 255–58
  libreta stores, 68–69, 144, 215, 256, 257
food shortages, 68–72, 79, 193, 258
foreign investment law, 134
14ymedio, 257
Fund for Cuban Studies, 187

garbage collection, 277–79, 281–82, 286
García Crego, Jorgito, 218, 219–20, 236, 267, 275
García Rodriguez, Juan de la Caridad, 303, 304
García Suárez, Joel, 77, 85, 87, 88
García Suárez, Jorge Félix, 77, 87, 88, 151, 153, 217–19
García Suárez, Juan Mario, 88–90, 93–94
García Suárez, María Victoria, 77, 307–8
  arrive in U.S. as refugee, 151, 152
  commemoration for *13 de Marzo* victims and, 119–20
  fired from job, 123
  interview contradicting government reporting on *13 de Marzo* tragedy, 102–3, 124, 127
  news conference of, in U.S., 185
  13 de Marzo tragedy and, 87, 88, 89–90, 93–94, 95, 96–97, 100–103
García y Villegas, Jorge Luis, 74
gasoline shortages, 68
gay marriage, 304, 308, 324
González, Armando, 226–27, 228, 229, 230, 302–3
González, Elián, 139, 186
Gore, Al, 186
Granma (newspaper), 103–4, 124, 126, 127, 204, 214, 223, 236
Granma (yacht), 14, 126
Guanabacoa
  Álvarez family home in, 43–44, 46
  architecture along José Martí Avenue, 41

Assumption of the Virgin Mary procession and, 301–4
belief systems in, 229–31
conditions in, 6
crumbling infrastructure of, 226–29
garbage collection in, 277–79, 281–82, 286
history of, 39–40
Hurricane Irma and, 1–5
tornado hits, 324
Guerra, Caridad, 304–7
Guevara, Ernesto "Che", 25, 26
Gutiérrez, Gustavo Martínez, 125–26

Havana
  building efforts in, 56
  Castro's takeover of, and repurposing of buildings in, 56
  ferry service of, 241–42
  Leal's restoration of Old Havana, 134
  tornado hits, 324
  waterfront rebuilding, for tourist trade, 241–42
  See also Guanabacoa
health care system, 157–58, 181, 261–62
Hermanos Ameijeiras Hospital, 158, 160–61
Hernández, Fedencio Ramel Prieto (Ramel), 78, 86–88, 94, 95
Hernández, José Durand, 260–63
Hernández, Maria Luisa Durand (Lili)
  as caregiver for elderly father, 260–63
  Castro's death and, 221, 222–23
  elections of 2018 and, 265–66
  faith in and support for Castro and revolution, 166–68, 213–14, 265–66
  father's death and, 263–65
  garbage collection issue and, 282, 286
  Hurricane Irma and, 4, 236
  libreta and, 258
  marries Carlos Castaño, 213
  May Day celebrations, attendance at, 166–67, 221, 222–23, 283–86
  realities of communism and, 261–62, 263, 322